"Harry Lee Poe's biography of Lewis's early years is an engaging book filled with glimpses of the celebrated author that cannot be found in any other biography of Lewis."

Lyle W. Dorsett, Director Emeritus, Marion E. Wade Center; Billy Graham Professor of Evangelism Emeritus, Beeson Divinity School; author, *And God Came In* and *Seeking the Secret Place*

"'The Child is father of the Man.' Anyone who doubts this observation by Wordsworth should read this excellent new biography of C. S. Lewis. Poe goes into great depth, drawing heavily on unpublished sources, recounting the first two decades of Lewis's life in splendid detail. Even seasoned readers of Lewis will find much that is new and illuminating in this readable biography."

David C. Downing, Codirector, Marion E. Wade Center

"A unique coming-of-age biography of C. S. Lewis that stands out in revealing how his early life shaped the future Lewis: body, mind, and soul. It vividly captures the whole person of Lewis—not only an aspect of him but also the variety and depth of his defining features. The result is an eye-opening, important, and rich portrait that benefits from the teeming knowledge and thorough research of the author. It includes the often-neglected, lasting significance of the people who impacted the often-solitary young Lewis, with illuminating flash-forwards to the future Lewis."

Colin Duriez, author, *C. S. Lewis: A Biography of Friendship* and *Tolkien and C. S. Lewis: The Gift of Friendship*

"Harry Lee Poe's *Becoming C. S. Lewis* breaks new ground in the study of Lewis's life. Specifically, Poe concentrates on the early years of Lewis's life—an area largely neglected or glossed over by other biographers—and explores in rich detail the people, ideas, and experiences that shaped Lewis's adult life. Mining the fertile cache of material available in the Lewis Papers—the eleven-volume archive compiled by Lewis's brother, Warren—Poe offers convincing arguments about how Lewis's earliest interests find expression in his adult writings. The themes found later in Lewis's magisterial works had their inception in Lewis's youthful writings, particularly in his lifelong correspondence with his boyhood friend Arthur Greeves. Readers intent on obtaining a deeper understanding of the most important Christian writer of the last hundred years will find *Becoming C. S. Lewis* a welcomed treasure trove."

Don King, author, *C. S. Lewis, Poet*; *Plain to the Inward Eye*; and *The Collected Poems of C. S. Lewis*

"Many fans of C. S. Lewis will savor having so much detail on his early years gathered together in one biography. This portrait of an artist as a young man is based on remarkably rich information that we have concerning Lewis's formative experiences and influences. Harry Lee Poe adds much helpful context and commentary."

George M. Marsden, author, *C. S. Lewis's "Mere Christianity":
A Biography*

"Wordsworth famously wrote, 'The Child is father of the Man.' To better understand C. S. Lewis's tremendous achievements later in life—as a writer of imaginative fiction and poetry, a literary critic, and a Christian apologist—we should look to his formative years. Harry Lee Poe's *Becoming C. S. Lewis* is a valuable contribution to biographies of Lewis, providing a rich and comprehensive look at Lewis's early years and his important relationships with figures such as his brother, Warren Lewis, his friend Arthur Greeves, and his tutor W. T. Kirkpatrick."

Holly Ordway, Professor of English, Houston Baptist University;
author, *Apologetics and the Christian Imagination*

"The young Jack Lewis is the Lewis whom all admirers of the mature C. S. Lewis need to know. We find it highly fitting, then, that Harry Lee Poe, who has long been a devoted guide to Lewis and the Inklings, has chosen to illuminate for us so faithfully the ardent youth who was father to the man."

Carol and Philip Zaleski, coauthors, *The Fellowship: The Literary
Lives of the Inklings*

BECOMING
C. S. LEWIS

BECOMING C. S. LEWIS

A Biography of
Young Jack Lewis
(1898–1918)

HARRY LEE POE

CROSSWAY®

WHEATON, ILLINOIS

Becoming C. S. Lewis: A Biography of Young Jack Lewis (1898–1918)
Copyright © 2019 by Harry Lee Poe
Published by Crossway
   1300 Crescent Street
   Wheaton, Illinois 60187

Cover design: Josh Dennis

Cover image: C. S. Lewis ca. 1912, Courtesy of The Marion E. Wade Center; Tulip wallpaper design, 1875, Morris, William (1834–1896) / Private Collection / The Stapleton Collection / Bridgeman Images

First printing 2019

Printed in the United States of America

Hardcover ISBN: 978-1-4335-6273-0
ePub ISBN: 978-1-4335-6276-1
PDF ISBN: 978-1-4335-6274-7
Mobipocket ISBN: 978-1-4335-6275-4

Library of Congress Cataloging-in-Publication Data
Names: Poe, Harry Lee, 1950– author.
Title: Becoming C. S. Lewis: a biography of young Jack Lewis (1898–1918) / Harry Lee Poe.
Description: Wheaton: Crossway, 2019. | Includes bibliographical references and index.
Identifiers: LCCN 2019009167 (print) | LCCN 2019011376 (ebook) | ISBN 9781433562747 (pdf) | ISBN 9781433562754 (mobi) | ISBN 9781433562761 (epub) | ISBN 9781433562730 (hc)
Subjects: LCSH: Lewis, C. S. (Clive Staples), 1898–1963—Childhood and youth. | Authors, English—20th century—Biography.
Classification: LCC PR6023.E926 (ebook) | LCC PR6023.E926 Z839 2019 (print) | DDC 823/.912 [B] —dc23
LC record available at https://lccn.loc.gov/2019009167

Crossway is a publishing ministry of Good News Publishers.

LB		29	28	27	26	25	24	23	22	21	20	19
15	14	13	12	11	10	9	8	7	6	5	4	3	2	1

To
Don King, Nigel Goodwin, and Rebecca Hays,
who have stood alongside me
in the ministry of
the Inklings Fellowship

Contents

Acknowledgments

I had never planned to write this book, but it got ahead of me. On one of those odd days when I decided not to do what I should have been doing, I began to wonder what C. S. Lewis liked to eat. That he liked to eat food, he made abundantly clear. He enjoyed eating and he confessed that he ate more than he should. I decided to look through his letters to see what he said about the meals he enjoyed. As it turns out, he said precious little about the menu. He regularly mentioned eating, but he rarely discussed what he ate. When he first went to live with W. T. Kirkpatrick at Gastons, however, he mentioned that he had good old Irish soda bread.

By the time I had read that far in the letters, however, I realized that the early life of C. S. Lewis had been neglected. He expressed opinions in those letters, before he went off to war, that he might have included in any of his scholarly works. It also became clear that most of the things he liked and disliked had been settled by the time he was seventeen. It became clear to me why Lewis devoted so much of *Surprised by Joy* to his school days and his time with Kirkpatrick. As I read the letters, this book began to take shape in my mind.

I am grateful to my acquisitions editor at Crossway, Samuel James, for his interest in this book—the first of three projected volumes on the life of C. S. Lewis—and the support that he and his colleagues at Crossway have offered. Claire Cook and Josh Dennis in the creative department of Crossway have done a beautiful job

11

of creating the cover and the cover design of the book, which would have been of paramount importance to seventeen-year-old Jack Lewis. Thom Notaro has done an exceptional job of editing the text.

In his biography of Lewis, Alister McGrath made much of the fact that his was the first biography of Lewis that had taken all of Lewis's letters and diaries into account. The kind of research that he and I have undertaken would be quite impossible had not Walter Hooper done the tedious and meticulous work of editing those letters in three volumes and publishing the diary. Scholars and lovers of Lewis can now examine those letters at their leisure in their own studies without facing the massive expense of traveling to the research libraries and special collections that hold those letters. Hooper has done an enormous service to generations that will come after him.

Even with the vast amount of material that Hooper has edited, much remains unpublished at the Marion E. Wade Center of Wheaton College and in the Bodleian Library of the University of Oxford. I am indebted to the Wade Center and its staff for their great kindness, generosity of spirit, encouragement, and helpfulness during several trips for extended periods of research into the primary documents related to Lewis during his early years. Marjorie Lamp Mead has always been gracious to me and all those who come to use the resources of the Wade. Laura Schmidt and Elaine Hooker went out of their way to find things I did not know existed. David and Crystal Downing arrived at the Wade Center as the new codirectors while I was finishing my research, and they extended me the warmest of possible welcomes. I am delighted that they will be leading this important research library into the future.

I am also grateful to Oliver House, superintendent of the special collections reading rooms in the Weston Library of the Bodleian Library of Oxford, for enabling my research. Judith Priestman, curator of English literary manuscripts, and her staff helped me make maximum use of my limited time in Oxford so that I could focus on those Lewis papers not duplicated elsewhere. I also appreciate the help and courtesy given me by Rachel Churchill of the C.S. Lewis Company in securing permission to quote Lewis.

I have had the pleasure of dialogue with many colleagues over the years with whom I have shared an interest in Lewis. Insights often come in undocumented conversations long forgotten. I am particularly indebted to Don King, Colin Duriez, Rebecca Hays, Walter Hooper, William O'Flaherty, Dennis Beets, Barry Anderson, Malissa and Russ Kilpatrick, Stan Shelley, Nigel Goodwin, Joseph Pearce, and James Como. I could not undertake projects of this sort without the support of Union University, particularly our president, Samuel W. ("Dub") Oliver; the provost, John Netland; and the dean of the school of theology and missions, Ray Van Neste. The faculty awarded me a Pew Research Grant, which helped to cover the expenses of my research, for which I am most grateful. My wife, Mary Anne Poe, has long supported my interest in Lewis and has been a great encouragement in the writing of this book. Finally, to the many students who have taken my class on C. S. Lewis, and to those many participants in the retreats sponsored by the Inklings Fellowship over the past eighteen years, I am grateful for your support and interest in the life and work of C. S. Lewis.

I

Young Jack Lewis at Wynyard School

1908–1910

Between the death of his mother in 1908 and his war service in 1918, young Jack Lewis made the transition from childhood to adolescence to young manhood. He spent this critical period of development, like so many other boys of his social class in England and Ireland, in a variety of institutional settings. During his school days, the boy who would grow to become C. S. Lewis formed his most important tastes in music, art, literature, companionship, religion, sports, and almost every other aspect of life. While his ideas and critical thought about what he liked and disliked would change, his basic preferences came together during this period and formed the foundation out of which his later life grew. The things he liked at fourteen were the things that engaged his intellect and imagination thirty, forty, and fifty years later. The things that sparked his imagination when he was an arrogant, conceited boy were the same things that influenced and motivated his change of character in the context of his conversion to Christianity, when his teenage years were half a lifetime behind him.

The transition from childhood to adolescence to young adulthood also came with critical spiritual issues. All people face the spiritual issues of growing up, but each person must deal with those issues himself or herself. People rarely recognize that they are traveling from one phase of life to another in the midst of the journey, but looking back we can see the landmarks fairly clearly. So it was for Jack Lewis. He lost something from his early childhood when he grew from childhood to boyhood. He suspected that it was the same for all boys for whom those years represent the "dark ages" of life between the two glorious ages of early childhood and adolescence. In boyhood, Lewis thought, everything grows "greedy, cruel, noisy, and prosaic, in which the imagination has slept and the most un-ideal senses and ambitions have been restlessly, even maniacally, awake."[1] Lewis thought of his boyhood as a desert characterized by greed, cruelty, noise, and the mundane—a foreign land that had intruded into the flow of his life as an interruption that did not really belong.[2]

As he moved into his adolescence, however, Lewis recovered some important things from his earlier childhood that his later boyhood had forgotten. He recovered the sense of wonder that comes from an experience of the transcendent. For Lewis, this experience was the most important thing of life itself, and understanding the nature and source of it would eventually lead him to faith in the God of the Bible. His conversion would come long after his adolescent years had ended; but without the path he chose while dealing with the spiritual issues raised in adolescence, Lewis might not have come to faith. At least, he would not have traveled the same path to faith.

The period of adolescence in the United States roughly corresponds to the period from the seventh grade through the twelfth grade or the years of middle school and high school. It begins around the time of the onset of puberty, when the body begins to do such strange things, and it comes to a close as young people mature enough to assume the responsibilities of adulthood. For some people, the end of adolescence comes when they take their first full-time job. College life can actually prolong adolescence for many people who use college to keep responsibility at bay. Whether college would have prolonged the adolescent period for C. S. Lewis remains a speculative question because he did not have that option. At the age when most young men of his social class would have been settling into their first full year of college, Lewis was settling into the trenches on the Western Front as an eighteen-year-old junior officer in the British Army.

Of Names and Monikers

Christened Clive Staples Lewis, the little boy announced at the age of four that he was Jacksie, soon shortened to Jacks, and finally reduced to Jack.[3] For the rest of his life he was known to his friends as Jack. C. S. Lewis had a variety of nicknames as a teenaged boy. His friend Arthur Greeves called him Chubs because he was a bit chubby.[4] His father, Albert, and his brother, Warren ("Warnie"), began calling him "It" in their correspondence about the time Jack went to Malvern College. By 1910, Albert had added new pet names for his sons as he started calling Jacks "Klicks" and Warnie "Badge."[5] Once Warnie entered the army during the Great War, Jack began calling him "the Colonel." In childhood, Warnie had also been called Bruser (or Bruiser).[6] Nicknames seem to have come with being a member of the Lewis family. In their letters, Flora Lewis called her husband her "dear old Bear" or Lal, while Flora was Doli to Albert Lewis. Albert's father called him Al, while other close friends and relatives called him Ally or Allie.

Clive Staples Lewis's first name was actually a last name, the name of one of the great heroes of Victorian England, for Robert Clive of India had beaten the French and laid the foundations for the absorption of India into the British Empire. The nineteenth century saw many young middle-class boys named Clive in the lesser public schools (what Americans would regard as private schools). When Jack was a child, his extended family on his mother's side appear always to have called him Clive.[7] Many years later, however, in a letter to Warnie Lewis after Jack died, their cousin Ruth Hamilton Parker referred to him as Jacks.[8] He was also called Clive by his teacher W. T. Kirkpatrick, who prepared him for his entrance examinations to Oxford.[9] George Watson, a former pupil of Lewis and colleague at Cambridge, reminds us that the faculty chairman of the appointments committee at Cambridge, where Lewis had an exalted position as holder of a professorial chair, addressed Lewis as Clive.[10] As an adult, on formal occasions he only used his initials, so he is known to the world as C. S. Lewis. He appears to have first used this formal signature in his first letter to his friend Arthur Greeves from Great Bookham in September 1914.[11] Normally he signed his letters to Greeves from "Jack," but when he was in a particularly pompous mood, he would sign "C. S. Lewis." As an adult, however, he almost always signed his letters "C. S. Lewis" unless writing to close family and intimate friends. A notable exception can be found in his letters to Sister Penelope. He often signed these letters "Clive Lewis" or "Clive S. Lewis," instead of "Jack" or "C. S. Lewis."[12]

The middle name also had an important bearing on the boy who would grow up to be C. S. Lewis. Staples was a family name on his mother's side, a name with a pedigree. Flora Lewis was a Hamilton, and the Hamiltons produced a long line of clergymen in the established church, of which her father was one. Her grandfather, the Right Reverend Hugh Hamilton, had been a bishop. The bishop's wife was a Staples. It was an important marriage in a society where rank mattered, for Elizabeth Staples was the daughter of a member of Parliament. More important for family relations, Elizabeth's sister married the second Marquess of Ormonde! When Flora Lewis named her firstborn child, she had given him names from her family as well. Warren was the maiden name of her mother, Mary Warren Hamilton, whose father was Sir John Borlase Warren. Like his younger brother, Warnie did not have a first name as such; he had three last names.

Thus, we see that Albert Lewis married into a family of the lesser gentry of the Protestant Ascendency of Ireland, and the names of his sons bore witness to those important family relationships, which conveyed a status that his success in the law alone could never provide. These are the kinds of people about which Jane Austen had written almost a century earlier. While English society might have moved on somewhat over the decades, Irish society was still trying to catch up to their English cousins. Knights and baronets have the dignity of a title—and in the case of a baronet, a hereditary title—but they do not have the rank of a peer. They remain commoners, but rather grand commoners. Mary Warren Hamilton had a sister, Charlotte Warren Heard, whose daughter Mary married Sir William Ewart, the second baronet.[13]

Why Wynyard School?

With great expectations for continued prosperity of the family and the greatest possible opportunities for their children, families of the social standing of the Albert Lewis family would be expected to send their sons to England for the kind of education that would aid their advancement in society. Flora appears to have played a major role in the decision to send the boys to England for their education. Albert had suggested a school in Armagh, but Flora countered that Armagh would be no better than Belfast "as regards accent." For those in the Protestant Ascendency of Ireland, overcoming the Irish accent and learning to affect an English accent was a primary aspect of a middle-class education. After Flora died, the emotional and sentimental Albert would have no choice about sending the boys to England. Their fate was sealed by Flora's death. Albert could disagree with a living Flora, but a deceased Flora carried the argument.[14] She would continue to play the dominant role in any decisions about where the boys would attend school and in Albert's resistance to their pleas for rescue from Wynyard. Albert regularly appealed to his sons for forgiveness when he seemed harsh or difficult, and the tone generally followed the same pattern as that he expressed to Warnie in January 1910: "But if ever I appear harsh to you dear Badge, remember that I have come through great trouble and affliction, and though I may err in my methods, my one object in living is to start my sons in life as educated Christian gentlemen—worthy sons of their mother." The appeals to Flora's memory were endless.[15]

Boys of good background attended a preparatory school in preparation for admission to a good public school. An English preparatory school corresponded roughly to an American elementary school, and a public school corresponded roughly to American middle school and high school. In both cases, pupils normally boarded at the schools and returned home only during holidays. William T. Kirkpatrick began advising Albert Lewis on preparatory schools in October 1904. Kirkpatrick had been headmaster of Lurgan, the Irish public school that Albert had attended. Kirkpatrick began corresponding with Albert in 1901 after having seen him the previous summer. Kirkpatrick's letters overflow with sage proverbs, such as "A man who forgets his promise betrays a lamentable weakness of character," and "An old horse needs a kick to remind him to go on." Just as his acquaintance with Jack Lewis would coincide with the commencement of the Great War, Kirkpatrick's first letter to Albert coincided with the Boer War. In the Boer War, as in the Great War, Kirkpatrick took the view that the government and those charged with prosecuting the war had no idea what they were doing. He punctuated his first letter with the word "hopeless." He regarded the Boers as fanatical in their political and religious beliefs and thought that the only way they would stop fighting would be if they were all exterminated. Kirkpatrick believed that the war with the Boers would never end as long as the Boers had twenty men left to wreck a railway. The letter suggests the kind of clever remark about the ignorance of government ministers that Jack Lewis would find so entertaining in his mid-adolescence. It also demonstrates that W. T. Kirkpatrick could be wrong.[16]

From Kirkpatrick's perspective, there were no good schools. He was particularly dismissive of Campbell College in Belfast, near the Lewis home. Kirkpatrick claimed to have taught a former Campbell pupil more in three months than the boy had learned at Campbell in a year. Kirkpatrick gave Albert a catalog of his major teaching achievements, bordering on the miraculous, that he had wrought in his young scholars. On the surface, it sounds like bragging, but given the miracles Kirkpatrick would achieve with Warren, it was more a commentary on the status of public schools than on Kirkpatrick as a miracle worker. This view of Campbell College that Kirkpatrick embedded deeply into Albert's mind, however, suggests one reason why Albert did not let Jack stay at Campbell several years later.

As far as what Albert might do about securing the best preparatory school placement for his boys, Kirkpatrick recommended that he write to Gabbitas Thring & Company, educational agents, Piccadilly, London. The agency would find the best school for the boys. Kirkpatrick agreed with Albert that an Irish school would not do if the boys were to have any future at all. He added the telling comment, however, that from his writing, no one could tell that Albert, the product of an Irish school, was not a public school boy.[17] The faint praise would have reminded Albert that he had not arrived, but that his sons might. In later years, the Lewis boys took delight in mocking their father's Irish accent behind his back.

In response to Kirkpatrick's advice, Albert reasoned that if Warren got nothing from his education but "good form" and football, he would at least "learn the language" that marked a man as a gentleman.[18] Gabbitas Thring & Company made Albert aware of Wynyard School in Watford under the headmastership of Robert Capron, who wrote to Albert on December 12, 1904, to sweeten the deal by suggesting that a promising pupil who intended to work toward an entrance scholarship to a first-class public school could expect a reduction in fees. Capron added that his boys had enjoyed great success in winning scholarships.[19]

In choosing a school, Albert had other issues than the quality of education. He hoped to find a school whose fees amounted to no more than seventy pounds a year. Furthermore, he wanted a school noted for its strong discipline, owing to Warnie's "self willed and obstinate" nature.[20] Kirkpatrick considered the four recommendations of Gabbitas Thring & Company that fit the profile Albert had established. He rejected the first school because of misprints in their prospectus. He rejected the second school because it was too cheap. He rejected the third school because it was not so easy to get to from Ireland, while accepting the fourth school, Rhyl, because it was easy to reach from Ireland. In the end, Albert ignored all Kirkpatrick's advice and sent Warnie to Wynyard.[21]

Flora's Influence on Young Jacks

Before Warnie was sent off to his English school, the brothers lived a semi-idyllic existence at their home in the Holywood Hills of the Belfast suburbs with their parents and the servants. The end of Jacks's childhood and entry into adolescence might have been different had his mother lived, but Flora Lewis died when her second son was only nine years old. She was a remarkable woman in many ways. She attended Queen's College in Belfast and took degrees in logic and mathematics during the late Victorian era, when few women held college degrees. She even tried her hand at writing stories and magazine articles. While her husband was of a passionate and vacillating nature, Flora tended to have a steady and practical temper. Both she and Albert loved to read, but neither of them read to their children. This task was left to the nursemaid, Lizzie Endicott.

In the summers, Flora took her two boys to Castlerock, a seaside resort not far from Belfast in County Derry. During their visit to the sea in 1904, Flora wrote to Albert that Jacks was delighted with the water and that he looked so funny skipping around in his "bathing drawers." A little later, however, she wrote that Jacksie did not care so much for the water. Perhaps his perfidious attitude arose because, as often happens with little boys, something was wrong with him all summer—first his ear, then his skin, then his foot.[22] Illness and health complaints dogged Jacks throughout his childhood. During the holiday to Castlerock in 1906, Jacks suffered from "one of his nasty fever attacks."[23] Warnie caught enough shrimp in a net for them to boil for their tea, and he also began to swim without his water wings. Jacks, on the other hand, did not do well in the water, and Flora concluded that swimming did not suit him.[24]

Though Jacks was normally a well-tempered little boy, his older brother could throw him out of temper with his perpetual teasing. Flora complained in a letter to Albert that Warnie could be tiresome without actually being bad.[25] During the 1906 holiday at Castlerock, Flora took the boys to visit Dunluce Castle for the first time. It was not important to Jacks at the time other than as somewhere to run around as little boys will, but in the years to come it would become a place shrouded in the stuff of faerie.[26] These extended visits to the sea instilled in C. S. Lewis a lifelong love of the sea and swimming, even if it began with a few false starts, but also of trains, the standard means of transportation from Belfast to Castlerock.

Instead of the annual summer holiday at Castlerock, Flora took her boys on a trip to Dieppe, a French seaside resort, in August 1907. No one was seasick from the voyage, and Jacks loved the boat trip across the Irish Sea on their way to London for the first stop of the journey. Jacks fell in love with Trafalgar Square and all the green squares of London, which he thought was "a lovely place." Flora took the boys to the zoo in Regent's Park, where they saw all manner of animals, but Jacks was most delighted by the mice.[27] In keeping with tradition, he was again sick during the vacation. They stayed at an English hotel in France. Flora was concerned about the safety of the beach at high tide, and Warnie wrote to his father that the beach was not very nice when the tide was in. Despite his prejudice against France and the French, Jacks was delighted with the village, which Warnie described as "the real old sort."[28] On the return trip from France, Flora took the boys back to London. Warnie wanted to see the British Museum, and Jacks wanted to visit the Tower of London.[29] To illustrate how precocious his brother was at this age, Warnie Lewis recalled what Jacks had to say to his father upon their return. He told his father that he was prejudiced against the French. When Albert asked him why, Jacks replied, "If I knew why, it would not be a prejudice."[30]

During this period, Albert's father, Richard Lewis, lived with the family at their recently completed Leeborough house, also known as Little Lea. The declining health of Richard added an extra burden to the operation of the household in 1907.[31] The burden would soon increase. On Friday, February 7, 1908, Flora consulted with a doctor about a complaint that would be diagnosed as cancer. Flora's mother insisted that she surrender herself to the care of a certain general practitioner, but Flora tried to explain to her mother that she would follow the care of the best surgeon in Belfast. A second consultation followed on February 11. On February 12, the first nurse arrived. The operation came immediately afterward on February 15 and lasted for two hours.[32] With Flora's cancer, Albert could not look after his father as well. Richard Lewis left Little Lea on February 19, 1908, after a stay of almost eleven months.[33] He suffered a stroke on March 24, 1908, and died on April 2.[34]

During the spring and early summer, Jacks found himself all alone in the big house with the long corridors filled with books. The mother who had always been there to attend him now needed nursing care around the clock. From the stuff of his childhood, it would not have been difficult for C. S. Lewis to create the figure of Digory in *The Magician's Nephew*, except that Jacks had no playmate like Polly Plummer. Digory and Polly had a box room at the end of the attic where they could play, just like the little end room at Little Lea, where Jacks and Warnie played. Polly wrote stories, just like Jacks and Warnie. Digory had a mother who was being looked after because she was going to die, just like Jacks. Polly first encountered Digory when he was crying in the garden, but we have no written account of Jacks Lewis crying over the anticipated death of his mother. We can only imagine that C. S. Lewis knew firsthand what he was writing about.

Warnie, Albert, and Jacks Lewis, ca. 1908. Used by permission of the Marion E. Wade Center, Wheaton College, Wheaton, IL.

Warnie and his father exchanged deeply emotional letters almost daily until the end of June, when Albert ended the exchanges by saying he would not write again until he had news. By the end of July, Warnie was back home in Belfast waiting with his family for Flora's death.[35] As the inevitable day approached, Flora wanted to give each of her sons a Bible. Albert dared not leave her side to purchase the Bibles, so his brother Joe accepted the commission and sent the Bibles to Little Lea on August 18.[36] Albert noted in his notebook that Flora died "at 6.30 on the morning of 23rd August, my birthday." Warnie noted that the quotation for the day from Flora's Shakespearean calendar was a quote from *King Lear*: "Men must endure their going hence, even as their coming hither; Ripeness is all."[37] Fifty-five years later, Warnie would have part of this quotation placed on the gravestone of his little brother when C. S. Lewis died in 1963: "Men must endure their going hence." Ten years after that, the name of Warren Hamilton Lewis would be added to the stone when Warnie died, and the two brothers now share a common grave.

Flora's death did not end Albert's misery in his *annus horribilis*, for less than two weeks later, on September 3, his brother Joe died as well.[38] All in all, Jacks and his brother Warnie might have enjoyed a happy, secure home life during their childhood, but all of that changed when Flora died.

Life after Flora

Lady Mary Ewart took an active interest in the lives of Jack and Warnie after the death of Flora Lewis, who was Lady Ewart's first cousin. As a result, the boys learned how to behave in august company. Through their Ewart cousins, the Lewis boys did not learn how the other half lived; they learned how the other .01 percent lived. Lady Ewart's daughter Hope offered to accompany Jacks on his trip home for the Easter holidays in 1910. In a note to Hope thanking her for the kind offer, Albert mentioned that he had dined with her parents the previous Saturday night at Glenmachan, their substantial house near Little Lea. He also thanked her for taking Jacks to see a production of *Peter Pan*.[39] Hope also wrote to Warnie from Bad Nauheim in Germany, where she and her sister Kelsie had spent a month, with the news that she had seen six flying machines in a fabulous competition. With his love of ships and locomotives, the news of flying machines would have thrilled Warnie and filled him with a degree of jealousy.[40] Over the following years, the kindness was sometimes appreciated and sometimes tolerated by the boys, but their mother was dead and nothing could change the fact or make up for it.

The death of someone who is loved inevitably raises questions of a spiritual nature even if we do not dwell upon them. The death of a mother raises the question known to philosophers and theologians as theodicy, or the problem of suffering. It might be stated simply as "If there is a good, loving, all-powerful God, then why did my mother die?" Lewis would wrestle with this question in one way or another until the time of his own death. It is a good question, versions of which have been asked by almost everyone who has lived. For some people, it has been the guiding question of life, including the Buddha and Charles Darwin. The question raises doubt about the goodness of God, but it is an odd question. It is odd because one cannot question the goodness of God unless the category of goodness is already present, and where does the idea of goodness come from? Though many people wonder these things, not many people try to find the answers. The questions of C. S. Lewis that began to form in his mind during childhood and adolescence would compel him toward answers that resulted in his conversion to faith in Jesus Christ many years later. First, however, he had to make the journey.

School as a Concentration Camp

In September 1908, without benefit of trial by a jury of his peers, contrary to *Magna Carta*, and in the absence of habeas corpus, young Jacks Lewis found himself interred in a concentration camp known as Wynyard School for the crime of surviving the death of his mother.[41] Deprived of his liberty, he also found himself letting go of the *s* at the end of his nickname, which he omitted when he signed his first letter home to his father. The young boy alternated between Jack and Jacks in his correspondence at Wynyard School, but the final *s* would not completely disappear until he later went to Cherbourg School in Malvern in 1911. In a notable exception, Lewis revived Jacks in his last letter home from Malvern College on July 13, 1914.[42]

Jack and Warnie Lewis in the doorway of their home, ca. 1910. Used by permission of the Marion E. Wade Center, Wheaton College, Wheaton, IL.

Wynyard was a very good concentration camp, complete with severe beatings of the pupils and other forms of cruelty, but it was not a very good school. The enrollment had begun to decline in the aftermath of high court proceeding against Robert Capron, the headmaster of the school, following the particularly brutal beating of a child in 1896. Jack and Warnie Lewis failed in their attempts to convince their father that he should pardon them or at least transfer them to a minimum security prison. Warnie's sentence ended when he left for Malvern College in July 1909. In 1930, as Warnie prepared to return to his military post after leave, he wrote that the end-of-leave feeling may not be pleasant, but it was "but a pale ghost of the Wynyard feeling."[43] Upon leaving the family home at Little Lea for the last time after his father's death, Warnie wrote in his diary that "since the days of going back to Wynyard, I cannot remember feeling so depressed."[44] The brothers carried the misery of Wynyard with them all their lives. When Jack began keeping a diary on April 1, 1922, his first entry involved a local school show he attended that enacted a scene from *Nicholas Nickleby*, which succeeded in calling up the "Wynyard terrors."[45] Though Warnie left Wynyard in 1909, Jack could not leave until the school finally was forced to close in July 1910 because of the continuing decline in enrollment.[46]

The Reverend Robert Capron, whom his students called Oldie behind his back, established Wynyard School in 1881 at the town of Watford in Hertfordshire, about seventeen miles northwest of central London. For Jack's first journey to Wynyard, he and Warnie traveled on their own to and from school. This trip involved taking a ferry across the Irish Sea to Fleetwood in Lancashire, then taking a train from the sea to London, where they transferred at Euston Station to a train that would take them to Watford. Jack Lewis was nine years old when he first made the trip. One of the points of this book is to show that the habits and preferences of a lifetime often form during adolescence or before, and this was certainly the case with C. S. Lewis. Jack and Warnie developed a love of smoking at an early age. By the time they were making their unescorted trips between Belfast and school in England, they indulged themselves in one long wallow in tobacco. Warnie declared that they did not smoke to appear sophisticated and grown-up. He insisted that they smoked only because they liked it, but he failed to explain how and why they took up smoking in the first place. On later trips, the boys traveled by way of Liverpool, instead of Fleetwood, where they enjoyed stopping over at the Lime Street Hotel in order to eat lunch and smoke their hearts out.[47]

The idea of two children making such a trip is unimaginable in the twenty-first century, but that was a different time, when the vast resources of the British Empire existed seemingly for no other purpose than to ensure a safe passage for Jack and Warnie Lewis. As it turned out, Warnie had a terrible bout of seasickness, the likes of which would not be seen again until Eustace joined *The Voyage of the Dawn Treader*. Young Jacks described the journey in a letter to his father about the trip and his arrival in Watford, where he first met Mr. Capron, whom he thought "rather eccentric."[48] Two years earlier, in 1906, a brain specialist had already diagnosed Capron as insane.[49]

Danger Signs at Wynyard

Warnie, as the older brother, had already been at Wynyard for three years when Flora died. She had taken him there when he first enrolled in May 1905. Twenty years after his experience at Wynyard, Warnie wrote that a boy's letters home rarely give a true picture of their school experience: "School boys [*sic*] letters are not to be trusted—fear of their letters being overlooked, fear of them being opened, fear of half measures of redress on their parents part if they do complain, all conspire to make them untruthful, except in extreme unhappiness."[50] The exception to the unreliability of Warnie's letters would be the constant references to the coming holidays and how much he looked forward to going home. He almost always mentioned how many days were left before his vacation would begin and he could come home.

The timing of Flora's cancer coincided with a growing awareness on her part that things might not be well with Mr. Capron at Wynyard. Capron had told Warnie that his mother said he was a failure and that he was lazy. Upon hearing this devastating message, the little boy wrote to his mother. We do not have Warnie's letter, but Warnie preserved his mother's reply, even though she advised in a postscript to burn her letter because it might cause mischief with Capron.[51]

Though the Irish Ascendency aspired to social acceptance by the English establishment, the Irish tended to be looked down upon as a lower form of life by the English. Warnie's abuse by Capron included his first experience of the English prejudice against the Irish. In a letter to his mother after she had assured him that his father and she did not regard him as a failure in spite of Mr. Capron's assertions, Warnie began to tell her of other things Capron said, especially about his Irishness:

> For instance this is what he said this morning when I missed a question. "please, don't want any of your Irish wit". Now no sensible person objects to having his country laughed at IN FUN out of school. But when he says things like that to me in school when I cannot say anything to him, and puts down all my mistakes to my being "an Irishman" it is rather annoying.[52]

At this point, Flora no longer had the strength to protect her son, and it fell to Albert to sort matters.

During June 1908, Warnie finally summoned the courage to write to his father a long letter enumerating Capron's offenses, but it came at the worst possible time for Albert to deal with it, as Flora lay dying. Albert replied to Warnie's letter immediately, but the substance of his response dealt with the importance of always telling his father everything that troubled him because soon he would have only his father to tell.[53] Albert's unfortunate letter left Warnie without the assurance that his father would protect him while at the same time giving him his first clear understanding that his mother was going to die.

The anti-Irish bias of his schoolmaster continued to plague Warnie, and Jack would witness the abuse when he arrived at Wynyard. They learned well of the English prejudice through-out their dreary days at Wynyard. Warnie reported to Albert that Capron's son Wyn had hit him across the head for not changing clothes quickly enough after a football game. Capron then assigned Warnie fifty lines of Virgil as punishment for giving cheek to his son and then exclaimed of Warnie's rebelliousness, "Soon we shall have Irish home rule here."[54] Irish home rule had been the great political issue simmering in Parliament for decades, and it had begun to come to a head in the first decade of the twentieth century. In practical terms, it meant a local Irish government dominated by Catholics. This was anathema to the Protestant minority clustered in the north around Belfast. Capron, and many Englishmen like him, could not distinguish between Protestant and Catholic issues, and tended to regard all the Irish as troublemakers who needed to be kept in their place.

Warnie's stream of complaints finally had its impact on Albert, who must have been nearly crippled with grief at this point. He asked Flora's sister-in-law Annie Hamilton to go to Watford and investigate matters at Wynyard. She appears to have been a formidable lady, and Warnie soon wrote to his father, "Since Aunt Annie's arrival the matter has been greatly cleared up." The boys still wanted to leave Wynyard, but Warnie apologized to his father for adding to his burdens after his aunt explained "the reasins [*sic*] why we could not leave."[55] The reasons were left unstated.

Warnie included Capron's letters to Albert in the "Memoirs of the Lewis Family," which he compiled and edited following Albert's death in 1929, and juxtaposed as they are with the letters of Jacks and Warnie, they show how Albert might have doubted his sons' reports of life at Wynyard. Capron had sent Albert Lewis several notes of sympathy and concern during the last stages of Flora's illness and following her death. He was always diligent to remark how he looked forward not only to having young Warren return soon to Wynyard but also to having him joined by his younger brother "Jacko." How the headmaster got Jacks's name wrong is a wonder, since he had gone to so much trouble to ensure that he would get both boys as paying customers. Because he repeated this name in his letter of December 11, 1908, and in subsequent letters, he may have continued to believe that Jacko was Jacks's name. In Capron's letter of September 9, 1908, following Joe Lewis's death, he urged Albert to "bear up bravely for the sake of the boys" and included a bill for school fees totaling just over forty-seven pounds for the coming term.[56] Capron wrote elegant letters, solicitous for the welfare of Albert and his sons, and showing every concern for Warnie's well-being and how he might be made to improve his many character defects. Jacks's simple response to his father was "it is quite untrue, Warnie is not lazy."[57]

On October 27, Albert wrote a long letter to Capron, much like a legal brief, laying out the facts and the matters in dispute. In his draft of the letter, Albert had informed Capron that he intended to remove his boys from Wynyard at the end of the term, but he struck through this declaration and replaced it with hopes that matters might improve.[58] During the Christmas vacation following Flora's death, Capron wrote a clever letter to Albert recommending that Warnie cut short his vacation and return to school as soon as possible because "prolonged holidays are most baneful" to the boy's progress. Confident that the busy court solicitor could not take the time away from his work, he invited Albert to accompany the boys on their return to Wynyard so that he could see for himself what a fine school he had chosen. Then he added, "I believe that dear Mrs. Lewis had great confidence in my wife and myself, and I would like to prove to you that we merit yours."[59] Jack and Warnie preferred to return to Ireland and enroll in Campbell College even if Albert did not think the boys at Campbell were gentlemen. Warnie observed, "I think English boys are not so honest or gentlemanly as most Irish ones." The boys had had enough of English schools.[60]

Wynyard, however, was not the end of the matter. It was barely the beginning, for Albert's aim was to secure the best public schools for his sons. No sooner had he decided on the preparatory school than he began calculating where to send the boys to public school. By 1906, Albert had sought Kirkpatrick's advice on how best to assure Warnie a good public school in 1910 or 1911. He had narrowed the field to Rugby, Cheltenham, Repton, Shrewsbury, Rossall, Malvern, and Winchester. The truly great schools of Eton and Harrow were far beyond his means, but he wanted Warnie to have a decent education without turning him into "an ignorant prig." Albert was troubled by the enormity of the responsibility of choosing a good school when all he had to go by were the names and when general knowledge told him how bad some English schools could be.[61]

Kirkpatrick responded to Albert's query with his usual dismissal of schools in general. The whole atmosphere of an English public school mitigates against a pupil ever becoming a scholar, though the tone would help a boy become a snob, which had its advantages in English society. Compared with the "coarseness, vulgarity, and disregard for truth" of an Irish school like Campbell, however, an English school was worth the expense. Kirkpatrick regarded Winchester as more difficult than Eton, Rugby as very good, Shrewsbury as a school where one could do worse, and Malvern as a school that would do. Rossall would not do, and the other schools were unknown to him, which is to say, would not do. Though Kirkpatrick understated the case by saying that one could do worse than Shrewsbury, he spent most of his assessment extolling the virtues of Shrewsbury. In the end, Albert wrote to Rugby, Cheltenham, Malvern, and Shrewsbury to inquire if Warnie might have a place in the summer term of 1909 or early 1910.[62]

Rugby regretted that it could not offer Warnie a place. Malvern, on the other hand, offered him a place in 1909 or 1910.[63] In December 1907, Kirkpatrick wrote to Albert to inquire how Warnie was doing at his preparatory school and to ask if he was going to Shrewsbury, Kirkpatrick's obvious choice.[64] Kirkpatrick may have taken it upon himself to write to the headmaster of Shrewsbury, for the latter wrote to Albert several times in an effort to get a final word on his intentions of enrolling Warnie. Albert appears not to have replied to these letters.[65] Likewise, the bursar at Cheltenham wrote to know Albert's intentions.[66] Remarkably, Albert appears to have taken the recommendation of Malvern College from Robert Capron over Kirkpatrick's recommendation of Shrewsbury. Capron gave as his reasoning that the head at Malvern had been at Eton and that many of Capron's former pupils had gone to Malvern.[67] By the end of May 1908, the decision was finally made, and Capron began advising Albert on the house at Malvern in which Warnie should be placed.[68] Though Warnie loved his time at Malvern, he was disparaging of Capron's letter of advice in which he mentioned Edward Clifford Bullock as a head of house who would do a fine job. Warnie's memoirs include a note to Capron's letter in which Warnie commented that Bullock had done exceedingly well at Malvern but had only taken a third (what in the South was once known as a gentleman's C) at Oxford, suggesting that the best students at Malvern were ill-equipped for Oxford.[69]

Robert Capron's wife, Ellen, died on March 1, 1909. The Lewis boys liked her and felt sorry for her, as her life was not much different from the bleak life of the boys at Wynyard School. Her death depressed Warnie, for it reminded him of the death of his mother.[70]

As matters deteriorated at Wynyard and more parents withdrew their sons from Capron's care, the headmaster grew to regret his barrage of letters to Albert in which he had criticized Warnie and held him up as a hopeless case. For Capron, Warnie gone meant one less boy paying fees. Capron wrote to Albert during the Easter break of 1909 to say that he took back everything he had said about Warnie's behavior in the past. The boy was now everything that Capron could hope for, and he would be happy for Warnie to stay on at Wynyard rather than go to a public school. With the few boys at the school departing regularly, Capron needed all the boys he could keep to stay in business.[71] Alas, Capron's change of mind came too late. Albert already had Malvern on his mind.

Warnie left Wynyard for the last time on July 28, 1909, but poor Jacks would have to return on his own for the fall term.[72]

Love of Animals

Young Jacks Lewis would carry with him into adolescence a love of animals. At Little Lea, the boys had a canary named Peter and an Irish terrier named Tim.[73] In addition to these animals, in fact, Jacks had populated an entire world of imagination with the inhabitants of Animal Land. Before going off to Wynyard, Jacks had written and illustrated a collection of stories about Animal Land and its major citizens. He had shared with his older brother Warnie the game of making up stories about the imaginary world, and after Warnie went away to Wynyard in 1905, Jacks had written to his brother about developments in their imaginary world.[74]

His love of animals manifested itself as an early ethical dilemma at Wynyard when Jack began the study of entomology. In correspondence with his father, the question arose as to whether Jack would like a microscope for Christmas in order to advance his study of insects. On reflection, Jack thought he would rather have something else. It seemed to him that in order to study an insect under a microscope, it was first necessary to kill the insect. By the age of eleven, Jack thought the extermination of harmless insects purely for the "gratification of one's own whimsical tastes" was not a very nice thing to do.[75] By his criticism of the "whimsical tastes" of others, he indicated the tastes that his own independent mind had begun to mark out for him. In later years, this young judgment would lead Lewis to oppose vivisection, or experimentation on animals. Though his thought would grow in sophistication, Jack Lewis adopted the fundamental value of animals as an aspect of his character, and this valuing would find its way into his fiction.

In *That Hideous Strength*, C. S. Lewis painted a picture of value-free scientific experimentation in which caged animals stand alongside the revitalization of the decapitated human head of a homicidal maniac. In the end, the animals gain their freedom at the expense of their captors. A few years later, Lewis wrote *The Lion, the Witch and the Wardrobe*, in which a group of children travel magically to the land of Narnia, Animal Land grown up. Narnia is a world of animals where humans are the intruders and where one of the greatest expressions of cruelty occurs when humans treat animals as mere dumb beasts.

In addition to his fictional treatment of animal experimentation, C. S. Lewis wrote an essay "Vivisection" for the New England Anti-Vivisection Society in 1947.[76] In this essay, he departed both from emotional appeals that pity the suffering of animals and from emotional appeals that stress the suffering of humans. Instead, he explored the nature of suffering and the question of whether pain is an evil.[77] In the brief essay, Lewis moved from the question of right and wrong from a Christian perspective to a perspective free of values in which only a utilitarian naturalistic view prevails, with humans as fair game for experimentation as well as animals. The essay on vivisection repeats much of what Lewis wrote in a chapter titled "Animal Pain" in *The Problem of Pain* in 1940. This chapter explored a Christian view of animal pain in relation to Christian eschatology.[78] The chapter, however, came before he wrote *The Abolition of Man*, in which he warned of the danger of valueless science in a post-Christian world. Remarkably, the boy of eleven followed the same line as the man of forty-nine, for young Jack's reasoning had gone immediately to the insect's experience of pain.

The Literary Life of Boyhood

In the face of all the misery of life at Wynyard, Jacks and Warnie, together with a boy named Field, decided to start a book club.[79] This forerunner of the Inklings might look like a clique or "inner ring," but Lewis would later make an important distinction between a group like his boyhood book club or the Inklings, on the one hand, and a true inner ring, on the other. The self-selecting group comes together because of something they all like, and the secrecy is accidental, the exclusiveness an innocent by-product of shared interest. Lewis said of this kind of group, of which his then current involvement in the Inklings and his boyhood book club were examples, "This is friendship."[80]

As it turned out, Jacks's book club was more of a cheap magazine club. Warnie's description of it involved each boy subscribing to a different magazine that all the boys could share. Their friend Field would subscribe to *The Captain*. Peckover would get the *Royal*. Gerald Mears would take the *B.O.P.*, Jeyes would get the *London Magazine*, and Randolph Philip Bowser would subscribe to *The Wide World*. That left Warnie to take *Pearson's* and Jacks to take *The Strand*.[81]

A book club seemed a natural basis for association with other boys for Jacks Lewis, even at ten years of age. Books formed the environment in which he had spent his years at home in Belfast. The letters and diaries of Lewis and the diaries of his brother, Warren, flow with continual references to how much emotional and intellectual distance lay between their father and them, but books formed a bond across the generation gap in spite of the conflicts. Jacks regularly wrote to his father about what he was reading and what he thought about what he was reading. In 1910, at the end of the last term he would spend at Wynyard, Jack wrote casually to his father of this bond when he spoke of them as "Shakespearean students like you and I."[82]

In early adolescence, the most important relationship for a young person remains the relationship between parent and child. The greatest task of early adolescence is the development of a sense of self-confidence and self-respect. Children and teenagers have a great capacity for cruelty to one another, and the comfort and security of caring parents plays an important role in helping a child learn how to navigate the treacherous shoals of life. Deprived of his mother by death and his father by distance, young Jacks carried on a regular correspondence with his father throughout his teens, when he spent most of his year in England at school. There he found himself knocked about and downtrodden on a daily basis by the public school system of his day, in his case a school with a maniac for a head. The system did not encourage the development of a strong sense of confidence and self-respect. Wynyard aimed more at the destruction of its inmates. Jack's struggle with how he felt about himself under the onslaught of ridicule and humiliation would develop into a character of arrogance and pride—a sin that would dog him the rest of his life and about which he would write in *Mere Christianity* and *Surprised by Joy*. Before his conversion, he masked a bruised spirit with an outward veneer of pompous superiority to others.

In this context, the steady correspondence with his father at home created a lifeline, as well as a constant reminder that the term would end and he could go home for the holiday. Regardless of the habits of Albert Lewis that would annoy his young son, home remained the place of security where Jacks found his greatest encouragement and acceptance throughout his youth. Thus, he often wrote about the things he and his father had in common.

Jack's appeal to Shakespeare probably also had something to do with staying in the good graces of his father, who would remain a river of bounty to him until Albert's death. Jack was learning how to manage his father—a skill that would only grow over the next twenty years. His real literary tastes at this time of life went in an entirely different direction from Shakespeare. In *Surprised by Joy*, Lewis recalls of his years at Wynyard with embarrassment, "My reading was now mainly rubbish," like the "twaddling school-stories in *The Captain*."[83] *The Captain* was a boy's magazine published in London between 1899 and 1924. Boys always prevail as the heroes in its stories. P. G. Wodehouse published three serial novels about Ronald Eustace Psmith (with the *P* silent) between 1908 and 1910, when Jack was reading the magazine devotedly. Lewis explained that the attraction of these kinds of stories lies in wish fulfillment for the boy who would never be the hero at anything or the boy who intended to win at everything. While *Peter Rabbit* appeals to a child's imagination, the stories in *The Captain* appeal to a boy's ambition to be seen as a hero, to be admired, to have a following. Such ambitions are fanned and fulfilled vicariously through the stories of boy-heroes who become captains.

Having grown into a literary sophisticate and snob by the time he was seventeen, Jack looked back on his earlier literary ventures at Wynyard with contempt. He would judge some books as "going back to Henty."[84] George Alfred Henty published 122 historical novels for boys of the adventurous, derring-do variety. Most of his novels involved war and heroism that extolled the British Empire or those values that a good imperialist held dear, as when Henty took the side of the Confederacy over the Union in the American Civil War. After an education at Westminster School and Cambridge, Henty volunteered in the medical corps during the Crimean War. After that, he wrote as a special correspondent covering the Austro-Italian War, the British incursion in Abyssinia, the Franco-Prussian War, the Ashanti War, the rebellion in Spain, and the Turco-Serbian War. From this background, he wrote his tales for boys. His novels had such names as *By Sheer Pluck: A Tale of the Ashanti War*; *A Roving Commission, or, Through the Black Insurrection at Hayti*; *Jack Archer: A Tale of the Crimea*; *With Clive in India: The Beginnings of an Empire*; and *The Young Colonists: A Tale of the Zulu and Boer Wars*. At Wynyard, Jacks devoured these adventure stories.

Jacks also developed a taste for stories about the Roman world, such as *Quo Vadis*, *Darkness and Dawn*, *The Gladiators*, and *Ben Hur*. While all of these stories were efforts at "Christian fiction," the faith element of the stories had little impact on Jacks at the time. He read them for the "sandals, temples, togas, slaves, emperors, galleys, amphitheatres" that fired a boy's morbid, erotic imagination.[85]

Albert Lewis, who enjoyed a prosperous life as police court prosecuting solicitor, in addition to a number of other lucrative retainers, indulged Jacks in his love of books. During Jack's early days at Wynyard, his father gave him *The First Men in the Moon* (1901) by H. G. Wells. Whether Jacks had read science fiction before this volume, we do not know. What we do know is that after this volume, C. S. Lewis loved science fiction all his life to the point of trying his own hand at writing it, beginning with his first space adventure, *Out of the Silent Planet.*

In 1955, Lewis addressed the Cambridge University English Club in a lecture titled "On Science Fiction."[86] As the newly minted professor of medieval and Renaissance literature at Cambridge, he might have been expected to speak to this group about his area of specialization, with all the prestige attached to it. Instead, he spoke on science fiction, a genre held in contempt difficult to exceed among the literary critics of the time. He singled out *The First Men in the Moon* as the type of fiction he had read with pleasure since his childhood. He had loved this kind of story since before it even had a name, which he amplified by pointing out that only twenty or so years earlier had the name *science fiction* finally settled on this genre, which had earlier been called *scientifiction,* among other things.[87]

This lecture in Cambridge was not the first time he had reminisced in print about his early encounter with a literary form that would captivate him all his life. In 1947 when Lewis and Dorothy L. Sayers took on the project of issuing a book in honor of Charles Williams, with the proceeds to go to his widow, Lewis contributed a chapter "On Stories," in which he retells a portion of *The First Men in the Moon.*[88] Ten years earlier, Lewis had referred to the science fiction of H. G. Wells in his first science-fiction novel, *Out of the Silent Planet.* When Ransom found himself stranded and alone on Mars, his mind immediately went to Wells's descriptions of aliens as monsters, more like insects or worms than like humans, and as creatures bent on mayhem.[89]

The last interview C. S. Lewis gave was for the new science-fiction magazine *SFHorizons* at his rooms in Magdalene College,

Cambridge, shortly before his death.[90] Instead of the usual question-and-answer format of an interview, Lewis carried on a conversation with Kingsley Amis and Brian Aldiss that was recorded and transcribed. What we have is the only example of how Lewis conversed as one topic led to another in a bright exchange of ideas. The transcription provides a window into what an Inklings evening would have been like. What it reveals is a charm and delight with science fiction that years of critical scholarship of medieval and Renaissance literature did not diminish.

Nonetheless, the stories of Wells had not fed the imagination of Jacks Lewis or provided him with a touchstone for that experience he called Joy. He would renew that experience through the literature he discovered a few years later. Instead, the stories of Wells tended to work against the spiritual impulse with their coarse, strong appeal to something more visceral.[91] The comments about H. G. Wells made by C. S. Lewis in later life tended to highlight the defects in the stories of Wells, often contrasting what the two writers did with science fiction. Lewis went so far as to suggest that his space-travel stories worked to exorcise the ravenous taste of Wells.[92]

In the end, the idea of a book club failed. The great hope that the Lewis brothers had of a group of boys coming together was less than a hope. A counterforce was at work at Wynyard that would educate Jacks about human nature in a way that would remain with him all his life.

What a Fellow Hates

If Jacks Lewis had begun to settle upon the things he would love his whole life, he also began to judge things he would hate his entire life. One aspect of his later life first came to light at Wynyard School by virtue of his first experience of the company of many boys. Jacks and Warnie had not grown up having playmates their own age, which is one reason they were best friends to each other. The boys knew Arthur Greeves, who lived across the street, but

Greeves was three years older than little Jacks at a time of life when a single year marks a line of demarcation that few are willing to cross. The friendship with Greeves, therefore, would not blossom until a few years later. At Wynyard, however, the small group of boys in residence at the school were thrown together to create their own society with its own rituals and social structure. As in *The Lord of the Flies*, the boys of Wynyard had their insiders and outsiders. Warnie and Jacks were outsiders. In a letter to his father, Jacks related the elaborate drama of school life with a description of alliances and betrayals. Jacks noted that a tyrant named Squivy (sometimes spelled Squiffy) had started a secret club that included everyone but Warnie and Jacks.[93] Thus, young Lewis came to know at Wynyard School what he would later describe and call "the inner ring."

Lewis developed a lifelong abhorrence of the kind of cliques that develop in all societies for the control of others and the advancement of the inner ring. The menace of the inner ring formed a major theme in *That Hideous Strength*, but it appears in other mature Lewis works. A year before the publication of *That Hideous Strength*, Lewis delivered an oration titled "The Inner Ring" at King's College, the University of London, in which he declared that his audience had met the phenomenon of the inner ring "in your house at school before the end of the first term."[94] Lewis knew of the inner ring at the hands of Squivy at Wynyard, but over the years, he came to recognize it in almost every society of which he was a part. He was still writing about it when he penned *The Four Loves* at the end of his life. He continued to despise the "self-appointed aristocracy" of those who regarded themselves as the "*élite*" for as long as he lived.[95] The desire to be part of the inner ring provides one of Screwtape's most innocent-looking temptations and produces one of the most diabolic results in *The Screwtape Letters*. In his formative years, however, Lewis tasted the antifriendship dimension of the inner ring. It is a tawdry substitute for friendship, and not a very good imitation. The inner ring exists for exclusion, and Warnie and Jacks certainly felt excluded by the machinations of Squivy.[96] To make the pain of exclusion all the more severe and to elevate it to betrayal, Squivy was the school-chum name given to the Field boy who was to have belonged to the book club that Jack and Warnie tried to start.[97]

We have already noted the strain Warnie experienced in being an Irish boy in an English school. During the Wynyard days, the animosity that Jacks and Warnie felt toward the English became solidified into their own sociodemographic theory of value. Warnie called it the "Northern Theory," and it involved the idea that anyone who lived in the south of England was a bad person, but the farther north one traveled from the south of England, the better the people became. Northern dwellers were superior people to southern dwellers, and this observation explained the island of Britain. On these grounds, Bowser was acceptable because he came from Cumberland in the north.[98] Jacks named Bowser as his "great chum," largely because Capron mistreated him for being from northern England, calling him a "great north country lout."[99] Field, on the other hand, had all of the principal characteristics of the English, in Jacks's opinion: "selfishness, cruelty, pride, and underhand dealing."[100] A day boy named Boivie also merited the approval of Jacks because he was a Swede, therefore a northerner, and Boivie also loathed anything connected with the south of England.[101]

In a brief journal that Jacks attempted while at Wynyard, he elaborated the "Northern Theory" with several observations. People south of Norfolk cannot even appreciate good food. The people get nicer the farther north you travel, but they get nastier the farther south you go. In applying this self-evident truth to the boys in Wynyard, Jacks explained that Bowser was the nicest boy because he came from Cumberland. Jeyes was the second nicest boy because he came from Northampton. Mears was only middling since he came from Chiswick. Squiffy was the nastiest boy at Wynyard because he came from Worthing in Sussex![102]

Jacks's experience of church life during this period also accentuated the divide between the English Protestants and the Irish Protestants. The boys of Wynyard were marched each Sunday to nearby St. John's Church, where Capron's son and assistant often preached. St. John's Church represented the High Church wing of the Church of England. Jacks called it the kind of church "abhorred by respectful Irish Protestants," of which Jacks regarded himself one. Jacks cynically remarked that the church "wanted to be Roman Catholic, but was afraid to say so." His Irish Protestant judgment fell on the church with the declaration "In this abominable place of Romish hypocrites and English liars, the people cross themselves, bow to the Lord's Table (which they have the vanity to call an altar), and pray to the Virgin."[103] Remnants of this anti-Catholic, Ulster background would lead J. R. R. Tolkien in later years to speak of the "Ulsterior motive" of his friend C. S. Lewis.[104]

Jacks's experience at Wynyard also confirmed his conviction that he did not like school games. He made only one reference to school games in his letters home from Wynyard, but the singular reference tells the story: "If I cannot triumph over Squiffy [*sic*] in games and out of school, I will do my level best to triumph over him in work (which I *can* do), and which is perhaps a far better way of getting on."[105] In the struggle for self-confidence, Jacks had decided to work on what he was good at rather than to continue to fail in what he was bad at. He intended to feel good about something, and he realized that academic work was where he could stand above the Squivys of this world. It is most important to note, however, that Jacks judged sports in light of his experience with Squivy. In journal entries from his time at Wynyard, it is obvious that Jacks thought games could be fun. In one exciting game of rounders in which Jacks chose players, his team almost won, except "for a howling catch by Boivie, and another by Mears, and an idiotically risky run by me."[106] As time went by, it was not the games that Jacks hated so much as the treatment from the English boys when his poor playing elicited their ridicule of the Irish boy. Thus Jacks was taught not to like games, which he associated with misery.

Warnie had written to Jacks about the games at Wynyard long before Jacks arrived there. He said that he was not very good at cricket but hoped to improve. He even asked if Jacksie would like for them to play cricket during his vacation and suggested that they could invite Henry and Jack Stokes to join them.[107] The Lewis boys had never played sports as children at home, so they went to Wynyard without any basic knowledge or skill at organized sports. Wynyard did not help them in this regard. Normally, boys would learn to play the games so important at public schools during their years at preparatory school. In the case of Wynyard, the boys played games only once a week at the Hertfordshire County Cricket ground, some two miles from the school, but as enrollment declined at Wynyard, the weekly games were eliminated. Thus, Jack and Warnie received none of the most important preparation for public school for which preparatory schools existed: skill on the playing fields. At Malvern College, Jack and Warnie would take different paths in dealing with this educational deficiency. By the time Jack left Wynyard, he hated sports.[108]

It is important to note that Jacks had chums and acquaintances at Wynyard, but they did not satisfy the longing for friendship. He knew friendship only in its absence. The common experience he had with the other boys at Wynyard involved the survival impulse and the common enemy they shared in Mr. Capron. John Burnett, a day student, became friendly with Jacks, perhaps over shared misery at Wynyard. Jacks stayed with the Burnett family when he became sick at school and needed to convalesce, and John visited Little Lea during the summer of 1909.[109] Jacks wanted to bring his friend Philip Bowser to Little Lea for the Easter vacation in 1910, but the boy's father did not want his young son to make the trip.[110]

Reflecting on the nature of friendship in *Surprised by Joy*, Lewis remarked that friendship had been the chief source of his happiness in life, but that mere acquaintance had meant little to him. He even wondered why anyone would want to know more people than could be real friends. Ironically, at that point in his life, C. S. Lewis had collected an enormous number of acquaintances, but apparently not because he had wanted them.[111] Acquaintances drained him without giving back, but friends enriched him.

Lewis in later life professed an inability to do arithmetic or any of its academic cousins. Mr. Capron, who liked geometry and mathematics, ignored other subjects and punished his charges with brutal canings for mistakes made in math. Students tend to like the subjects taught by good teachers and despise the subjects taught by poor teachers. So it seems to have been with Lewis and Mr. Capron.[112] When Lewis began preparing for his entrance examinations to Oxford in 1917, his tutor, W. T. Kirkpatrick, remarked in a letter to Albert Lewis that young Clive not only had no taste for math but had an aversion to it.[113] Interestingly, Kirkpatrick did not say that Jack had no aptitude for math. Kirkpatrick was not one to spare the feelings of people, so he would not hesitate to mention if Jack could not do the work. He had been quite forthright in his letters to Albert Lewis about Jack's older brother, Warnie. Jack could have done the math if he had wanted to do the math, but he hated the math along with the monster who had first inflicted it upon him. It would not be the first time, nor the last, that a teacher had ruined a subject for a student.

This situation suggests the enormous responsibility that teachers have in the manner of their teaching. J. K. Rowling has portrayed this dynamic at work in Hogwarts School of Wizardry and Witchcraft. Some teachers make students love a subject, while other teachers can ruin the most fascinating subject. One of the funniest examples of this problem appears in the case of the Hogwarts history professor who was such a dull teacher that no one noticed he had died.

How the Lewis brothers came to be enrolled at Wynyard suggests another of Jack's dislikes that matured in his life as a scholar.

Albert Lewis prided himself in his ability to see beneath the surface and to read between the lines. In his exhaustive search for an appropriate English school to educate his Irish sons, it seems remarkable that Albert Lewis finally settled on Wynyard. C. S. Lewis reflected on this choice in his spiritual autobiography, *Surprised by Joy*, when he wrote of his father's method of interpretation:

> The obvious meaning of any fact or document was always suspect: the true and inner meaning, invisible to all eyes except his own, was unconsciously created by the restless fertility of his imagination. While he thought he was interpreting Oldie's prospectus, he was really composing a school-story in his own mind.[114]

In his life as a scholar and critic, Lewis had little patience for imaginative schemes of interpreting literature that amounted to little more than a projection of personal fancy upon the text. The tendency to read into a text what a critic was interested in grew to mammoth proportions in the twentieth century as this creative approach became not only acceptable but normative, to the dismay of Lewis, who fought the trend till his death.

In his early academic career in the 1930s, when he began to establish himself as a major figure in the study of English literature, Lewis wrote a series of articles published in *Essays and Studies* that dealt with one aspect of this tendency. The collection of essays, together with responses by E. M. W. Tillyard, was published in 1939 as *The Personal Heresy: A Controversy*. In this series, Lewis attacked the practice of reading an author's fiction as autobiography or of evaluating a work in terms of the author's moral character. He disliked the practice common in the 1950s of finding the hidden meaning to Tolkien's *Lord of the Rings* or of his own Narnia tales. This approach to interpretation leads to a kind of mischief he recognized early on in his father's self-congratulatory ability to read between the lines to disastrous results for Jack and Warnie at Wynyard.

Wynyard Revisited

Wynyard's town of Watford made an appearance in *The Great Divorce* over thirty years after Lewis left the market town, and the reference does not come as a compliment. In chapter 10, where Lewis describes the case of the wife who may forgive her husband but never forget his failure to conform to her demands, the wife insists upon improving their circumstances, which includes going house hunting in Watford. Watford is the kind of town where a resident of hell would want to live, but not Lewis.

Another dreadful Watford association entered the Narnia stories at the end of *The Last Battle*. In that story, the earlier visitors to Narnia make one last trip to Narnia from our world by means of a railroad disaster. Eustace and Jill, together with Lucy, Edmund, and Peter, joined by Digory and Polly, all enter the bliss of Aslan's country when a railroad train on which Digory, Polly, Lucy, Eustace, and Jill are traveling crashes into the station platform on which Peter and Edmund stand waiting.[115] In 1910, when Lewis was still at Wynyard School, just such a railroad catastrophe occurred when two Watford trains collided, resulting in death and mayhem. The episode was well reported in the national press, and one cannot help but wonder if young Lewis contemplated that he might have been riding on one of those Watford trains or standing on the platform when the wreck occurred.

The eschatological association of a Watford train wreck and the train disaster in *The Last Battle* might be mere coincidence, but a year before he published *The Last Battle*, Lewis published *Surprised by Joy*, in which he wrote of his Watford experience as preparation for death and paradise. He said, "Life at a vile boarding-school is in this way a good preparation for the Christian life, that it teaches one to live by hope."[116] Lewis found that the expectation of the coming vacation gave him the necessary hope to carry on through the misery of each term at Wynyard under the tyranny of an insane schoolmaster. He even referred to the end of term as the "Last Day." In *The Last Battle*, Lewis reprises this idea as Aslan explains to all: "'There *was* a real railway accident,' said Aslan softly. 'Your father and mother and all of you are—as you used to call it in the Shadow-Lands—dead. The term is over: the holidays have begun. The dream is ended: this is the morning.'"[117] As bad as Jacks's experience of Wynyard had been, however, his brother Warnie declared that he had escaped the worst of Capron's brutalities because he amused the headmaster, who made Jacks his pet.[118] For Jacks, however, this indignity may have been the worst brutality of all.

The End of Wynyard

Albert confided to Warnie in February 1910 that Jacks continued to be dissatisfied with Wynyard and that, for some reason, the school continued to decline. He even suggested that he might have to remove Jacks and place him somewhere else.[119] Capron saved Albert the trouble of thinking about removing Jacks when he wrote to Albert on April 27 to acknowledge receipt of a check for Jacks's fees. He then informed Albert regretfully that he must give up his "school work." He had hoped to sell Wynyard School as a going concern but feared that he would have to sell the property merely as a private house. He took the opportunity, however, to urge Albert not to allow Jacks to attend a day school in Ireland.[120] The contrary Albert reacted by enrolling Jacks in a day school in Ireland. Jacks would go to Campbell College near Little Lea.

Most biographies of C. S. Lewis go through his school years as quickly as possible in order to get to the important things, but in *Surprised by Joy*, Lewis devoted the greatest part of the book to his childhood. He seems to have understood that his childhood formed him. At one level, his later conversion seems to be the inevitable consequence of a number of decisions he made in late childhood and adolescence about what he liked and what he did not like. The Wynyard experience was brief, but in these few short years Lewis developed tastes that would last his lifetime and would affect his understanding of matters he never even considered in his youth. The Soviet state did not exist in his youth, but his evaluation of communism derived from his time at school. He once explained to J. B. S. Haldane, the communist scientist known for his Soviet apologetics, that he had a miserable life as a public school student where "mammon was banished," much as, in the Soviet state, the few favors one could hope for came from either servility or force. Such a society had been for him "the most wicked and miserable" he had known, and he thought Soviet communism would be equal.[121] During his time in Malvern and the later three years he spent with W. T. Kirkpatrick, Lewis would complete his basic life preferences. His experience suggests the critical importance of the school years for children and how adults can help them grow through those years, if only they will.

2

Off to Malvern

1910–1914

After leaving the dreadful Wynyard School in July 1910, Jack earned a brief reprieve from a renewed English incarceration when his father allowed him to spend the fall of 1910 at Campbell College near his home in the Protestant suburbs of Belfast. If Jack wrote to his brother Warnie during this period, no letters survive to tell us of his experience.

Campbell College

Jack attended Campbell College for only one term, but rather than live at home, he boarded at the school. The striking feature of this period of Jack's life as he recalled it as a middle-aged man was his dread of solitude. Loneliness was his greatest enemy, and the great weakness of Campbell, despite its more humane character compared with Wynyard, was that it offered him no sense of belonging or community—not even the community of the totalitarian prefect system. Due to illness, he withdrew from Campbell College halfway through his only term there. Living at home, he experienced the closest relations with his father that he had during boyhood. Without the presence and influence of Warnie to get into mischief, he had none of his usual conflict and adversarial relations with his father. Recalling this time with his father at home, Lewis observed, "I remember no other time in my life of such untroubled affection; we were famously snug together."[1]

Campbell College, Belfast

For the most part, Jack's reading habits had not changed significantly from his time at Wynyard. Years later he reflected, "Many of the books that pleased me as a child, please me still; nothing but necessity would make me re-read most of the books I read at [Wynyard] or at Campbell."[2] During this period, however, Jack's literary interests began to develop in one respect beyond Henty, Wells, and Rider Haggard. His love of poetry appears to have emerged at Campbell College, where he read Matthew Arnold's *Sohrab and Rustum*, which wrapped him in "an exquisite, silvery coolness, a delightful quality of distance

and calm, a grave melancholy."³ Arnold's long poem retells a
Persian story in which the warrior Rustum unknowingly kills his
long-lost son in single combat. We do not know how the young
Jack Lewis came to read the poem, though it may have been an
accident owing to the theme of war and adventure that had run
through his recreational reading during the previous few years.
Only years later would Lewis learn to appreciate the poem as
tragedy in the tradition of Homer's *Iliad*, for when he came to
read the *Iliad* with W. T. Kirkpatrick, Homer's epic reminded
him of *Sohrab and Rustum*.⁴

Alan Jacobs has called attention to the significance of the part
played by Lewis Alden, Jack's English teacher at Campbell, in
Jack's sudden infatuation with narrative verse. Jacobs observed,
"Jack became acquainted, perhaps for the first time, with the
power of poetic language, especially the rhythm and propulsion
it can give to a story."⁵ The combination of meter, rhythm, and
rhyme actually added to the story to make it more exciting. For
Lewis, the sound of poetry would always provide the stirring
import of its power, as he wrote about his early enjoyment of
Homer's *Odyssey*: "The music of the thing and the clear, bitter
brightness that lives in almost every formula had become part of
me."⁶ One must imagine Alden reciting dramatically to his class
to gain a glimmer of the theater of the experience for Jack, who
had always loved a good show at the opera house in Belfast. Jack
was learning not merely to read the lines of poetry but also to hear
them ringing in his ears even when reading silently. Remarkably,
Jack's lifelong love affair with poetry had begun with only a few
weeks of class with Alden before his father removed him from
Campbell College.

On November 13, 1910, Jacks returned home from Campbell
College with a severe cough. Dr. Leslie advised against sending
him back to school until he was completely well. In a letter to
Warnie, Albert pondered whether the air in Malvern might be
better for Jacks's health than the air of Belfast.⁷

Cherbourg School

In January 1911, Jacks traveled with Warnie to Great Malvern in Worcestershire, where Warnie continued his studies at Malvern College and Jacks entered nearby Cherbourg School.[8] Cherbourg was a short-lived project, an example of educational institutions that quickly arose and just as quickly disappeared throughout the Victorian era and into the early twentieth century. Educated men often set up their own schools when they did not gain a good appointment to a college or good living with a parish. Wynyard had been a similar establishment that arose and disappeared with its only headmaster. Arthur Clement Allan founded Cherbourg School in 1907 and operated it in Great Malvern until 1925, when he relocated the school to Woodnorton, Evesham, until his retirement brought an end to the school in 1931.[9]

The town of Great Malvern had a strong appeal to Jacks with its impressive medieval priory built along the side of the Malvern Hills. He told his father that he thought Great Malvern was "one of the nicest English towns" he had seen. During the eighteenth century, it enjoyed renown as a fashionable spa, like Bath, because of its mineral waters. As a resort town, Great Malvern developed a prosperous residential district, which reflected its prosperity. Lewis thought that the Malvern Hills, which encompassed Great Malvern, were beautiful, though not as beautiful as the hills of Ulster.[10] At the top of one of these nearby hills lie the remains of a pre-Roman settlement known as the British Camp. Extensive earthworks crown the hill. One romantic legend holds that the British Camp was the location of the Roman defeat of the British chieftain Caratacus. Atop Holly Bush Hill near British Camp lie the remains of an Iron Age hill fort. Thus, the hills combined the natural beauty that Lewis was beginning to love with the kind of historical antiquity associated with legend.

Years later, Lewis returned again and again to Malvern on holiday. He wrote to Arthur Greeves that Malvern was "an exquisite, unchanging place" and that he would like to "end my days" there.[11] He loved the Tudor Hotel for the way it catered to gentlemen by providing them with a little room far away from all the other guests where they could sit and smoke, and because it lacked all the "silly" modern luxuries of modern hotels. When Maureen Moore married a schoolmaster at Malvern College, the young couple provided Jack with a place to stay when he visited the hills. Maureen was the sister of Edward "Paddy" Moore, the friend Lewis made during officer training at Keble College in 1917 and who was killed in the war. Paddy's mother lived with Lewis from the end of the First World War until her death in 1951. Maureen lived with them from her teenage years until her marriage. Thereafter, when Maureen visited her mother at the Kilns, Jack's house near Oxford, she offered her house at Malvern to Jack and Warnie as a break from the care of Mrs. Moore. On those visits, Lewis still loved to tramp the Malvern Hills with "larks singing in a blue sky, lambs bleating, the wind rustling in the grass."[12]

At Wynyard, ten-year-old Jacks had spoken of the other "boys," but once at Cherbourg School in the shadow of Malvern College, where his older brother was enrolled, twelve-year-old Jack had learned the new slang and referred to his fellow inmates as the other "chaps." Reflecting years later in *Surprised by Joy*, Lewis said that he made his first real friends at Cherbourg, but not friends of the first order.[13] He simply learned how to be friendly and to receive friendliness in return. It might seem a contradiction that sixty-five pages after telling his readers that he made his first true friends at Cherbourg, he claimed to have made his first friend in Arthur Greeves several years later.[14] Rather than contradicting his earlier statement, Lewis actually began to clarify the different types of friendship. This clarification of friendship would form part of his book *The Four Loves* (1960).

He had not yet hit upon his adolescent rebellion against God when he first arrived at Cherbourg, and his first letters home reflect a willful attention to the disciplines of religion. He could not find his prayer book among his things, so he asked his father to look for it at home.[15] Within a few weeks of arriving at Cherbourg, he attended a performance of Handel's *Messiah* with great pleasure.[16]

By the time he arrived at Cherbourg School, long walks had become a great source of pleasure and pride for Jack Lewis. In his second letter home, he described a long walk across the fields at the base of the Malvern Hills when, all at once, a Malvern College cross-country race intercepted his party, and who should run past him but his brother Warnie.[17] In the same letter he claimed to have had a "ripping walk" that took him into Wales and back![18] His enthusiasm marks the beginning of a lifelong love of long walks, for this adventure would have taken him some thirty miles.

The long walks were on his terms, but organized school sports were drills in which Jack lost his autonomy. During his first term at Cherbourg, Jack attempted to keep a diary once again, beginning on March 11, 1911, but he kept it up only until March 19. His comments reflect a marked difference between playing games at Wynyard and the tone of sports at Cherbourg. They were no longer boys playing. They were chaps training. His most common description? "Rotten." He was rotten at sports training. He was rotten at the long jump (2 feet, 11 inches). He was rotten at hockey. In boxing, however, he was not rotten. He "got a tremendous knocking about."[19] A great task of early adolescence involves developing a strong sense of confidence, and the knocking about that Jack received in the course of games at Cherbourg did not contribute to his self-confidence. He was rotten, and he hated it.

Forty-five years later, Lewis wrote in *Surprised by Joy* of these days at school. He remembered his longing and anticipation for each distant vacation. His memory appears to have preserved his intense feelings about school, for in his first letter to his father upon arriving at Cherbourg, he wrote hopefully and enthusiastically that he had only seventy-nine more days until the end of term.[20] In his next letter, Jacks expressed delight that he had only nine more weeks until vacation.[21] Several years later, as he began to anticipate leaving Cherbourg for Malvern, however, he noted that he did not regard the passage of time toward end of term with his usual eagerness, because Malvern was unknown ground— Lewis did not like change and unknown ground. Besides, in spite of fierce and long drawn-out arguments with teachers and other boys, in retrospect he had rather liked Cherbourg.

The Lewis family group on the beach in Scotland, August 1911 vacation. Used by permission of the Marion E. Wade Center, Wheaton College, Wheaton, IL.

After Jack's first term there, during the summer of 1911 Albert took the boys to Scotland for a holiday with Albert's third brother, Richard Lewis, known as Uncle Dick. They went to a small coastal village in the southeast of Scotland, where they stayed at a pub instead of a proper hotel. The food was bad and the beds were worse. Jack and Warnie shared a bed that was so uncomfortable, they tossed to see who should sleep in the bed and who should sleep on the floor. The loser got the bed. Deprived of his daily ration of hot roast beef, Albert sank into a state of despair and bad temper. Warnie noted that the miserable holiday only served to remind him of the happy times with his mother at Castlerock. Flora was never far in the background.[22]

A Growing Love of Literature

In his last letter from Cherbourg, on July 8, 1913, Jack expressed his thoughts and feelings about what suggests an elementary attraction to a literary life while reflecting on how the postman had assigned him essay topics on which to write when he was still a little boy. The wonder is that the little boy undertook to write them. Young Lewis was amazed by the role played by an uneducated postman in preparing his little mind for composing essays that would eventually lead to his scholarship to Malvern College. From the postman, he then reflected on the influence of his father and their family, "a race rich in literary feeling and mastery of their own tongue, and in that atmosphere of culture which has always shrouded the study both at Dundela and Leeborough."[23] In *Surprised by Joy*, he simply says that he grew up in a house full of books. At the age of fourteen, however, he had already felt what that environment meant, even if he did not yet know what it would come to mean later.

The literary life expressed itself at Cherbourg in 1912 and 1913 with the first published works of Lewis. From writing for the postman, Lewis graduated to writing for the *Cherbourg School Magazine*. For the November 1912 issue, he combined his love of walking with his literary bent in an article titled "The Expedition to Holly Bush Hill."[24] The next year, he turned his pen to addressing the greatest evil in the world, sports, with an article that asked and answered the question "Are Athletes Better than Scholars?"[25] For his third and final contribution to the school magazine, Lewis returned to a more pleasant topic with a second article about walking to Holly Bush Hill, which had the same title as the first.[26]

Writing essays for the postman represented just one aspect of a larger literary life that Lewis had appropriated by the time he went to Cherbourg. We have seen that in his last letter to his father from Wynyard School, Lewis had identified himself and his father as "Shakespearian students." Many biographies of Lewis have emphasized the distance between C. S. Lewis and his father, but the literary connection between them formed early. Perhaps the love of books, and in this case Shakespeare, provided a bond between father and son, or perhaps it provided a way for young Lewis to gain or seek approval. Without speculating on the psychology of the dynamic, we may simply observe that Lewis and his father enjoyed Shakespeare. When Lewis wrote of being a Shakespearian student, he referred not to school studies but to pastime pleasures. A traditional classical education like his did not focus on English literature the way more recent approaches to education have done. School studies meant Latin, French, algebra, and history. Shakespeare and all other English literature from Dickens to the Romantic poets belonged to pleasure reading. Later, at Malvern College, Jack would have the option of taking a class in Shakespeare or in drawing for his recreational class.[27]

Going to a Shakespearian play in 1911 for Lewis would have been like going to the movies for someone today. It was a form of popular entertainment. People who attended church understood Shakespeare's English because of the ubiquitous King James Bible throughout the English speaking world. The service of the Church of England preserved the language of Shakespeare. Even all extemporaneous prayer poured from the tongues of clergy and devout laity in the Elizabethan cadences of the King James Bible. In mid-May of his second term at Cherbourg in 1911, Jack wrote to his father that he was looking forward to attending *The Merchant of Venice* at Malvern's theater the following week. He remarked that the theater had a very good offering from the traveling theater companies that made the rounds of the smaller cities and towns of Britain in the days before feature-length films. Jack ventured to make a severe judgment about the Malvern theater: it was "rotten."[28] At one level, Jack Lewis was merely a snob, but at another level, he rendered a comparative judgment about the theater in Malvern: it did not measure up to his idea of what a theater should be based on his previous experience of theatergoing in Belfast. Albert Lewis had made it possible for his sons to attend the theater enough for it to be a routine and familiar experience. The offhand remark represents something that Lewis came back to at the end of his life in *An Experiment in Criticism*. Everyone makes judgments about the things they like, and they have some criteria for evaluation, regardless of how aware they may be of their own thought process.

In January 1913, Lewis wrote again of a visit to the local theater. This time he saw F. R. Benson's company in *Julius Caesar*. He gave a more detailed critical review of the play than he had done previously. Though he enjoyed the play, he found Benson's performance overdone with a tendency to sing rather than speak his lines. He provided several examples of words that Benson over dramatized.[29] The rest of the company did a good job, from Lewis's perspective. Then, we find Jack doing something that he had not done before. He expressed a negative remark about Shakespeare by invoking no less an authority than his brother, Warnie. While Jack did not go so far as to condemn Shakespeare as Warnie did, Jack thought that Shakespeare tended to miss the realism of modern drama and the stateliness of Greek drama.[30] Lewis had begun to experiment with new opinions. The mature Lewis would move beyond such a preoccupation with the realism of modern drama, but fourteen-year-old Jack had met the new fashionable opinions about drama, art, literature, and religion.

In a letter to Warnie in July 1913, Jack remarked on the pleasure of a visit to the hippodrome or the opera house.[31] He also demonstrated a familiarity with the stage by referring simply to "Benson," who would star in *The Merchant of Venice*. Sir Frank Robert Benson was a Shakespearian actor who had managed his

Off to Malvern

own traveling theater company for almost thirty years when Lewis saw him on stage in Malvern. One other comment from Lewis at the close of his letter emphasizes the considerable pleasure that drama provided Lewis. He had enclosed a photograph of the actors in his school play from the previous term that included Jack Lewis.

The day after that letter to Warnie, Jack wrote to his father after winning a classical scholarship to Malvern College. Albert had asked Jack what he would like to have as a reward for winning the scholarship (which would have saved Albert a considerable amount of money in tuition). Jack wrote that he most wanted a nice edition of Kipling, whose poems he had just begun to read. The suggestion is that he had already read most, if not all, of Rudyard Kipling's stories and novels. At the age of fourteen, he was taken by the poems and wondered why he had never read them before.[32] Warnie amplifies the significance of Jack's winning the scholarship by examination, noting that the day Jack was scheduled to take the exam, he was sick in bed again with a high temperature. Despite the fever, Jack wrote his exam paper from his sick bed. Given the circumstances, Warnie considered it the greatest triumph of his brother's career.[33]

C. S. Lewis would come back to Kipling again and again throughout his life, but something troubled him about Kipling. The mature Lewis thought that Kipling's stories suffered from an apparent absence of an overarching sense of justice in the face of a human system in which people were disciplined not to seek their rights. In Kipling's world, the incompetence of the ruling class creates misery and futility, waste and ruin for those who do the actual work. Kipling offers no hope that, in the end, it will all have been worthwhile. This offense to his sense of justice left Lewis feeling suffocated by Kipling's world. Though he enjoyed much of Kipling, after a few days reading him Lewis was left feeling "sick to death, of the whole Kipling world."[34]

In an address to the English Association many years later, C. S. Lewis expressed the view that Kipling's continual stress of the importance of discipline, of raw recruits and apprentices being "licked into shape," amounted to Kipling's doctrine of humanity, which resembles the doctrine of original sin.[35] Kipling's world was the world not of the liberal arts but of work, routine drudgery, and sweat that allows the rest of the world to enjoy the freedom to pursue diversions. What Kipling really loves is the intimacy of a closed circle of self-interested people who benefit from the toil of others.[36] He loves work not as an end in itself but as the context and occasion for professional brotherhood. Lewis observed that in Kipling's world, what really matters is "to belong, to be inside, to be in the know, to be snugly together against the outsiders."[37] Lewis calls such a confederacy of Kipling's imagination an "inner ring."[38] As we have already seen, Jack had learned early in his school days of the sinister dynamics of an inner ring.

Changing Views on Religion

The great change in Lewis's views of religion came unintentionally as a by-product of several events during his first year at Cherbourg. The matron at the school was Miss Cowie, a lady for whom Lewis had a high regard. When she was forced to leave Cherbourg and was replaced by Miss Gosling in the spring of 1912, Lewis observed to his father only that Miss Gosling was not as decent as Miss Cowie.[39] He wrote a great deal more about Miss Cowie in *Surprised by Joy* over forty years later, when he spoke affectionately and tenderly of her. He insisted that "no school had a better Matron" and that all the boys loved her for her care and attention shown them when they were ill—especially him, the orphan.[40] From her, Lewis received the kind of affection and attention that would normally come from a mother. Perhaps for this reason, he took note of Miss Cowie's spiritual wanderlust, for she explored all manner of occult practices in vogue at the time, such as theosophy, Rosicrucianism, and spiritualism. As she tried first one approach to spirituality and then another, it seemed to Lewis that Christianity was also just another approach to spirituality. Christianity no longer seemed to him to deal with matters of truth but now seemed only speculation, like so many other vague approaches to religion.[41]

Miss Cowie's spiritual experimentation came along when Lewis was reading Virgil in his studies. Virgil took Lewis into the midst of a world full of rival religious ideas. Today we speak of this phenomenon as religious pluralism. In 1912, Lewis experienced religious pluralism not only through his readings of the ancient pagan religious ideas of Virgil's Roman Empire; he experienced the same thing in his own British Empire at its height. Within the empire, around the globe, religious pluralism in the British colonies challenged the truth claims of Christianity, from the Buddhism of Asia to the Hinduism and Islam of India to the traditional religions of Africa. Miss Cowie provided the occasion, but it is hard to think of a clever boy like Jack Lewis not wondering why Christianity should stand above all the many other religions of the world.

To complicate matters in a way that militated against Lewis finding answers to his unarticulated ponderings, theological scholarship of the preceding few decades had taken up the comparative-religion approach to theology in an effort to make theology more scientific. This approach did not explore the truth claims of Christianity so much as it compared Christianity with other religions in a way that made religion an evolutionary phenomenon. This approach also fit with another popular trend in theology at the time that concerned viewing religion not from the perspective of a divine encounter but as a human phenomenon that takes different shapes in different times and places under different conditions. Such approaches drain Christianity of any transcendent dimension and provide no reason why Jack Lewis should not regard the old Christian faith as just another bit of speculation. Reflecting forty years later on the experience of his journey away from faith, Lewis wrote:

> All those teachers and editors took it for granted from the outset that these religious ideas [of the Romans] were sheer

illusion. No one ever attempted to show in what sense Christianity fulfilled Paganism or Paganism prefigured Christianity.
. . . Little by little, with fluctuations which I cannot now trace,
I became an apostate, dropping my faith with no sense of loss
but with the greatest relief.[42]

Yet, even as Lewis dropped religion, he took up a new interest
that would eventually lead him to find the answers to just the sort
of questions and doubts that had arisen in his mind over the old
pagan myths.

Finding Norse Mythology

In his radio broadcast to Iceland for the Joint Broadcasting Committee in May 1941, Lewis stated that when he was fourteen years
old, he had discovered the old Norse myths.[43] It happened by accident. One aspect of Lewis's growing interest in literature involved
his regular browsing through *The Bookman*, an English literary
magazine similar to the *Times Literary Supplement* or *The New
York Times Book Review*. As he flipped through the pages of the
Christmas issue of *The Bookman* for 1911, Jack's eyes fell upon an
elegant edition of the old Norse tale of Siegfried and the fall of the
gods, based on Richard Wagner's libretto of the story for his fabulous four-part opera *Der Ring des Nibelungen* (*The Ring of the
Nibelungs*). The Nibelungs were the dwarfs of Norse mythology
who lived under the earth, mined its riches, and crafted its metal.

J. R. R. Tolkien complained that fairy tales had been relegated
to the nursery in modern times. We might equally say that opera
has been relegated to the most sophisticated of the upper class in
the early twenty-first century. It was not the case in 1911. Opera
belonged to the masses as a form of popular entertainment on the
eve of World War I, just before the feature-length movie first came
into its own. Opera had enjoyed a great run for over two hundred
years by combining drama and music in the telling of great stories.
Wagner's *Ring* cycle represents the high-water mark for opera,

after which it suffered a sudden decline. In 1911, however, every town of any consequence, from Malvern to Silver Dollar City, Utah, had its own opera house, where traveling opera companies visited.

Though based on the old Norse sagas and the *Nibelungenlied*, Wagner wrote his four-opera cycle as a celebration of Germanic culture. Begun in 1848, the cycle was completed in 1874, just three years after the unification of the German Empire at the close of the Franco-Prussian War. Thus, it not only inspired young Jack Lewis and his future friend J. R. R. Tolkien but also inspired a new generation of Germans growing up in a single empire, such as Adolf Hitler. Wagner's story involves the competition between several rival races: the Nibelungs or dwarfs, the gods, the giants, and men.

The Story of the *Ring*

Wagner's first opera is *Das Rheingold* (*The Rhinegold*). As the story opens, the dwarf Alberich has gone to visit the Rhine maidens who guard the golden treasure of their father, the water god. Alberich longs for the love of one of the maidens, who only flirt with and torment the poor dwarf. As they laugh at him, they reveal the secret of their father's gold, which may be forged into a powerful ring by which its owner can rule the world if he or she will only foreswear love. In his anger at being ridiculed, Alberich rejects love, steals the gold, and forges it into a ring that allows him to rule all the other dwarfs, whom he compels to amass a great treasure for him.

Meanwhile, the king of the gods, Wotan, has made a bargain with the giant brothers Fafner and Fasolt. In exchange for building him the great stronghold of Valhalla, Wotan will allow the giants to take the goddess Freia. It was an unfortunate bargain for the gods, because Freia is the goddess who tends the golden apples that bestow on the gods their immortality. Without the apples, they will die. Loge, the god of fire, offers an alternative bargain. Having heard of Alberich's great treasure, he proposes that the giants accept a pile of gold high enough to completely hide Freia. They agree to the exchange, and Loge accompanies Wotan to the underworld of Nibelheim, where they hope to trick Alberich out of his treasure. Among the ring's many powers is that it enables a person to change shapes. Loge tricks Alberich into turning himself into a frog, in which shape he is captured and not allowed to go free until he has turned over the ring and the treasure to Wotan. When Wotan piles the treasure before Freia, she is almost completely hidden, except for one trace of her golden hair. Wotan is forced to add the ring to the pile. Freia is set free, but the giants immediately begin to quarrel over the ring. Fafner murders Fasolt and claims the ring and treasure for himself. The ring allows him to turn himself into a dragon, in which form he seeks a secluded place to guard his treasure. The first opera closes with the gods crossing a rainbow bridge to enter the golden halls of Valhalla to await their doom.

Wagner's second opera is *Die Walküre (The Valkyrie)*. Many years have passed since the action of the first opera. The driving force to the plot is Wotan's desire to possess the ring. Because he is the god who protects bargains and treaties, he cannot violate his own treaty with the giants. He resolves to father a race of mortals known as the Wälsungs, who will accomplish the task for him. The result of this plan is the twin boy and girl Siegmund and Sieglinde. The twins are separated from birth and wander in the wilds, shunned by other people for their wildness. The daughter, Sieglinde, is taken for the wife of Hunding, the chief of the Neiding tribe. Years later, during a furious storm when Hunding is away from his hall, Siegmund wanders to the door and seeks shelter of Sieglinde. The two fall in love and run away together with the help of Brünnhilde, the most cherished of Wotan's nine Walküre daughters. The Walküre ride through all the world seeking out the greatest warriors who fall in battle to carry them to Valhalla, where they will help defend Valhalla from the doom that awaits the gods. The Walküre are Wotan's daughters through his affair with Erda, the goddess of the Earth, who lives in a perpetual sleep by which she dreams the fate of all, whether men or gods.

Wotan's wife, Fricka, is the goddess of marriage and is horrified that Wotan's two illegitimate children have dishonored the marriage of Hunding by their illicit love. To make matters worse, Wotan's illegitimate daughter Brünnhilde has helped them escape. Fricka forces Wotan to agree to punish all of his wayward children. Siegmund dies in battle. Sieglinde dies in childbirth, but not before giving birth to Wotan's grandson Siegfried. Brünnhilde is stripped of her immortality and forced to sleep a deep sleep. No longer a great warrior, she will be cursed to fall in love with whoever wakes her from her sleep. In the end, Wotan agrees to surround her sleeping byre with a wall of fire that only the bravest of warriors would dare to pass. The second opera closes as the flames guarding Brünnhilde grow and spread to protect her sleep.

Wagner's third opera is *Siegfried*. It opens in the cave of Mime, the brother of Alberich, who found the infant Siegfried and raised him. In addition to the infant, Mime collected Siegmund's sword from the battlefield where Wotan caused it to shatter in obedience to his promise to Fricka. Mime hopes to recover the ring and the treasure through Siegfried, but first he must reforge the enchanted sword. It can be wielded only by a great warrior who does not know the meaning of fear. Siegfried has nothing but contempt for his foster father, who has kept him away from all contact with any other person. Eventually, Siegfried decides to reforge the sword himself and go off on an adventure to discover the meaning of fear. He slays the dragon Fafner, takes the ring in ignorance, and seizes the magic helmet Tarnhelm, which provides a cloak of invisibility to its wearer.

When Siegfried slays the dragon Fafner, the dragon's blood burns his finger, which he puts to his lips to cool it. Upon tasting the magical dragon blood, he acquires the ability to understand birds. A passing bird tells him of the sleeping woman, and Siegfried rushes off to find her in hopes of learning from her the meaning of fear. Along the way he meets Wotan in disguise, who seeks to block his way, but Siegfried is rude to the old man and breaks Wotan's great spear. Wotan is reconciled to his fate and to that of all the gods, who will pass away to be replaced by the race of men. Siegfried falls in love with Brünnhilde, the first woman he has ever seen. When he wakens her with his kiss, she falls in love with him, and the opera ends.

Wagner's final opera in the *Ring* cycle is *Götterdämmerung* (*The Twilight of the Gods*). Having secured his bride, Siegfried is ready to go off on another adventure while Brünnhilde stays home. Meanwhile, Alberich the dwarf has not given up his desire to recover the ring. He has fathered a son by Grimhilde, the wife of the king of the Gibichungs, whose name is Hagen. Hagen's half-brother, Gunther, is now the king. Neither Gunther nor his sister, Gutrune, has married. Alberich and Hagen conspire to ruin Gunther, Gutrune, Siegfried, and Brünnhilde. When the royal party meets Siegfried on a hunt, Hagen gives Siegfried a drink containing a potion that causes him to forget Brünnhilde and fall in love with Gutrune. He agrees to fetch Brünnhilde to be Gunther's bride. Brünnhilde believes Siegfried has broken faith with her. In the end, Hagen fatally stabs Siegfried and then kills Gunther. Brünnhilde finally realizes what has happened and rides her horse into Siegfried's funeral pyre to be consumed by the flames after throwing the ring into the Rhine, where the Rhine Maidens rescue it. Hagen dives into the Rhine to gain the ring, but he drowns in the attempt. The opera ends with the Rhine Maidens rejoicing while Valhalla and the gods are consumed in flames.

King Ludwig II of Bavaria built a great opera house in Bayreuth specifically to produce the four *Ring* operas. A Wagner festival at Bayreuth began under the leadership of Richard Wagner upon completion of the opera house and has continued to the present day. Wagner and his music became an international sensation.

Rackham's Illustrations

William Heinemann rode the crest of the wave of the *Ring's* popularity with the publication of a two-volume set of Wagner's libretto translated into English by Margaret Armour in 1910–1911. To maximize his profits, Heinemann produced a limited edition and a trade edition. The publisher reserved a thousand copies of the edition for sale in Britain while allowing only 150 to be sold in the United States. The limited edition created scarcity, boosting demand for the popular trade edition, which went into many printings. Most important of all, however, Heinemann commissioned the famous illustrator Arthur Rackham to provide thirty-four color illustrations plus fourteen black-and-white drawings. The illustrations provided a stunning complement to the early gramophone recordings of excerpts from Wagner's *Ring* and offered those who could afford them a multimedia extravaganza. Jack Lewis wanted the extravaganza.

Lewis's casual survey of the 1911 Christmas issue of *The Bookman* began a lifelong obsession/delight/preoccupation that would be formative for his life in almost all of its dimensions. It formed the basis for his most important friendships, and it played a critical role in his conversion to Christianity. The Norse tales gave Lewis pleasure but also something more profound. The tales had an effect on him at an affective level. Lewis acquired the precious volume of *Siegfried and the Twilight of the Gods*, and by November 1913 he was in heavy negotiations with his father to obtain *The Rhinegold and the Valkyrie* to complete the set.[44] Adding to the longing for "northernness" about which Lewis would later write, no doubt, was Arthur Rackham's decision to depict the Rhine Maidens in his beautifully executed color paintings without a stitch of clothes.

Lewis's love of Rackham's illustrations also goes a long way to explaining his reaction to Walt Disney's animated *Snow White and the Seven Dwarfs* (1937). His disdain for the depiction of the dwarfs did not rise to the level of hostility, but he thought Disney had missed them completely. Disney had profaned the image of dwarfs created by Rackham, and such a desecration could not be forgiven. Disney's dwarfs were comic figures, but the dwarfs of Wagner made visible by Rackham were dangerous, self-possessed creatures to whom the term "jolly" did not apply. In fairy stories, dwarfs should be ugly, and they would never play the kind of music that Disney's dwarfs played. Nonetheless, Lewis approved of the overall storyline and thought "all the terrifying bits were good."[45]

We know how Jack Lewis felt about Wagner and his northern operas not only from the memories of C. S. Lewis written many years later but also from an essay on Wagner he wrote for class at Cherbourg. Jack called Wagner the "great Bayreuth master," for he aimed not at writing pretty music but at producing mental feelings and sensations in the hearers that corresponded to the story in the libretto. Young Lewis believed that Wagner's *Tristan and Isolde* exceeded anything the world had seen to that point, but it came before his greatest work, the *Ring* cycle.[46] Jack acknowledged that the great mass of the public did not appreciate Wagner but that the true "musical public," of which no doubt he was a representative, appreciated Wagner's music, which was not simply a collection of melodies of varying value but "the best and truest means of expressing character, scenery and emotion."[47]

The Utility of Education

None of the matters I have just discussed involved Jack's formal education at Cherbourg. We may think of the mature C. S. Lewis as interested in learning for its own sake; true education does not have a pragmatic purpose as measured in some utilitarian benefit. The young Jack Lewis had no such high view of formal education. He was at Cherbourg for one reason: to earn a scholarship to Malvern College. While pleasure reading was for pleasure's sake, schoolwork was for the prize. In addition to the scholarship, Jack also looked forward to the tangible reward from his father for

doing well—in this case, a "nice edition of Kipling."[48] His few letters to his father over the remainder of his time at Cherbourg dealt
with his progress toward winning the scholarship or his concern
over his brother's troubles at Malvern.

During his time at Cherbourg and later at Malvern College,
Jack Lewis still had only one friend—his brother Warnie. He
would not become friends with Arthur Greeves until the Easter
vacation of 1914. Warnie's misdemeanors at Malvern College had
grown in enormity until he was in danger of expulsion and ruin,
because the successful completion of public school was the necessary means to the next rung on the ladder of success in the British
Empire. If Warnie lost his place at Malvern College, then his future
prospects looked quite dark. Until this point in their lives, Warnie
had looked after Jack and smoothed the way for him. From this
time forward, Jack would gradually assume the role of the more
responsible brother who looked after Warnie. For the next twenty
years, their relationship would tend to be on an even footing without any morbid codependency or pathetic inability to function.
Following Warnie's last hurrah at Malvern College, however, Jack
would no longer be the younger brother in the way he had been.

What had happened this time? Warnie had been caught smoking! Malvern College did not allow smoking. As a boy, Warnie's
smoking represents a typical expression of independence from
authority on the road to developing his own identity. Existentially,
smoking was a thrill. He and Jack had the habit of climbing out
their bedroom window at home and sitting on the bow roof over
their father's study to sneak a smoke.[49] Warnie had been a prefect,
but this honor was withdrawn following the smoking incident in
June 1913. Though he was not expelled, he was not allowed to return to Malvern after that term.[50] The timing was bad, for Warnie
had settled on a career that made education utilitarian. He wanted
to serve in the Army Service Corps, which meant that he needed to
be accepted as a cadet at Sandhurst, which meant that he needed
to prepare for the entrance exam. Jack's letter to his father about

Warnie's career choice suggests that Albert Lewis did not think a career in the Army Service Corps was good enough, but Jack stood by Warnie's decision and loyally put it in the best light: "congenial work and mixing with other gentlemen."[51]

Being sent down meant that Warnie would not overlap Jack at Malvern College. As Jack prepared for his first term there in September 1913, Warnie prepared to spend the next segment of his life under the tutelage of W. T. Kirkpatrick at his home in Great Bookham, Surrey, where he tutored private students in preparation for university entrance exams.[52] Warnie lived with Kirkpatrick from September until December of 1913.

Kirkpatrick, who had never approved the choice of Malvern for Warnie, had anticipated that Warnie would come to study with him eventually. When Kirkpatrick wrote to Albert back on October 4, 1909, he acknowledged that he had failed to send condolences about the death of Flora, since condolences are the "most ineffective things in the world," worth absolutely nothing. On the other hand, human sympathy must count for something. Thus he managed to dance around the idea that he could not say, "She is in a far better place," as all the other letters of condolence would normally do. Apparently, the pious Albert never realized that Kirkpatrick had left the faith in the intervening years since he was Albert's schoolmaster, and Kirkpatrick always avoided the subject with him. He also acknowledged that Albert had sent his son to Malvern. After making rather severe judgments about the difference in quality of the public schools of England, Kirkpatrick now only remarked that it really does not make any difference where a boy goes to school, and Malvern had the advantage of good scenery. Faint praise, indeed! Instead, Kirkpatrick, with remarkable prescience about what would happen at Malvern, made an unusual offer: ". . . and it may even be within the bounds of possibility that I could be of some service to you in the future when you come to face the problems of his future career, and the special preparation which may fit him for it." Graciously, he did not tell Albert back then that he was wasting his money by sending Warnie to Malvern.[53]

When Albert began to explore sending Warren to study with Kirkpatrick, as Kirkpatrick had suggested would eventually happen, Jack had just won his scholarship to Malvern. Kirkpatrick again predicted the future in his estimation of Jack's achievement in winning the scholarship based on an essay. He remarked: "But if a boy of the age of your second son send up an essay unequalled at Malvern Entrance—THERE is something to be proud of, and you would be more—or rather less—than human if you were not. If education does not contain the promise and potency of the future, what is the good of it?"[54] But Kirkpatrick rarely let an opportunity pass to denigrate the academic quality of Malvern College. He regularly mentioned the "literary genius of [Albert's] younger boy," perhaps in anticipation of the time that Albert would inevitably recognize that Jack should not be sent to Malvern, a school that Kirkpatrick often reminded Albert had ruined Warnie.[55]

Why did Kirkpatrick take on boys like Warren in his retirement when he could have been enjoying life? Largely because he was not enjoying the life of retirement. In his letters to Albert, he had expressed his envy for the drudgery of Albert's work, for he missed having an occupation. The money he received for his boarding pupils certainly eased his finances, but he did it because "the work was congenial and gave [him] an interest in life."[56] Teaching saved Kirk from depression in old age. It also saved Warnie. Kirkpatrick's evaluation of Warnie's character, temperament, personality, and abilities was the diametric opposite of what Capron had told Albert about the boy. Warnie's only real deficiency was his poor grasp of mathematics, the subject taught by Capron that also appears to have created the lifelong dread of the subject in Jack.[57] To his credit, Albert consoled Warnie with his own experience with math when he had faced his examinations. He confessed that he had done miserably with a fourth. Albert offered nothing but sympathy and encouragement to Warnie as he faced his exams and assured his son that doing his best was all one could ask. The only things that counted to Albert were character and industry, and he knew that Warnie had both.[58]

Despite Albert Lewis's anxiety over the entrance exams to Sandhurst and his son's uncertain future, Warnie placed twenty-first out of 201 candidates who were accepted at Sandhurst in 1914. His performance earned him a prize cadetship, which included half fees and a fifty pound bonus when he took his commission.[59] Kirkpatrick was not only prescient in academic matters; he was also not above saying, "I told you so," as he did to Warnie after the entrance examination results for Sandhurst were posted.[60] Kirkpatrick was particularly pleased that Warnie had done better on the exam than any of the Malvern candidates. He took particular delight that a Malvern man stood 201st out of 201 candidates.[61]

Jack's letters to Warnie during this period make explicit the way the two brothers practiced the art of working their father. In other words, they were like most other teenage boys. While Warnie lived with W. T. Kirkpatrick, cramming for his Sandhurst entrance exams in November 1914, the brothers plotted a scheme to persuade their father to pay for Warnie to visit Malvern. At one point, Jack sent Warnie a sample letter that he would send to their father on Warnie's behalf in which he would argue that most of the other boys would have friends coming to visit them for the end of term, and that if Warnie came for a visit then, Jack would not have to travel home all by himself. To sweeten the deal, he added that the assistant headmaster had been hoping that Warnie would return for a visit.[62] Wise to their tricks, Albert Lewis did not bite.

Malvern College: Being Irish in England

Once again, Jack was on his own. He went up to Malvern College a few days after Warnie went to stay with Kirkpatrick. C. S. Lewis had difficulty thinking of anything good that came out of his time at Malvern, but one thing stood out in his mind many years later.

He had learned to read wherever he happened to be on the long journeys between Belfast and Great Malvern by train and ferry. He first read Christopher Marlowe's *Tamburlaine* on the train between Larne on the Antrim coast, where the ferry landed, and Belfast while traveling in a thunderstorm. He first read Robert Browning's *Paracelsus* by candlelight on the ferry crossing the Irish Sea.[63]

Malvern College, front

During this period, Jack also took up reading George Bernard Shaw, simply because he found Shaw on his father's bookshelves and possibly because Shaw was Irish. At that time, Shaw was one of the lions of the "literary world," but Jack did not know that anything like a literary world even existed. He read Shaw for pleasure, and not because everyone who is anyone read Shaw. Books written in English continued to be a source of pleasure because English literature was not a course taught in any self-respecting school in that day.[64] Little else besides remained to give C. S. Lewis warm memories of his time at Malvern College.

From his correspondence, Jack appears to have liked Malvern upon his first arrival in September 1913 through February of 1914, but then everything turned sour. In a letter to his father on March 18, 1914, Jack complained that all the prefects detested him and went about venting their spite on him. Jack made clear that he was the brunt not of *mere* prefects but of "illiterate, ill-managed *English* prefects."[65] Many people today think of C. S. Lewis as English, but he was not English at all. He came from Belfast in Ulster, a territory now known as Northern Ireland. In 1914, however, Ireland had not yet gained independence from the United Kingdom, and Belfast was as much Ireland as Dublin and Cork were Ireland. Furthermore, Jack Lewis self-identified as Irish. He had a partisan regard for Irish weather over English weather, Irish landscapes over English landscapes.[66] Finally, although Jack and Warnie made fun of their father's Ulster accent behind his back, Jack Lewis still spoke with an Irish accent in 1914. In *Surprised by Joy*, the middle-aged Lewis admitted that he assumed an instant hatred of England and all things English on his first trip to Wynyard School, and this hatred "took many years to heal."[67]

Malvern students with Lewis in the center, 1914. Used by permission of the Marion E. Wade Center, Wheaton College, Wheaton, IL.

Jack's fagging—the practice of forced labor imposed by upper-class prefects on their juniors—which he reported to his father, came at the time of the Home Rule Bill crisis in Britain. Ulster Protestants opposed the Home Rule Bill, which they derided as the Rome Rule Bill. The crisis had been building for decades, but 1914 was the critical year. In March, a number of British army officers from Ulster had let it be known that they would refuse to act against Ulster Unionist leaders who resisted home rule. The long-standing and deep-seated prejudice of the English against the Irish, coupled with the home rule crisis, may have accounted for a sudden surge of hostility against young Lewis. Albert and Kirkpatrick exchanged ideas about the Irish question throughout their correspondence in 1913–1914 when Jack was experiencing such a bad time at Malvern.[68]

Interestingly enough, the next letter Jack wrote to his father on March 22 began with a discussion of the Irish situation. James Craig, the local member of Parliament who played a major role in the crisis and would become the first prime minister of Northern Ireland in 1921, lived just a few houses away from Albert. The Lewis family was not indifferent to the great question of Irish home rule. On March 15, 1913, Albert had delivered a speech in Ulster Hall at a meeting of the West Belfast Anti-Home Rule Association in which he spoke vigorously against the Home Rule Bill and in support of the continuation of the Unionist principles.[69] Jack said that it was a good thing that Craig had not been arrested, or Mr. Lewis might have been in trouble too! Furthermore, Jack could not leave school early for the short vacation but would have to remain at school to attend the house supper because all the Irish boys were staying, since it was the headmaster's last term. He concluded this letter with the observation that "the people here" did not "grasp the Ulster situation."[70] By "the people here," Jack meant the English. To the English, all of the Irish were troublemakers, whether Catholic or Protestant. Toward the end of his time at Malvern College, Jack wrote philosophically to his father of the trials of being Irish in England: "Perhaps all this unpleasantness in a foreign land has its use, in that it teaches one to love home and things connected with home all the more, by contrast."[71] He complained of being "cooped up in this hot, ugly country of England."[72]

It is surprising that Jack largely escaped severe fagging for so long. The fagging system in English public schools like Malvern College was the norm. Early on, Lewis had smugly written to his father that he had not come in for any degree of fagging because the prefects enjoyed picking on "that fat beast Lodge, whom everyone hates."[73] In those first months, Malvern was "very pleasant" or "very enjoyable," and Jack was "having a very good time."[74] In the many references to prefects until March 1914, they were merely prefects, but in his pleading letter of March in which he begs his father to "please take me out of this as soon as possible," he calls them *English* prefects.

Until he was on the receiving end of the brutality of the fagging system, Lewis failed to express any sympathy for the other boys who fell prey to harsh treatment. In his March letter, however, all of that changed. His heart went out to every "poor creature" who had suffered continually like himself without any relief in sight. The headmaster could not help. He would only make matters worse, and any intervention by Albert Lewis would prove lethal to Jack. The repercussions would be too horrible to contemplate.

Sports, Clumsiness, and Withdrawal

The issue that Lewis discussed in *Surprised by Joy* that set him at odds with the social structure at Malvern College focused on sports. The most important qualification for recognition as a "blood" at Malvern was athletic skill.[75] Those without it suffered the humiliation of exclusion and persecution in the fagging system, in which the unworthy endured endless physical and psychological punishment for the crime of not being athletic.[76] Lewis was not athletic, but this crime was punished more severely at Malvern than it had been at Wynyard, where the boys were too terrorized by the headmaster to develop as severe a hierarchical system as Malvern possessed. Lewis confessed to a general clumsiness that came naturally, but also to never having learned to play sports growing up or at Wynyard.[77] The clumsiness came in part from a physical disability that probably had a major effect on his ability to play sports. He and his brother inherited a genetic peculiarity from their father—they had only one functioning joint in the thumb. The upper joint near the nail was present, but it would not bend. As a result, he was no good with a tool, a bat, or a gun. He could not make model ships or cut paper with scissors as a boy.[78] This self-identification of clumsiness is one he would carry throughout his life. He mentioned it in his preface to *Essays Presented to Charles Williams* (1947).[79]

Though Warnie had the same physical handicap, he dealt with it in a different way. Writing in his diary in 1961, Warnie still spoke of Wynyard as a hellhole, but even worse to him on reflection was the experience of comparative poverty at Malvern, where other boys were three to five times as rich as he, and where money mattered. For this social pain, Warnie blamed his father, who "never denied himself anything" but did not have the same generous spirit toward his sons, in Warnie's estimation.[80] Warnie had no sympathy with Jack for not liking sports because he had found a way to deal with his own athletic failure. He played the clown. He threw himself into school games in a play for acceptance despite his inferior economic standing. Warnie regarded Jack a failure at the important social skill of feigning interest in something that bored him to death. This failure or refusal to seem interested in what interested other people contributed significantly to Jack's unpopularity at Malvern, in Warnie's opinion. Not only did Jack not put up the show of interest; he made his boredom "glaringly obvious to all."[81]

Whereas the great spiritual issue throughout Jack's life was pride, a pride so fierce he could not tolerate being bested at anything by anyone, Warnie's great spiritual issue was envy.

Writing of this period in 1947, Warnie admitted to himself that he had spent his youth filled with discontent and envy—envy of those who were good at games especially. He also had room to envy the boys with refined manners who wore tailor-made clothes, owned motorbikes, and were better looking.[82] If Warnie could not excel at sports, he would play the clown and make people laugh. He would pull pranks that earned him attention. If Jack could not excel at sports, he would not play. Warnie might enjoy having the school laugh at him, but not Jack.

For C. S. Lewis, the greatest expression of evil and suffering in his life did not involve the death of his mother. A mother's death brought sympathy and attention. For him, the greatest example of the universe red with tooth and claw came from his clumsiness. His efforts at tying a knot or trying to make something straight always had a comic effect, and when things have a comic effect, people laugh.[83] Lewis was the cliché of the clumsy oaf. In the Harry Potter stories, he would have been Neville Longbottom, not Harry.

Lewis became the object of a blood demonstration of power early on at Malvern when one blood told him that his group would not play games on that afternoon. As it turned out, the blood had lied, and Lewis was beaten for not turning out.[84] The incident Lewis described was as fresh as if it had happened the morning he wrote it. It is not difficult to see why the idea of right and wrong, of justice and injustice, should play such an existential part in his moral argument for the existence of God a decade after his conversion. Jack became a marked man for fagging, and not least of which because he was big for his age and had the kind of face that a prefect would react to by saying, "And take that look off your face too."[85]

The desperate plea for rescue that Jack sounded in his March letter began with quite a different issue. Academic reports had gone out and Albert Lewis was not pleased. The brutal fagging he had received, which he now disclosed to his father, came as

Jack's excuse for why he had not done well on his grades. This was the second report that did not meet Albert's expectations. The first had come in November 1913 with midterm reports, and the subject that had disappointed was Jack's favorite subject with his favorite teacher: classics and English under Harry Wakelyn Smith, known to the students as Smewgy.[86] Jack's letters had been filled with praise of Smewgy and how well Jack was doing in his classes. Jack had a simple explanation for why he had not done well with his Greek. Everyone else had already covered Greek grammar three or four times, but it was all new for him. What he had learned at Cherbourg did not really count because he had learned the Greek grammar there only in order to pass the exam, and he had promptly forgotten it all.[87] His concluding point, however, provides a window into how Jack's manipulative manner had developed. He assured his father that he need not fear about future reports because "I get on well with Smugy [*sic*], and really that is half the battle."[88]

But things did not get better. Albert Lewis exchanged letters with Warnie over the situation, which both regarded as very serious. The foremost proposal seemed to be the removal of Jack from Malvern College and his placement with W. T. Kirkpatrick as a private tutor until he was ready for university some three years later. Warnie had hoped that Jack would flourish at Malvern, as he himself had done and reap a rich bounty of lifelong friends and happy memories. Instead, Jack grew increasingly insular as he countered any perceived air of English superiority with a stronger manner of intellectual and cultural superiority on his part. By nature, Jack Lewis was an introvert and preferred as little company as possible interspersed with long spans of solitude. While the neglect of the students at Wynyard School had allowed him time and space of his own, Malvern kept him busy every moment with a rigorous supervised schedule of activities. He had no time to study once the fagging began in earnest, much less time to immerse himself in pleasure reading.

Warnie did not sympathize with Jack's misanthropic way of disparaging what everyone else enjoyed, like a house victory in games. Of these events, Jack only said, "I saw a lot of boys throwing their caps in the air and making unpleasant noises: yes, I suppose it is an interesting study."[89] As far as Warnie was concerned, Jack had burned his bridges, and it made no sense to stay at Malvern College. Jack was interested in music and books, but his school companions dwelt on cricket and food.[90] Besides being too intelligent for his form at Malvern, Jack had an independent mind, which for schoolboys amounted to heresy of the worst kind. Warnie observed of the boys at Malvern that they "detest nonconformity, and there is no mercy shown to one who refuses to move with the herd."[91] Warnie seemed to relish the thought of the little intellectual snob trying his superior manner with W. T. Kilpatrick, as he wrote, "There would be no one there except Mr. and Mrs. K for him to talk to, and he could amuse himself by detonating his little stock of cheap intellectual fireworks under old K's nose."[92] Albert Lewis feared that if Jack spent three years in isolation from the company of boys his own age, his worst faults would become exaggerated, and he would grow into a worse hermit than he already was.[93]

At a time when Jack felt completely alienated from the other boys at Malvern, he also felt a hitherto unknown alienation both from his father and from Warnie over the issue of Malvern. Not only did they not take his side; they blamed him. In 1913, Albert and Warnie began referring to Jack as "It" in their correspondence. This terminology coincided with Warnie's removal from Malvern College and Jack's arrival there. Jack's deprecation of Warnie's beloved Malvern, joined with Jack's newly acquired priggish style, left father and brother despairing of "It."

Years later, Warnie challenged Jack on his treatment of Malvern in *Surprised by Joy* and forced him to admit he had been wrong in his characterization of the school. Warnie had known most of the prefects that Jack described as brutes, and Warnie thought they were all "very pleasant fellows." Surely they were very pleasant fellows to Warnie, who was also a prefect, but prefects did not treat first years the way they treated one another. Warnie also challenged Jack's suggestion that forced sexual favors commonly were extracted by the older boys from the younger. Warnie doubted it and took the position that the relations between older and younger boys who had formed an attachment were purely platonic and sentimental. To Jack's charge that sex was the only topic of conversation among the boys at Malvern, Warnie insisted that the boys also talked about such things as musical comedy, actresses, horse racing, and clothes. Though Jack confessed to Warnie that he had been clearly wrong in his description of Malvern, one cannot help but wonder if the confession were not the simplest way to end the discussion and keep the peace at the Kilns.[94]

As Warnie very well knew, however, the problem of sex between older and younger boys was a problem in public schools, and it had come to the attention of Albert in connection with Malvern. In May 1910, Albert discovered that the son of a reputable man known to him had removed his son from Malvern and placed him in another school. Mr. Sinclair would not say why he had removed his son, so Albert assumed the worst and immediately wrote to Warnie, not as his father but as his "best friend." He advised Warnie that in every school "there were bad, vicious boys who tried to introduce sinful, unhealthy, disgusting, criminal practices." Albert begged Warnie to tell him if anything of the kind happened at Malvern and pleaded for Warnie's promise "for Mammy's dear sake." Such a promise to his father was easy to give and ignore.[95] Warnie assured Albert that nothing of the sort went on in his house, which had "a good reputation for cleanliness."[96]

In a separate discussion of how Malvern had affected him, however, Warnie was less charitable toward his alma mater. He said that four years at Malvern had made him a cynic, and not simply a cynic of the "young poseur" variety but a cynic produced by a "lax atmosphere." He also believed that Malvern had played a part in his development of an inferiority complex because of its laissez-faire methods—the very system that Jack hated, whereby the older boys, and not the schoolmasters, ran the school. Furthermore, Malvern had instilled in him the public school code as a rule of life, which he came to realize, while studying with Kirkpatrick, was "inadequate." Finally, Malvern had simply failed to give Warnie the education for which his father had paid good money.[97]

In the end, Albert Lewis begged Kirkpatrick to take Jack and prepare him for his entrance exams to Oxford. Kirkpatrick was reluctant and recommended that Jack be sent back to Campbell College in Belfast, but he relented and agreed to take Jack in September.[98] In the meantime, Albert Lewis told Jack to stay at Malvern through the end of term in July as an experiment. Jack stayed until July, but he did not like it. He had learned at Wynyard School to fall back on his intellect for self-confidence and a sense of superiority to the mere brutes who were good at sports, but his intellect had failed him at Malvern College. He worried that he had fooled himself and that he was no better than any of the other boys at schoolwork. He confided to his father:

> And the worst of it all seems to be that I am not getting on too well in form. It's discouraging. Whether it is that I haven't time to do it, or that I'm losing my mental faculties, or the fact that it is getting harder, I don't know: but the fact remains that things aren't as they should be. Goodness knows, I work as hard as I can. But it's all uphill.[99]

The excuses had disappeared. He was a little boy whose only friend in the world had gone off to Sandhurst to become an army officer. His retreat to academic superiority had failed him. The wolves had sensed that he was crippled, and they had attacked to tear him to pieces. In that deep moment, he began to ask the kind of questions that would eventually lead him to become an entirely different person than what he was, having become the sort of chap that Bertie Wooster might call an obnoxious little git.

Looking back on this period forty years later, C. S. Lewis speculated that the real reason that his father allowed him to leave Malvern to study with Kirkpatrick was Warnie's experience at Malvern. Warnie had loved Malvern and drank deeply of its worst aspects. Albert had wanted his sons to attend proper English public schools to become proper English public school boys who would grow into proper English gentlemen, but when Warnie followed the plan, Albert did not like the result. Warnie had grown "flippant, languid, emptied of the intellectual interests which had appeared in his earlier boyhood, immovable, indifferent to all real values, and urgent in his demand for a motor-bicycle."[100] The more Warnie assumed the affected speech of the public school boy, the more Albert intentionally mispronounced words and exaggerated his Irish accent. No, Jack would not stay at Malvern. Jack would go to Kirkpatrick. After all, Kirkpatrick had succeeded in knocking the public school manner out of Warnie in a matter of weeks. Perhaps he could knock some sense into young Jack. It is little wonder that the Lewis men sometimes referred to Kirkpatrick as "the Great Knock."[101]

C. S. Lewis devoted a major portion of *Surprised by Joy* to his miserable time at school—172 out of 224 pages. Until now, the biographers of Lewis have not regarded his adolescence as of any great importance. Roger Lancelyn Green and Walter Hooper, in the first full biography of Lewis, devoted 30 pages of their 308-page book to this period of his life. Alan Jacobs gave 45 pages out of 342 to this period in the life of Lewis. George Sayer was a bit more generous with 54 pages out of 252, but Sayer wondered at the seeming disproportionate use of space by Lewis: "The account of his misery at school takes up a third of the book. Why is it so exaggerated?"[102] Sayer is not alone in dismissing Jack's account of school as an exaggeration. In his biography of Lewis, Alister McGrath commented on the "implausibility" that Malvern and Wynyard were worse than the "death-laden trenches" of France.[103] McGrath gave 44 of his 308-page biography of Lewis to the school days.

We should recall, however, that Sayer's perception of an exaggeration came from the perspective of someone who spent his entire career as a teacher at Malvern College. To Sayer, life at Malvern was perfection itself. He had not walked in the shoes of Jack Lewis. Nor does it matter that Lewis's account of his time in school was regarded as "unbalanced and exaggerated" by his study mate whose later career led him to the exalted position of air chief marshal, Sir Donald Hardman, C.B.E., K.C.B., D.F.C.[104] They could not identify with Jack's experience any more than Warnie had done, even though Warnie might have done so. Sayer, Hardman, McGrath, and the others do not seem to know what it means to live with a physical handicap that prevents a chap from performing according to the expectations of the culture. In some cultures, Jack would simply have been put in a situation in which he would have died.

In the United Kingdom, the United States, Canada, and several other English-speaking countries, it can seem like the validity of a boy's right to exist depends upon the boy's ability to hit a ball, kick a ball, catch a ball, throw a ball, and do innumerable other things with a ball. Manual dexterity is critical. Boys who cannot do a passable job at sports played with balls simply do not count in some circles. Boys who do well, such as Air Chief Marshall Sir Donald Hardman, C.B.E., K.C.B., D.F.C., do not notice the problem. Rarely do they notice their persecution of the boy who cannot play. At a time in life when a boy's self-image and his further development into a man were at stake, Jack Lewis had the legs kicked out from under him by the other boys. It is a primitive practice that ensures the survival of the fittest. The one thing C. S. Lewis did not do was exaggerate how horrible his experience was at school and how much worse it felt than his experience at the front during the war. At the front, he would do his duty and show courage under fire. He would be wounded. He would be honored. He would have self-respect. None of this would come on the playing fields of public school.

I easily identify with the experience of Jack Lewis at school and have long been amazed that his friends and biographers could not see what he had gone through. But seeing was how I saw. I have amblyopia, often referred to as lazy eye. In short form, it means that I have only one eye that works properly. The other eye is overexerted so that it does not work when the good eye is open. When the good eye is closed, I can see vague images. I can tell if something is a house or a tree. I can even tell if I am looking at a person, but I cannot tell who the person standing in front of me might be. Two eyes allow us to triangulate the position of objects. We can gauge distances. We can estimate where a flying object might be in space. A boy with only one eye cannot hit a ball, catch a ball, throw a ball, kick a ball, or do much of anything at all with a ball. A boy who is more likely to be hit in the head with a baseball than to catch it has seemingly no validity in some contexts. In the adolescent struggle for self-understanding, I found other things that I was good at, and I learned to find my sense of self-worth within me rather than from the crowd. Jack Lewis did the same thing.

Looking back on the experiences he had and the choices he made during his youth, Lewis would observe that they were like arrows shot at him rather than something he worked up within himself. Not until he surrendered in faith to God when he was over thirty years of age would he begin to understand who had been shooting the arrows.[105]

At the end of a long, despairing letter to his father, Jack mused: "I wonder is there any truth in the idea that a wise man can be equally happy in any circumstances. It suddenly struck me the other day that if you could imagine you were at home during the term, it would be just as good as the reality."[106] The apostle Paul had made the claim in his letter to the Philippians (4:12–13). It would be many years before Jack Lewis found his answer. Self-awareness had begun to creep ever so slowly into the life of fifteen-year-old Jack Lewis as he reasoned, "To get on well at one of these [English public schools], one needs to have a constitution of iron, a hide so thick that no insult will penetrate it, a brain that will never tire, and an intelligence able and ready to cope with the sharp gentlemen who surround you."[107] With these words, Jack Lewis described the mystery of conversion that would engulf him in as many more years as his total life up to that point. In describing all that he was not at fifteen, he described all that he would become as one of the great men of Oxford, where his iron constitution, thick skin, and able intellect allowed him not only to survive but to flourish.

Jack Lewis also noticed something else of critical importance to him later. It is difficult for people to see when they are doing evil to others, but it is remarkably easy to see when others do evil to us. The sense of fair play that C. S. Lewis would talk about in the opening pages of *Mere Christianity* was something he had missed growing up at Malvern. He had not been treated fairly, and that matter of injustice bothered him as much as the mistreatment. In the coming years he would have his own world of experience, and he would have the world of ideas introduced to him by W. T. Kirkpatrick. He had good experiences like the pang of Joy that greeted him from time to time, and he would have the bad experiences of injustice that also came upon him unawares. His experiences would play as critical a role in his spiritual journey as the ideas he considered, and in the end, his experiences would help him decide between the many ideas he would encounter.

In this darkest hour since the death of his mother, Jack Lewis experienced something new and glorious that had never happened to him in his entire fifteen years of life. He made a friend. By an act of unpremeditated kindness during the Easter vacation, Lewis accepted an invitation to visit the boy across the street from his father's house. Arthur Greeves was an older boy, the same age as Warnie, whom Jack had known for years, but only as a casual acquaintance. Arthur, who was sick in bed, sent word to Little Lea that he would appreciate a visit from Jack. Because of a weak heart, Arthur Greeves spent most of his life in a quiet way and did not go away to public school as Jack had done, so news that someone near his age had returned to the neighborhood for vacation may have prompted his initiative to seek some company in an otherwise lonely existence. In *Surprised by Joy*, Lewis stated that he could not remember why he accepted the invitation. It was an uncharacteristic act of the introvert. But for some reason, he crossed the street where he discovered the great joy of having a friend.

3

Making a Friend

Spring 1914

Until he entered Arthur Greeves's bedroom during the Easter break of 1914, Jack Lewis had all the makings of an ax murderer. His father and brother had worried for some time about his isolation and growing antisocial tendencies. Though Lewis had always been terribly close to his older brother and would be his closest friend until death, he did not go through the process of making a friend of Warnie. Warnie had always been there. If anything, Warnie had adopted Jack. By the Malvern years, however, his only friend had been taken from him simply by virtue of their age difference. Society had separated them. Albert and Warnie had no idea what to do about Jack. He seemed helpless and hopeless as he retreated further into his arrogance and sense of superiority.

Lewis had known Greeves for many years as merely the older boy down the lane. He had no interest in forming a friendship with Arthur Greeves, and only reluctantly went across the street to visit him when word came to Little Lea that Arthur was ill and would appreciate some company. Arthur had made overtures to the Lewis boys several times over the years, to no avail. When Arthur died, Warnie noted in his diary with some guilt and regret that his

> most enduring recollection of him was of the early days at Leeborough when to both of us he was simply that most exasperating boy across the road who loafed in at unseasonable hours to interrupt us in our games, drawings, writings, the wholy [*sic*] busy world of Boxen in fact—and would not take the most brutal schoolboy hints to go away.[1]

Greeves had been at Campbell College during the brief time that Jack was there, but they did not cross paths. Before Jack could have a friend, however, something had to happen to Jack Lewis. Lewis had no material out of which to form a friendship when Arthur had initially tried, but by Easter break 1914, he had a storehouse that would form the basis of his friendship with Arthur and all of his most important friendships in the years to come.

Enter Norse Mythology

In *Surprised by Joy*, Lewis described how his deep, lifelong friendship with Arthur Greeves began through their shared love of Norse mythology. Although they had known each other for many years, the friendship between Lewis and the older Greeves, who was Warnie's age, had never developed until this common interest emerged. The fascination born of Lewis's casual encounter with Rackham's illustrations of Wagner's *Ring* shown in the Christmas 1911 issue of *The Bookman* had grown far beyond Wagner by the time Lewis crossed the street to visit Greeves. Lewis had the sort of attachment to Norse mythology that boys of his age would have had for cowboys at one time, or superheroes at another. For boys not interested in sports, this sort of enchantment is not at all unusual.

Most people are blessed not to remember every incident of every day of their lives. We tend to remember moments that have a particular significance we may not even realize at first. Looking back at his early encounters with Norse mythology more than forty years later from the vantage point of his newly acquired Chair of Medieval and Renaissance Literature, Lewis recalled his first tastes of northernness with a vividness that testified to their significance for who he would become. First, Rackham's pictures had engulfed him in "a vision of huge, clear spaces hanging above the Atlantic in the endless twilight of Northern summer, remoteness, severity. . . ."[2] This experience of northernness sparked a memory of a similar experience he had years earlier, which Lewis placed sometime before his mother's death. He had grown fond of Longfellow's *Saga of King Olaf*, and while thumbing through this volume, he came across Longfellow's translation of *Tegnér's Drapa* with the lines

> I heard a voice that cried,
> Balder the beautiful
> Is dead, is dead—[3]

Both experiences with Norse mythology had aroused in young Jack a powerful emotion reinforced by the memory of having experienced the emotion before. In later life, Lewis would call this experience Joy, probably influencing J. R. R. Tolkien, who wrote that grace does not deny the existence "of sorrow and failure: the possibility of these is necessary to the joy of deliverance; it denies (in the face of much evidence, if you will) universal final defeat and in so far is *evangelium*, giving a fleeting glimpse of Joy, Joy beyond the walls of the world, poignant as grief."[4] Joy as poignant as grief captures the intensity of what Lewis felt as an "unendurable sense of desire and loss."[5]

The Norse mythologies had presented the moment in which Lewis had an experience that dominated his memory, and he wanted to have the experience again. He found that he could not re-create the experience or cause it to happen again, but he could remember that he had had the experience, and he nurtured that memory of a memory, even if it was not the feeling. As a teenage boy, like most other teenage boys before and since, Lewis liked music. In 1912 the options for records were rather limited, but Albert Lewis had indulged his sons with the gift of a gramophone of their own. Lewis poured over gramophone catalogs and came to consider himself an expert at music. While leafing through *The Soundbox*, a standard catalog of the day, he found a synopsis of Wagner's *Ring*, and then he heard "Ride of the Valkyries" at a local record shop. Until then, his highest musical experience had been Gilbert and Sullivan. He had never heard anything like Wagner, and for a while, all of his pocket money went to buy recordings of Wagner's northern operas.[6] To the pictures and the music, Lewis added the words of the *Ring* when he found the very book that *The Bookman* had only reviewed. While visiting his older cousin, Hope Ewart Harding, he found *Siegfried and the Twilight of the Gods* on the drawing room table.[7] Even then, it was Arthur Rackham's images rather than Wagner's words that he desired. Warnie went halves with him, and they bought a cheap edition of the prized volume. Years later, Lewis recognized that Warnie had come up with the extra money "purely through kindness, as I now see and then more than half suspected, for he was not enslaved by Northernness."[8] Warnie was always that way with his little brother.

The Norse stories grew into Lewis's great obsession. He could not get enough of them. Though he did not believe in the Norse gods as actual divine beings, they were much more important to him than the God of the Bible. They made him feel a certain way that his old religion had never done, even if they were not real. He did not feel the loss of his old religion, but he would have felt the loss of the Norse gods most poignantly if they had been taken from him. Years later, Lewis would ponder this youthful fascination with Norse gods and wonder if God had sent him the false gods so that he could acquire the capacity to worship the real God when he made himself known.[9]

To Wagner's interpretation of the Norse myths, Lewis added H. A. Guerber's *Myths of the Norsemen*, Donald A. Mackenzie's *Teutonic Myth and Legend*, and Paul Henri Mallet's *Northern Antiquities*.[10] Once at Malvern, which had an admirable library, Lewis found *Corpus Poeticum Boreale*, F. York Powell's edition of the mythological poems known as the *Elder Edda*. From this last work Lewis "tried, vainly but happily, to hammer out the originals from the translation at the bottom of the page."[11]

It is only a brief step from futile efforts to translate Old Icelandic by the use of footnotes to embarking on writing one's own great Norse poem. Lewis began writing his epic "Loki Bound" during the summer of 1914, just after making friends with Arthur Greeves over Easter vacation.

Living in the semimythological landscape of Ireland, Lewis acquired a newfound appreciation of his own world, and he began to sense that in just such places the old Norse gods used to rummage and cavort. During a cycling holiday, he began to imagine how the mountains and hillsides might belong to Wagner's world, and that he might come upon Mime, Sieglinde, or Siegfried in the next glade. Nature did not merely remind him of the deep experience he had when he first encountered the illustrations by Arthur Rackham. Nature itself created the mood that reminded him of the experience.[12]

Unfortunately, this newfound interest in northernness that soon took over his internal life had no place at Malvern College. No one at Malvern had any interest in whether Balder the beautiful had died. Who cared? Jack's interest managed to cut him off from the others in his school even more than their interest in sports had done. Because of the association in his experience between the world of Norse mythology and an unknown longing that had come upon him powerfully several times in his brief life, this interest went beyond a mere hobby. Somehow it meant life itself, but he had no idea how. He was pursuing not an intellectual idea but the return of a feeling he could not conjure.

The discovery of northernness coincided with Jack's growing isolation from the other boys at school. Neither his brother Warnie nor (later) his former pupil and close friend George Sayer could ever bring themselves to sympathize with the depth of Jack's hatred of the public school experience. In a sense, it was the inverse of Br'er Rabbit's briar patch. Br'er Fox could not imagine any horror worse than the torture of being cast into the briar patch, but to Br'er Rabbit—for whom the briar patch was home—it was the greatest delight. Warnie had an entirely different attitude toward games than Jack did. In his lavishly illustrated *Through Joy and Beyond*, Walter Hooper includes a sketch by Jack of Warnie playing cricket in 1930.[13] Warnie thought Malvern a wonderful place because the boys got to play cricket and rugby every day of the year! Warnie appears to have enjoyed various games. He wrote in his diary of winning at tennis in 1922.[14]

Though Warnie was not enslaved by northernness, he had an inkling of what his younger brother had experienced. When Warnie accompanied Jack in 1946 to the University of St Andrews in Scotland, which conferred upon him an honorary doctoral degree, Warnie wrote in his diary of the Scottish landscape with an overwhelming sense of "all that 'northernness' which was my first love and will be my last."[15] What Jack had found in literature, Warnie had found in nature. That same spring, Warnie wrote of a "restless melancholy discontent" which came upon him every spring. It was one of his oldest feelings, and he wrote:

> I can remember feeling it in days when I looked *up* into the delicious fragrant mass of flowering currant at the old house. For years I thought it a materialist phenomenon—that the discontent would be instantly cured by a change of station, more money, more leave etc. But I begin to suspect that it is spiritual, a subconscious longing for another world.[16]

In 1967 he noted in his diary that the currants were in bloom, and it took him back to life at Dundela Villas, probably before the birth of Jack, when the flowering of the currants was his first aesthetic experience. He wondered if the experience pointed to a better world. On All Saints Eve in 1948, Warnie attended services at St. Cross, where Charles Williams was buried. Warnie noted in his diary that "whilst waiting for it to begin, I had one of those blinding flashes of exquisite happiness which come and go like lightning. Always a mysterious thing, and must I think be a direct individual intimation of heavenly bliss—and a strong hint to strive for it."[17] Thus, Warnie had a point of reference for appreciating Jack's experience of northernness, but he could not share it. When Arthur Greeves died, Warnie wrote that "there was much of [Jack's] imaginative life which only Arthur could share with him, all that 'Northernness' as they called it, to which I could not respond."[18]

Sharing a Common Interest

In his state of isolation, Jack Lewis crossed the street during Easter vacation 1914 to visit Arthur Greeves, who was sitting up in bed, delighted to have a visitor. Years later, in *The Four Loves*, Lewis would reflect on the odd nature of friendship that does not depend on people being alike. Unlike romantic love, in which two people focus on each other, friendship begins with a focus on a common interest that draws people together. Only later does it become what the Greeks called brotherly love. As Lewis entered the bedroom, he saw on the bedside table the book *Myths of the Norsemen*, H. A. Guerber's study of Norse mythology, which he had been reading. Lewis recalled the exchange between himself and Greeves that revealed their common interest when, forty years later, he wrote in *Surprised by Joy*:

"Do *you* like that?" said I.
"Do *you* like that?" said he.

Describing in *The Four Loves* how friendship begins, Lewis went back to this first moment of making his first friend: "The typical expression of opening Friendship would be something like, 'What? You too? I thought I was the only one.'"[19] When such a thing happens to two or more people, Lewis reflected, "instantly they stand together."[20] Thus, Walter Hooper took this last phrase from Lewis as the title for the edited volume of letters from Lewis to Greeves, *They Stand Together*.

And so began a deep friendship that would last for just a few months shy of fifty years. The depth of the friendship remains evident more than a half century after Lewis's death, because most of what we know of Lewis behind the facade of his intellectual stamina comes from the trove of letters he wrote to Greeves, in which he talked about most of his most personal matters.

Norse mythology would remain an important part of their friendship, but it also became a factor in other relationships and episodes throughout Lewis's life. Another example of how Wagner and the *Ring* provided a touchstone for relationships appears in a letter from Lewis to Greeves when Lewis was billeted at Keble College in June 1917 while in the Officer Training Corps. Lewis had spent the afternoon on the river with his cousin Cherry Robbins, who turned out to love Wagner and Arthur Rackham's illustrations as much as Lewis and Greeves did. Not only had she seen *Die Walküre* at Covent Garden, but she had read the *Ring* libretto in Lewis's beloved Rackham edition. In the final analysis, however, Lewis sadly judged that she was not beautiful enough for him.[21]

A month later in another letter to Greeves, Lewis mentioned that he had read *Siegfried* in German, which had stirred his enthusiasm for Wagner to the extent that he wanted a gramophone. Even as he discussed the wildness of Wagner's poetry and the majesty of the music, Lewis acknowledged that a great deal of his pleasure in the *Ring* came from Rackham's pictures.[22] In 1918, a month before the Armistice, Lewis expressed his disgust that the Germans would dare to name their great defensive trench system the Siegfried Line. He wrote, "Anything more vulgar than the application of that grand old cycle to the wearisome ugliness of modern war I can't imagine."[23]

When Warnie Lewis decided to organize the Lewis family papers after his retirement in 1931, together with a sketch of everyone associated with the family, Jack reluctantly undertook a sketch of Arthur Greeves, but only after Warnie's effort had missed the mark.[24] Fortunately, Jack's concise sketch of Arthur provides a picture of the man from his youth: his character, his habits, his preferences, his virtues, and his vices. Otherwise, we would know little of Arthur Greeves because only a few of his letters to Jack have survived. We are left to infer from the almost three hundred letters from Jack to Arthur what Arthur thought and felt and did.

An Unlikely Friend

From Jack Lewis's description of Arthur Greeves, it seems the two boys could not have been more different. Greeves had a bad heart condition from childhood and experienced poor health throughout his life. Though a despiser of organized team sports, Lewis enjoyed robust health and vigorous exercise in the form of brutal thirty-mile hikes, as well as early morning swims in icy cold ponds. Lewis self-identified as a scholar, but by this term he probably meant its original meaning: a person who had earned a scholarship. By comparison, Lewis said that Arthur was "a dull boy" without "ideas."[25] At first glance, this remark sounds like a severe insult of someone who had been Jack's best friend for over twenty years. In fact, the insult is a boomerang, for Lewis had learned a great deal about himself since first becoming friends with Arthur.

In *Surprised by Joy*, Lewis referred to his younger self as a "prig." American English has no equivalent. *Nerd* and *geek* simply come nowhere near the mark. Terms like *obnoxious little twit*, *intellectual snob*, and *stuck-up smarty-pants* come closer, but lack the full import of the single word *prig*. Needless to say, Jack was not a pleasure to be around, and his father and brother were concerned. If Lewis thought of himself as a boy when he wrote The

Chronicles of Narnia, he would not have seen himself as noble Peter, the high king. He was Eustace Clarence Scrubb, the little boy who almost deserved to have a name that no right-thinking boy would ever want to use, like Clive Staples Lewis.

To all appearances, the relationship between Jack and Arthur might seem one-sided, but Lewis received much more from Greeves than Greeves received from Lewis, in spite of Jack's continual stream of pedantic instruction. Lewis wrote, "I learned charity from him and failed, for all my efforts, to teach him arrogance in return."[26]

Charity for Lewis did not mean mere philanthropy. Jesus dismissed mere philanthropy in the Sermon on the Mount as a matter that easily devolves to self-interest (Matt. 6:2–4). The adult Lewis chose his words carefully. He did not mean that he found Arthur merely generous or magnanimous. In *The Four Loves*, which Lewis wrote some forty-five years after his friendship began with Greeves, he explored three forms of natural love mentioned by Edmund Spenser, to which Lewis added the selfless love of divine origin found in the New Testament, most famously in 1 Corinthians 13. Friendship is the form of love that the Greeks called *philia*. *Charity*, on the other hand, is the word used by the translators of the King James Bible for the divine love known in Greek as *agapē*. The divine love bestowed upon a person allows that person to love what is naturally unlovable.[27] It also allows a person to give to the needy apart from self-interest. In other words, Arthur Greeves presented to Lewis in his most virulent atheist years a form of love that flew in the face of the materialistic view of the world he had adopted. In *The Four Loves*, Lewis spoke of the supernatural dimension of charity that defied mere natural selection and the quest for advantage.[28]

To friendship and charity, Lewis added that Greeves had introduced him to the love of what Arthur called the homely—the charm of everyday life so easily taken for granted or overlooked. He loved the bright hearth, the ducks in a barnyard, a row of cabbages, and anything else characteristic of the "love of home." In *The Four Loves*, Lewis came to describe this kind of love as affection, the English equivalent of the Greek word *storgē*. The homely involves the love of places, people, sights, sounds, smells, and anything else associated with our roots.[29] To round out Arthur's influence on providing Lewis with the basic ingredients of *The Four Loves*, Greeves became Lewis's only confidant in the exploration of his adolescent ideas about sex, to which Lewis gave the more dignified designation of *eros* in the book. Though Lewis would take the outline to *The Four Loves* from Edmund Spenser, he had learned of them and found much of their embodiment in Arthur.[30]

In *Mere Christianity*, Lewis insisted that the habit of giving to the poor constitutes "an essential part of Christian morality."[31] Lewis spoke these words in a radio broadcast over the BBC on September 27, 1942.[32] After discussing the importance of gauging the amount one gives in terms of the degree to which it might infringe on one's pleasures, he said that the real reason people give less is their fear of insecurity. Whether that is the problem for anyone else, it was certainly a fear that beset Jack and Warnie Lewis. Giving did not come naturally to Jack Lewis, yet he gave away the royalties from his books and more. He had learned this kind of generosity from Arthur Greeves.

Lewis wrote that Arthur had acquired a love of money by heredity and training, for he came from a wealthy family and never worked for a living throughout his life. Yet, Arthur overcame this vice, becoming the sole support of an unemployed man, and helping Lewis when money was short.[33] The period when Lewis needed financial help probably fell during the years 1919 through 1925. During this period after the Great War when Jack returned to Oxford to complete his education, Albert Lewis provided ample support for his son. Jack's financial expenditures, however, went far beyond his own needs for he had undertaken the support of Mrs. Janie Moore and her daughter Maureen, the mother and sister of Lewis's roommate in the Officer Training Corps, Paddy Moore, who was killed in the last year of the war. Jack and Paddy had become acquainted during officer training before leaving Oxford for France in 1917. They had promised each other that if one of them should die and the other live, the survivor would care for the parent of the deceased.[34]

Lewis had made a noble promise befitting the generosity of Arthur Greeves but without the resources of Greeves to back it up. Jack Lewis kept from his father the domestic circumstances of the trio in Oxford, so he could not rely on financial aid from that quarter. Apparently, Arthur came through. While he managed to keep his father in the dark about Mrs. Moore, Jack mentioned her regularly in his letters to Arthur, even suggesting that Arthur partner with Mrs. Moore in a poultry farm in Headington.[35] Perhaps Arthur decided it was easier to send money.

Books, Music, and Country Walks

Jack wrote his first letter to Arthur Greeves from Malvern College on June 5, 1914, after returning to school from his Easter break. He made the usual apologies one makes for taking so long to write, then bounded into a long exposition of how he felt about Malvern. He cataloged the faults quickly under sports, schoolwork, and food. The worst feature of life at Malvern, however, was the absence of any interest in music and books among the "brainless English schoolboys."[36] Not only was Arthur interested in such things, but he also shared with Lewis the virtue of not being English. The greatest positive feature of Malvern was its library, and through this library, Lewis had discovered the Irish poet W. B. Yeats, whose works brimmed with what Lewis told Greeves was "our old Irish mythology."[37]

In addition to sharing a love of Norse mythology, Lewis and Greeves found that they shared a love of the Irish countryside. This first letter to Greeves reminisces about County Down and the Holywood Hills. Lewis inquired of Greeves's favorite places to go walking. He began planning their walks together when this term, which had just begun, would finally come to a close. Lewis and Greeves would walk the hills of Ireland together for decades to come, and these kinds of walks in the company of Arthur Greeves would become a lifelong passion. He had taken solitary walks, but he began to anticipate how wonderful it would be to hike with people who enjoyed the same kind of walks.

Over time, however, Lewis learned that he and Arthur enjoyed their walks in different ways. Lewis had no interest in dissecting nature any more than he had been interested in dissecting frogs in school. He had revolted at the idea of killing the frog in order to study it, and he equally revolted at the idea of fragmenting nature in order to appreciate it. He wanted to experience the out-of-doors as a whole, which had an effect on him the same way he expected a novel or a poem to work on him. During his adolescence he established the habit of charging across the countryside, over hill and dale, through the brambles and the bushes, bounding through the whole of nature as it embraced him. Here he had experienced Joy, and here he was reminded of the experience even if he could not re-create it or compel it. Thus, when Tolkien joined him and other Inklings on walking vacations later in life, Lewis always left Tolkien far behind as the latter insisted on stopping to examine flowers, twigs, and anything else that caught his eye. For Lewis, it was like having a botanist along. Writing almost half a century after making friends with Arthur Greeves, who would grow up to become a landscape painter, Lewis observed without mentioning Greeves, "If you love nature in his fashion, a landscape painter is (out of doors) an even worse companion than a botanist."[38]

A Lifelong Correspondence

The first letter to Arthur from Jack at Malvern College is also the last letter Jack wrote to Arthur from Malvern. By early August, the term was over, and Jack Lewis would never again return to Malvern College as a pupil. He would complete his education preparatory to the Oxford entrance examinations with W. T. Kirk-patrick. This first letter appears to have been prompted by one from Arthur, because Jack responded to Arthur's news that he was learning music theory and that he had undertaken the job of having Jack's gramophone repaired.[39] This kind of specific reply averted a problem that frequent correspondents may face when their letters cross in the mail.

When people frequently write to each other, they need to find some way to clarify which letter they are answering. Lewis solved the problem by addressing specific incidents within Arthur's letters. Though we do not have what Arthur wrote to Jack, Jack's reply allows the reader to infer what Arthur had said and done. Over time, it is possible to construct a fairly solid picture of Arthur's beliefs and habits by reading Jack's responses. As an example, one of Jack's earliest letters to Arthur, on October 6, 1914, stated that Jack would begin by answering Arthur's questions. From Jack's answers we may infer what questions prompted each one. The apostle Paul took this approach of answering questions in his first letter to the Corinthians. More to the point of the development of Jack Lewis into C. S. Lewis, the correspondence with Arthur taught Jack how to write the book known as *The Screwtape Letters*.

Arthur Greeves is not the subject or inspiration for *The Screwtape Letters*, but the long practice of writing to Arthur in a continuing dialogue taught Lewis a literary technique that is deceptively difficult. The reader of *The Screwtape Letters* can easily infer the situation with the young demon Wormwood and his "patient" by reading the instructional letter from the senior tempter Screwtape. It is all there without seeming to be in any way artificial. This kind of correspondence is a literary skill that occasional letter writing does not tend to develop, but it is a critical skill for correspondents who might follow a subject or train of thought across several exchanges, especially when letters cross in the mail. Arthur Greeves provided the context in which Lewis learned this skill in a way that Jack's casual writing to his father, with whom he did not explore great questions or share deepest thoughts, could never have done. Letters about the weather and what I did today might be written to anyone or no one at all.

Letters to Arthur also taught Lewis an important skill without which he would not be broadly known today. Granted, he still would have been the author of *The Allegory of Love, A Preface to Paradise Lost, The Abolition of Man, English Literature in the Sixteenth Century, An Experiment in Criticism,* and *The Discarded Image,* and he would have a place of standing in a community of several hundred scholars worldwide. Without this skill, however, he could not have written the radio broadcasts that became *Mere Christianity.* He could have written *Dymer* and *The Pilgrim's Regress* without this skill, but he could not have written *The Screwtape Letters, The Great Divorce,* The Chronicles of Narnia, or the Ransom trilogy.

Because Arthur was not a deep intellectual, Jack had to learn to talk about huge ideas in small ways. Though wealthy and educated, Arthur needed extra help in following the thoughts of Jack Lewis, so Jack learned how to make himself understood to someone who had not done all the hard work of thinking through difficult problems. Though given to artistic tastes, Arthur Greeves remained the common man, and C. S. Lewis would make his reputation on his skill at explaining the biggest ideas of the last twenty-five hundred years to the average person on the street. He might have learned this skill later in some other way, but most of his colleagues at Oxford and Cambridge never did. They might have done so, but their friends tended to be like them. Jack's first friend was not like him. Jack was learning that true friendship depends not on being like someone else but on liking what someone else likes.

Arthur Greeves started Jack Lewis down a dangerous path that led him to the conviction by 1941 that there is no such thing as an *ordinary* person, the *mere* common man. In a sermon he was asked to give in the University Church of St Mary the Virgin on

June 8, 1941, even as the Battle of Britain was coming to a close, Lewis declared that it is in light of the possibility of glory that "we should conduct all our dealings with one another, all friendships, all loves, all play, all politics."[40] In this conclusion to this sermon titled "The Weight of Glory," Lewis went on to say that the matter becomes even more heightened when one's neighbor is truly a Christian, because the one who glorifies has taken up residence in that person, and the neighbor becomes "the holiest object presented to your senses" after the blessed sacrament itself.[41]

During all the early years of their friendship, when Lewis had adopted a fierce atheistic perspective on the world, Greeves remained a Christian unshaken by Jack's latest and most fashionable arguments for why God could not possibly exist and why the Jesus story was only a myth. Greeves would be susceptible to a variety of fringe groups and sects that preyed on the devout but simple, yet in all his many explorations, he did not linger long in the hinterland. Like Bunyan's Pilgrim, he always returned to the narrow road. Arthur Greeves showed Lewis what the hope of glory looks like. Greeves was the effect of what Lewis would not give serious consideration until double his lifetime from when they first met. Looking back in 1941 from the pulpit of St Mary the Virgin in Oxford, Jack realized that it had been Arthur Greeves who had treated him as one who might inherit glory, regardless of how little Jack had valued glory at the time. Long before he became a Christian, Lewis recognized something different about Arthur Greeves, so that beginning in May 1915, he often addressed Greeves as Galahad in his letters. Sir Galahad was the son of Sir Lancelot and Lady Elaine in Malory's *Le Morte d'Arthur* (1485), who, alone among all the knights of King Arthur's round table, found the Holy Grail because of his purity.[42]

Young Artists

Arthur played the piano and fancied himself a composer in the same way that Jack fancied himself a poet. By October 1914, Jack had conceived the idea for an opera that the two would produce together with Jack writing the libretto and Arthur composing the music. "Loki Bound" would be a grand opera of Wagnerian proportions in the style of Greek tragedy, though dealing with the Norse gods. Thus, he proposed combining their interest in things northern with their respective love of poetry and music.

In Jack's prologue, Loki, the god of fire, explains how he fell out with the other gods over the creation of humans, which Loki regarded as a bad idea. Odin, the ruler of the gods, has enslaved Loki. To aggravate the conflict, Loki had persuaded the gods to enter a contract with the giant Fasold, who agreed to build a wall around the godly dwelling of Asgard in exchange for the goddess Freya, who would become his concubine. With the wall almost completed, the gods now regret their bargain and blame Loki. At the insistence of Thor, Odin agrees to punish Loki if he cannot find a way out of the contract before the wall is completed. In dialogue with the chorus, Loki conceives a plot to send a spirit of madness into the horse of Fasold, which bears the brunt of the labor in building the wall. During the last night before the term of the contract expires, Fasold and his horse drag the last great stone toward the wall when Fasold strikes up a conversation with the chorus about his hopes and fears over his approaching acquisition of the beautiful goddess Freya. Suddenly the spirit drives the horse wild. It breaks its bonds, kicks its master, and gallops off as the dawn begins to break. Fasold has failed to keep his side of the bargain and Freya is safe. All the gods rejoice over their defeat of Fasold except Odin, who realizes that doom awaits them all. The power of the gods rests on their treaties governed by honor. Because they have cheated Fasold and defrauded him by trickery, "the twilight of the gods" is upon them. As this reality sinks in, Loki scorns the gods who had treated him ill and tells them that their doom has been his plan all along. Because no god has the power to kill Loki, the gods persuade Odin to chain him to a rock. In the final scene, Odin returns to Loki to offer forgiveness. Unlike all other beings,

Loki is not created by Odin but created with Odin by the Fates. Loki is the only one who can be a friend to Odin, but Loki rejects the offer and the tragedy ends.[43]

The story has all the power of Norse mythology. Jack based it on the same traditions that Wagner used in composing his *Ring* opera cycle. If one did not fear violating what C. S. Lewis called "the personal heresy" in his literary critical dispute with E. M. W. Tillyard in the 1930s, one might recognize a shadow of Jack Lewis in Loki, the cleverest of the gods, who endured abuse and scorn from lesser beings before he finally got back at them all. One might also recognize the yearning for friendship and the pain of loneliness that Jack Lewis had felt for so long as the boy who was different and did not fit in. While the story is about something that Jack knows well, it is not about Jack, who did not reject the offer of friendship when it came from someone that a prig would regard as beneath his dignity. Jack was learning that true friendship has no such "dignity."

Jack did not stop with laying out his part of the partnership. He went on to suggest the musical treatment for each character and scene, ranging from the "somber and eerie" opening song of Loki to the "swinging ballad" of the giant to the "inexpressibly sad, yearning little theme" in which Odin describes his loneliness.[44] Arthur replied with approval of the project, but apparently expressed his fears of inadequacy at preparing a full orchestral score for such a grand opera. Jack replied that he need not worry about the score. They would have a "hireling" tend to the dirty work.[45]

From musical questions, the boys went on to the problems of the set. Jack confessed that he was not as good as Arthur was at music and at painting, so he deferred to Arthur to produce the actual illustrations to accompany the opera. Having deferred, however, he then proceeded to tell Arthur what his illustrations should look like: "First of all, the vast, dreary waste of tumbled volcanic rock with Asgard gleaming high above the background thrown out into sharp relief by the lurid sunset: then in the fore-ground there is the lithe, crouching figure of Loki, glaring with satanic malignity at the city he proposes to destroy."[46] Arthur may have begun producing the illustrations, for in a letter a week later, Jack sympathized with the difficulty that Arthur had with drawing a horse—presumably Fasold's horse.[47]

The early letters from Jack to Arthur indicate that the friendship sparked the creative powers of the teenage boy that had lain dormant since the days of his private fantasy worlds known as Boxen and Animal Land. Talk of "Loki Bound" only led to ideas about other grand projects he might undertake. Once he had finished his Norse opera, he thought of writing an Irish drama or narrative poem.[48] The dull, practical talk of grownups suggested an allegorical treatment of Irish mythology. The earliest gods of Ireland were the Formons: monstrous, hideous brutes. They were overthrown by the light and beautiful Shee. At this point, it is impossible to defend Lewis against "the personal heresy," for he made clear that he and Arthur were the Shee who talked about art, literature, science, and music, while the adults were the monstrous Formons with their stern, ugly, money-grubbing talk.[49] In his next letter, Arthur must have asked what a Shee was, for Jack's reply began with a long, technical, etymological discussion of the linguistic background to the word and the relationship between the Celtic and the Teutonic.

As the weeks passed, Jack inquired in vain about the progress of Arthur's musical composition and illustrations for the opera. Though they liked some of the same things, Arthur never rose to the level of Jack in terms of talent or energy to exercise what talent he had. Arthur dreamed of writing music, but he never went so far as to actually compose any of the music he dreamed about. Jack continued to encourage, praise, compliment, and cajole, but it must have become apparent that Jack would not have a collaborator with Arthur. Without a musical partner, Jack abandoned his Loki opera. He would have greater success encouraging J. R. R. Tolkien to complete *The Lord of the Rings*.

During the Easter break of 1915, however, Jack had turned his hand to writing poetry in earnest. During the two years before going up to Oxford, he wrote fifty-two poems, fourteen of which he included in *Spirits in Bondage*, the collection of poetry that would become his first published book.[50] By June he suggested that Arthur might illustrate his lyric poems and then proceeded to instruct Arthur on how the pictures should be drawn: "You can begin a picture of my 'dream garden' where the 'West winds blow'. As directions I inform you it is 'girt about with mists', and is in 'shadowy country neither life nor sleep', and is the home of 'faint dreams'."[51]

Over time, Jack became less instructive and more accepting of his new friend even as friendship began to have its own impact on him.

4

Jack and War Come to Great Bookham

Fall 1914

Jack Lewis arrived in Great Bookham on Saturday, September 19, 1914, to study with W. T. Kirkpatrick. While the experience of meeting the tall, lean, bewhiskered logician might have been unpleasant to many young boys, the mature C. S. Lewis would recall that it was like "red beef and strong beer."[1] Having departed from Ireland, Jack arrived in London at Euston Station and then transferred to Waterloo Station, where he caught a train to Great Bookham.[2] Traveling down through Surrey from London, Lewis passed the rugged and quaint countryside that suggested to him the very idea of "Happiness" and filled him with a desire for a domesticity that had eluded him until then, but which he would find in abundance during this next period in his life. He found comfort, security, nurture, stimulation, challenge, and satisfaction in the home he was about to enter.

Forty years after he went to live and study with W. T. Kirkpatrick, C. S. Lewis described in *Surprised by Joy* their first meeting at the train station in Great Bookham, Surrey. In his stumbling effort to make conversation, young Lewis commented on how surprised he was to find such wild country in Surrey. Kirkpatrick immediately set about to organize the way Lewis thought. Had he ever been to Surrey? Had he read about the topography of Surrey? What grounds had he for any expectation about the countryside of Surrey? Jack Lewis's introduction to logic had begun. What would follow were three years of critical training during every waking moment and in every setting, from breakfast to supper every day. Until Kirkpatrick, education had meant learning information. With Kirkpatrick, education meant learning how to think about information one had encountered.[3]

The description of his first encounter with Kirkpatrick leaves Lewis appearing rather simple and doltish. It demonstrates a skill in writing that some authors never develop. He creates an effect or impression in his audience without expressing it overtly. He wanted his audience to admire the teacher to whom he knew that he owed so much. He accomplished this task at his own expense. He gave the impression that he had no grounds for being surprised by the wildness of the Surrey landscape when, in fact, he had a reason for his assumption, however poorly grounded.

Lewis actually had read about Surrey before meeting Kirkpatrick, but he accepted the view of a person whom he should have regarded as highly unreliable in her opinions. By reading Jane Austen's *Emma*, Jack Lewis would have acquired the idea, quite uncritically, that Surrey was a garden and not a wild landscape. Upon meeting Emma, Mrs. Elton remarked that Surrey was "the garden of England." Emma attempted to contradict her, but Mrs. Elton stood her ground. Though Jack did not mention *Emma* specifically in his correspondence until two years later, he had probably already mastered all of Jane Austen's novels by the time he arrived in Great Bookham. In *Surprised by Joy*, Lewis mentions that under the influence of Arthur Greeves, he had read the best of Sir Walter Scott's Waverley novels, all of the novels by the Brontë sisters—Charlotte, Emily, and Anne—and all of Jane

Austen's novels.[4] Within a few days of his arrival at Kirkpatrick's house, he made a familiar reference, in a letter home, to what Jane Austen would have said about the local vicar.[5] By the end of his second week in Great Bookham, Jack had made the trip to what he called "the famous Boxhill," where Emma and her friends went for a picnic.[6] To add to the Jane Austen connection, St. Nicolas Church in Great Bookham, which dates from before the Norman Conquest, had been the parish where Austen's godfather, the Reverend Samuel Cooke, served as rector, and where she often visited during her time in Surrey.[7] Cooke had married Cassandra Leigh, first cousin to Jane Austen's mother. Austen visited the Cookes at Great Bookham in 1799 and 1814. In *Emma*, Austen mentioned not only Box Hill but also Dorking and Guildford, which became favorite haunts of Jack during his years with Kirkpatrick.

Lewis began his first letter home to his father from Great Bookham with two literary allusions. His first ramble into the countryside had brought him to a large forest that reminded him of Shakespeare's *As You Like It*.[8] In this play, the heroine, Rosalind, flees her uncle who has seized control of her father's duchy. She finds refuge in the Forest of Arden, just as Prince Caspian would find refuge from his uncle in the forests of Narnia. This comic love story continues to have huge entertainment value, and Jack Lewis would have read it for fun instead of as a school assignment. A little over a decade later, an older Jack Lewis would undertake his first important scholarly work, *The Allegory of Love*, which explored how the love story came to play such a prominent role in Western culture.

The second literary allusion came as Jack described to his father his first impressions of the village of Great Bookham. It was the kind of village he had read about but never actually seen. He recognized it at once as a place that might have come out of Oliver Goldsmith's *The Vicar of Wakefield*, with its red-tiled cottages, old inn, and early church, dating back to the Norman Conquest of 1066. Goldsmith's novel revolves around the changing fortunes of a wealthy clergyman who loses all due to a dishonest broker. He and his family undergo a number of privations and hardships at the hands of unscrupulous landlords and disreputable characters who send the vicar to debtors' prison and stain the reputations of his daughters before all is put right in the end and the fortune is restored.

Mr. and Mrs. Kirkpatrick lived in a house called "Gastons," and Lewis wrote of his new situation there with extravagant superlatives. He liked Mrs. Kirkpatrick "exceedingly." He was "thoroughly satisfied" with everything about the town, the house, and the Kirkpatricks. He considered the new move a "brilliant success."[9] His initial impression would not diminish materially during his two-and-a-half-year stay with the Kirkpatricks. In Warnie's estimation, however, Kirkpatrick was not a happy man and had married only to obtain a housekeeper after his sister married. As far as Warnie or Jack could see, Mr. and Mrs. Kirkpatrick had no common interests. He found recreation in gardening, Schopenhauer, and Fraser's *Golden Bough*, while she took pleasure in tea parties, bridge, and gossip. Warnie took the view that "Romanticism is essential to happiness, and if a man is an anti-Romantic, he must needs fall back, as I suspect Kirk did, on dispising [*sic*] happiness."[10]

While Jack had given his father an assessment of Great Bookham and life at Gastons, Warnie gave a description of the place that he regarded as

> the most beautiful corner of Surrey, with it [*sic*] wild, oak studded common, its silent stately woods, and its quiet lanes—its hotel where no guests ever seemed to come or go, and its ribbon of road running from the station to "Gastons" with wide stretches of turf separating it from the solid, discreet, tree-enclosed houses on either side.[11]

By the end of his first week at Gastons, Jack had walked the six-mile round trip to the neighboring village of Leatherhead to get his hair cut. He thought the news of a haircut would gladden his father's heart, though it left him looking like a convict, in his own opinion.[12]

The Great War

Over the summer of 1914, between the time Lewis left Malvern and the time he arrived in Great Bookham, the world had slipped into the greatest war it had ever known. In June, Archduke Franz Ferdinand, the heir to the throne of the Austro-Hungarian Empire, had been assassinated in Sarajevo, part of Bosnia, which the Austrians had formally seized from the Ottoman Empire in 1908. The assassin belonged to a terrorist organization known as the Black Hand, which strove to advance the interests of Serbia in creating a single Balkan nation out of many small states, as the Italians and Germans had succeeded in doing only a few decades earlier. The Austrians made a number of demands on Serbia, which involved Austrian involvement within Serbia in the investigation and prosecution of conspirators. Serbia viewed this demand as an unwarranted encroachment on Serbian sovereignty and rejected the critical demands.

The great danger arose because Austria had its eye on Serbian territory, while Russia regarded itself as the historic defender of Slavic nations. To complicate matters, Russia, France, and England had entered into a series of alliances between 1904 and 1907 that called for mutual defense in the event of an attack on any one of the three. In short order, Austria declared war on Serbia on July 28, at which point Russia mobilized its forces, followed by Austria, France, and Germany. Germany declared war on Russia on July 31. On August 3, Germany declared war on France. On August 4, England declared war on Germany. On August 6, Austria declared war on Russia. Over the next four years, nation after nation would join the conflict, with the United States finally entering the war on April 6, 1917.

Within less than two weeks of Jack's arrival in Great Bookham, Warnie Lewis suddenly ended his studies at Sandhurst and was commissioned a second lieutenant in the Royal Army Service Corps. While Jack and Albert were proud of Warnie for obtaining a commission as second lieutenant after only nine months at Sandhurst, when it normally took a minimum of two years, Kirkpatrick only fumed cynically that the government had refused to prepare for the inevitable war during the previous eight years. Warnie's commission was not so much a compliment to his ability as a condemnation of an incompetent government that was sending young officers off to war who were deplorably underprepared.[13] Despite his service as a junior officer, Warnie continued to accept financial assistance from Albert, who paid the bills but never hesitated to warn his son of the pitfalls of army life, including "the dangers of drink." Warnie ignored the warning and fell into the pit that would hold him for the rest of his life, to the despair of his little brother.[14] Albert promised Warnie a supplementary allowance of five pounds per month, but Warnie soon asked for more, to the exasperation of Albert.[15] The allowance continued, supplemented by regular parcels with cigarettes in lots of a hundred, together with cans of pipe tobacco and all manner of cakes, chocolates, and other food. Along with the physical comforts he could send, Albert also sent long letters seasoned with verses of Scripture in a concerted effort to encourage Warnie's spiritual development and faith.

When Jack Lewis arrived at Gastons, he found that the Kirkpatricks' only son, Louis, had been posted to a camp near Great Bookham. He had volunteered almost immediately. Conscription would not come until the winter of 1916. Louis dropped by Gastons to see his parents on the day after Jack's arrival, so Jack met the entire family in short order.[16] Only a few weeks after Britain entered the war, Jack observed that the little village of Great Bookham was in the full swing of war preparedness, with its "sewing meetings and all the usual war codotta."[17] With the success of the Germans in their invasion of Belgium, Great Bookham joined many other English villages in preparing cottages to host Belgian refugees, but Jack ridiculed the effort as being done in a "typical fussy 'Parishional' way."[18] By October 18, the ladies of Great Bookham had a family of seven Belgian refugees in their refugee cottage. Jack tried his French on the mother, but the other members of the family spoke only Flemish. Undaunted, he tried a phrase book on them. The war came closer to Great Bookham, however, through the reports of Louis Kirkpatrick, who described unloading a train full of wounded soldiers who confirmed the newspaper stories of German atrocities, including mutilating nurses and killing wounded soldiers.[19]

The dismissal of the Belgian refugee project as something done in a parishional way, followed by a quip that Kirk had some funny comments about the effort, suggests the strong influence that Kirkpatrick had begun to exercise over the mind of Lewis. His letters to his father are full of comments about Kirk pointing out this or anticipating that or knowing a good deal about thus and such. When he heard that his Ewart cousins believed the rumor that a million Cossacks from Russia had been secretly sent to Britain to fight on the Western Front, Jack said that their "Russian delusion" was an example of how "primitive man" constructed their mythologies and other "nonsense," as Kirkpatrick had pointed out.[20] When the Sunday *Times Literary Supplement* printed an article suggesting that Nietzsche's teachings could not in any way be construed to support the war, Jack wrote to his father that "it just shows how we can be duped by an ignorant and loud mouthed press," because Kirkpatrick knew a great deal about Nietzsche, and he thought the article a great blunder.[21]

Subtle Philosophy

The comment about Nietzsche is particularly telling because heretofore Jack Lewis had not been given to reading obscurantist nineteenth-century German philosophers. He had entered that dangerous period of adolescence when a young person, male or female, might be prone to hero worship of an adult who stood out from the crowd and showed him or her some attention. That had certainly happened between young Lewis and old

Kirkpatrick. Lewis had drifted away from the church and God in an insubstantial way while at Cherbourg School, but now he had the Great Knock—a nickname for Kirkpatrick from Albert's school days—who could provide an intellectual foundation for his newfound atheism. Apparently, in their time spent reading Homer in Greek, Kirkpatrick introduced Jack to Nietzsche by way of his first great book, *The Birth of Tragedy*, which deals with a reinterpretation of Greek culture in terms of the Apollonian tendency and the Dionysian tendency. The Apollonian tendency involves order, rationality, restraint, and harmony and is named for Apollo, the Greek god of truth and light. The Dionysian tendency, on the other hand, involves disorder, drunkenness, frenzy, and freedom from all restraint and is named for Dionysus, the Greek god of wine and madness. Nietzsche identified with Dionysus and came to regard the Dionysian tendency as a synthesis with the Apollonian instead of standing in opposition to it. The real opponent was Jesus Christ. Notably, Nietzsche saw in his contemporary Richard Wagner the rebirth of tragedy, a connection that Jack Lewis would have recognized.

Nietzsche's philosophy did not share with Plato the view that rationality and truth would lead to the good condition of people. He saw no reason for optimism and every reason for pessimism. A brute materialist, Nietzsche saw no rational grounds for morality. Nature just exists; it is neither good nor bad. Morality has no place in a universe of brute matter. Thus, Nietzsche advocated nonconformity as the path to becoming oneself. In order to be himself, Nietzsche realized that he even had to break off his friendship with and regard for Wagner.

Nietzsche's most important philosophical idea is probably the concept of "the will to power." Julius Caesar earned the admiration of Nietzsche for his self-mastery in becoming himself rather than in his achievements as a conqueror. He might just as easily have excelled as a poet. For Nietzsche, the true achievement was in being himself. Such a person stands out as the *Übermensch*, variously translated as "overman," "beyond-man," or (most famously) "superman." The universe of Nietzsche had no place for spirits or gods of any kind. As far as he was concerned, they were not rational and were highly inhibiting to someone wanting to be himself. Thus, Nietzsche coined the phrase "God is dead." While Jack Lewis thought he was doing his Greek, something else was being slipped in alongside it. Years later, C. S. Lewis would recognize the same thing taking place in the form of an English literature textbook for high schools. That later situation became the occasion for him to compose a series of three special lectures he was invited to deliver at the University of Durham. The lectures were published as *The Abolition of Man.*

Another important point about Nietzsche for the later C. S. Lewis concerned Nietzsche's profession. Though known for his philosophy, by training he was a philologist, and his academic post was as professor of philology at the University of Basel. As a young adult, Lewis had rejected Nietzsche by the time he met J. R. R. Tolkien, who was also a philologist. In remarking on the beginning of his friendship with Tolkien, Lewis quipped that having grown up in Ulster, he was suspicious of Catholics, and that upon joining the English faculty at Oxford, he had been warned of philologists. Tolkien was both.[22] Tolkien proved to be an acquired taste for Lewis.

Kirk, as Jack usually referred to Kirkpatrick in his letters to Belfast, had come to be the final authority. Jack ridiculed his father's fears of an invasion as another of Albert's hyperboles. Britain could depend upon her navy; and, besides, Kirk said that the war would end with the complete exhaustion of one side, "or more likely both parties." In the case of the British Navy and the final end of the war, Kirkpatrick proved to be correct. The powerful intellectual influence of Kirk through his infallible logic left Jack bragging to his father that he had a "genuine philosopher" for a son. It was a big change, for he had once thought of himself as a poet.[23]

Trying to Ignore the War

War would not be the preoccupation of Jack in his letters home to his father and to Arthur Greeves, but the war formed the ever-present backdrop of his life from his first arrival in Great Bookham until the Armistice in 1918. While his father fretted about Jack in Great Bookham in the event of a German invasion, Jack reflected that "the truest service that we who are not fighting can do is to conduct our lives in an ordinary way and not yield to panic."[24] In the context of war, Jack Lewis received his most important intellectual stimulus and education. In the context of war, he would read the great books of the Western tradition from Homer through Trollope. And in the context of war, he completed the formation of his tastes, his preferences, his values, his likes, and his dislikes. As for the war itself, however, Jack determined not to let it intrude into his life until such time as he had to go and fight. Until then, he would not think about it.[25]

Thus, Jack seldom commented on the war in his letters home to his father or to Arthur unless something had happened that offended his sense of justice or intelligence. Just such an offense occurred early in the war when Prince Louis of Battenberg had been forced to resign as First Sea Lord because of his German origins. Prince Louis had a complicated lineage. His father was Prince Alexander of Hesse and by Rhine, the younger brother of Grand Duke Louis III of Hesse-Darmstadt. His German-Polish mother, Julia Hauke, was the daughter of a newly created Russian count who had fought in Napoleon's army. Because she was not considered to have sufficient rank to marry someone in the line of succession of the grand-ducal land of Hesse-Darmstadt, the marriage was designated as morganatic, which meant that neither she nor her children could share her husband's princely title. Grand Duke Louis granted her the title of countess but eventually raised her dignity to princess of Battenberg without the right of succession to the grand-ducal title.

Prince Louis's connection with Britain began at the age of fourteen, when he joined the British navy and became a naturalized subject through the intervention of his family's royal connections. Queen Victoria took an interest in him, and he eventually married her granddaughter, Princess Victoria of Hesse by the Rhine, his first cousin once removed. At the beginning of World War I, Prince Louis had risen to the rank of First Sea Lord, the commanding officer of the entire British Navy. British public opinion was so fiercely anti-German, that Louis was forced to resign his post by the end of October 1914.[26]

Jack was outraged by the injustice of it all. From what he had heard, and one wonders where he might have heard it unless from Kirkpatrick, Prince Louis was the most capable man in the navy. He had fallen victim to

a number of ignorant and illiterate clods (who have no better employment than that of abusing their betters). . . . This is what comes of letting a nation be governed by 'the people'. 'Vox populi, vox Diaboli' [the voice of the people is the voice of the Devil], we might say, reversing an old but foolish proverb.[27]

Throughout his life from this point, Lewis recognized the weaknesses of democracy and cherished a romantic attachment to monarchy. On the eve of his sixteenth birthday, however, something else was at work in Lewis that is less attractive. He expressed the view to his father that he hoped a few people from the Low Holywood Road would clear off to the front where they would be much improved by shooting. This callous effort at humor was undergirded with an appeal to Kirk, who feared that one consequence of the war would be "the survival of the *un*fittest."[28] Jack was drinking deeply of Kirk's understanding of social-Darwinian thought, and this understanding would form a critical aspect of his view of reality for more than a decade. Yet, he held on to his romantic notion of the courageous soldier going off to war to be shot, but that left him with the moral and physical dregs of society to carry on afterward.

Despite the war and its promise of horrors to come, Jack felt no great sympathy for the sufferings of those engulfed in its early phase. He observed his lack of feelings for those in distress as he contemplated his own self-satisfaction with the comforts of life away from Malvern. He thought that perhaps he ought not to have such an utter absence of feelings for the plight of humanity, but he also felt that he could no more alter his feelings than alter his height or the color of his hair. His disposition was what it was. He thought it wrong of him to pretend to any false sense of sympathy to interrupt his complacency. He was at a loss to explain himself as he pondered, "Whether this is the egotism of youth, some blemish in my personal character, or the common inheritance of humanity, I do not know."[29] To ponder such questions would prove dangerous to the young atheist, for such questions have unavoidable spiritual implications.

For the time being, however, Jack did not ponder the spiritual implications of his disposition. Instead, he developed a philosophical position to justify himself before his father in what would prove to be a continuing discussion through the mail about whether Jack would have to enter the army and fight. These speculations began about the time Warnie was sent to France in November 1914.[30] Albert Lewis fretted that his younger son would soon be sent off to the front, where only death awaited him, for Albert Lewis tended to expect the worst. Jack, on the other hand, wished only to enjoy the earthly paradise he had found at Gastons and did not want an Irish father spoiling it for him by his continual fretting. Jack referred to the subject as "the controversy of the paradise and inferno."[31] His avowed philosophical argument declared that if evil cannot be avoided, it is best to close your eyes to it and pretend that it is not there.[32] This early attempt at logic appears to have carried little weight with Albert, who would not drop the subject from his correspondence until Jack was at the front as Albert had predicted.

With Arthur, he raised a new philosophical question that occurred to him: Is it always best to tell the truth? Jack decided that always telling the truth was not advisable and could as often as not be criminal. While he acknowledged to Arthur that telling the truth had a certain utility in everyday life, it could lead to sad, unsound conclusions. This sort of discussion, and the reasoning that it reflects, provides a shadow of the discussions Lewis was having with Kirkpatrick about the great philosophical questions of the last twenty-five hundred years. Such questions plagued the ancient Greek philosophers that Jack would read with Kirk. For now, Lewis had only just begun to practice thinking, and he confessed to Arthur that it was sometimes hard to tell when he was thinking.[33]

Imitating Kirkpatrick

Another important change in Jack occurred when he came under the tutelage of Kirk, and it is reflected in his correspondence. Until he moved to Gastons, Jack's letters home began with thankfulness for letters and the inevitable gifts of money, books, and other largesse that flowed from his father. Once he came under Kirk's influence, his letters to his father, his brother, and his only friend began with a severe critique of their previous letters. He pointed out their failure of logic, their ignorance of language and literature, their poor grammar, and anything they might have mentioned in their previous letter. Then with a grand air of magnanimity, he forgave them their shortcomings and assured them of his eternal affection. Jack was imitating his mentor, for better or worse, as teenagers in search of themselves often do.

In a brief sketch that he wrote for Warnie's collection of the Lewis family papers years later, C. S. Lewis said that Kirkpatrick probably had no consciousness of how offensive his own manner must have been to others, whether at a bridge party, at a tea party, or over dinner. Preoccupied by his pursuit of truth as Kirk was, Lewis thought that his mentor would appreciate correction of his own errors and assumed that others would be grateful to him for correcting their failures in thought. Young

Jack appears to have been mimicking Kirk but with the hackneyed skill of a dilettante.[34]

Jack's attitude toward the war and those who would be immediately affected by it had its most personal connection with Warnie, who had left England for France. Albert expected, and Jack had agreed, that the two brothers would meet and say their goodbyes before Warnie departed. Warnie appears to have written to Jack about meeting, but according to Jack, Warnie neglected to designate a time and place, so the farewell meeting never took place.[35] Warnie's tendency toward irresponsibility usually took on a comic strain in Jack's letters to his father, even as Jack made a feeble effort to console his father's fears that his firstborn might soon die in France. Jack often disparaged his brother by affording him exalted titles, like "this great man" or "the colonel."[36]

Kirkpatrick maintained a regular daily routine, which provided Lewis with a structure to develop the discipline necessary to succeed at his studies. Jack told Arthur Greeves of his schedule early on:

8:00	Breakfast
9:15	Greek lessons
11:00	Break
11:15	Latin lessons
1:00	Lunch and free time
5:00	Lessons
7:00	Break
7:30	Dinner and English literature

In middle age, Lewis looked back nostalgically and regarded Kirk's daily schedule as the ideal that he would prefer for himself as a "normal" day.[37] In the Kilns, presided over by Janie Moore, however, a normal day with an uninterrupted routine eluded him. Though Kirkpatrick assigned some reading in English literature, the readings tended to be critical discussions about literature, such as Lewis would write in his *English Literature in the Sixteenth Century* (1954). Kirkpatrick started Lewis on H. T. Buckle's *History of Civilization in England* (1857). Of course, Kirkpatrick allowed Lewis to read all the novels he wanted during his free time, but they had nothing to do with his education from Kirkpatrick's perspective because they did not involve facts.[38]

Visitors to Gastons

Life at Gastons had plenty of action. The Kirkpatricks appear to have kept open house with a constant flow of company for tea and overnight guests. Former pupils regularly turned up. During Jack's first week with the Kirkpatricks, Oswald Smythe spent the week at Gastons. Jack reckoned that Smythe was about twenty-five.[39] He had studied with Kirkpatrick before 1905 for a year and a half, whereupon he had won a first-place entrance to Woolwich School.[40] The Smythes belonged to the larger Lurgan connection of which Albert Lewis was a part. When Warnie had studied with Kirkpatrick, Oswald's mother had come for a visit. She was the sister of Stanley and Howard Ferguson, friends of Albert from his Lurgan days. Mrs. Smythe had taken Warnie to see a moving-picture show in London.[41] Within a few weeks, Smythe's older brother, Gerald, lost an arm and was coming home. The elder Smythe eventually returned to France and by July 1916 had been wounded on two more occasions.[42] This sudden connection with the war in France left Jack reflecting that "it begins to come home to you as a personal element, doesn't it?"[43]

Soon after Jack's arrival, Mrs. Kirkpatrick entertained her theatrical friend by the name of MacMullen, who brought a maid, a bulldog, and a bath chair for her weeklong visit.[44] Miss MacMullen visited Gastons regularly while Jack was in residence, and she usually brought her own brand of drama with her. In July 1915, she enlisted Jack as her "patient" so that she could practice wrapping him in bandages. She treated him in turn for a broken arm, a sprained ankle, and a head wound. He was a good sport about it all, despite having to endure an evening's share of small talk.[45]

Lewis learned by his second week at Gastons that he was expected to learn to play bridge, which had become the great new popular card game made fashionable on trans-Atlantic ocean voyages.[46] Bridge requires four people to play, so it provided a sociable means of entertaining a visitor to Gastons, though Lewis had not yet developed his social skills to a degree that he thought of bridge as an inviting pasttime. Bridge, however, formed part of the broader education of Clive Lewis that Mr. and Mrs. Kirkpatrick intended.

For afternoon tea, Jack had learned to expect a regular visit by the ladies of Great Bookham. He could also expect that his presence was required at tea by Mrs. Kirkpatrick but that Mr. Kirkpatrick was not expected at tea and would not appear. Helping Mrs. Kirkpatrick entertain the ladies became one of Jack's responsibilities as part of his broader education. At tea, Jack had the privilege of learning what Mrs. Grant-Murray would do were she Lord Kitchener. He also discovered all about Mrs. Mile's new maid.[47] Mrs. Crutwell liked to see young people enjoy themselves, which by implication meant that she liked to see Jack comply with how she wanted him to attend to how she enjoyed herself.[48] Jack abominated the "grown-up" conversation that went along with tea. To Arthur Greeves he confessed his contempt for discussions of politics, what happened at the office, golf, war, and the kind of anecdotes that made up typical adult conversation; and forty years later, he had the same view.[49]

Jack's loathing of grown-up talk did not arise as a whim while living with Kirkpatrick. For Jack, grown-up talk usually found its root in the political conversations between Albert and his friends at home in Little Lea. Warnie explained Jack's attitude in terms of the heated political discussions among Albert's like-minded, upper-middle-class set. The talk was never true conversation in terms of an examination of different points of view. Rather, the rantings tended more toward a competition between the participants over who could make the most insulting remarks about the liberal government that proposed home rule for Ireland. The greatest tongue lashing was not aimed at the Irish Catholic, who tended to be dismissed as "a poor ignorant bogtrotter who was too stupid and priest-ridden to understand the blessings of English rule." Instead, the grown-ups aimed their vitriol at the English liberal, who was "an impudent blockhead officiously intervening in an Irish domestic quarrel." Warnie accused Prime Minister Asquith of attempting a *dragonnade* in Ulster in 1914 (the *dragonnade* was the policy of Louis XIV to use force against the French Protestants), which fanned the Ulster Protestant dislike and distrust of the Liberal Party into hatred. Warnie vowed that the very word "liberal" still stank in his nostrils fifty years later.[50]

Because Mrs. Kirkpatrick often had other ladies of Great Bookham to tea, she just as often went to tea at the homes of her friends, which left Jack free to enjoy tea by himself. Though Kirk disdained tea as an institution or a meal, Jack enjoyed it immensely, especially if he could combine the pleasure of food with the pleasure of reading. At tea, he preferred reading something that he could dip into at any point, like Boswell, Andrew Lang's *History of English Literature*, which he was reading for Kirk, or a novel like *Tristram Shandy*.[51]

Roger Lancelyn Green suggested that the character of Mr. McPhee in *That Hideous Strength* derives from Kirkpatrick.[52] Mrs. Kirkpatrick may have played a major role in the development of Jack's caricature of women that ornamented portions of *The Screwtape Letters*, *The Great Divorce*, and *That Hideous Strength*. She certainly provided a model that Mrs. Moore and Edith Tolkien would reinforce, leaving the inexperienced Jack to conclude that they represented the totality of their sex.

Time for Writing

One of the few complaints about life at Gastons that Jack expressed to Arthur early on involved his freedom to write. He felt inhibited at Gastons simply because he did not have the freedom to write whenever he wanted. Ideas did not come to him according to Kirk's routine schedule, and when an idea came, he wanted to write it down immediately. He realized that he could not be pulling out his manuscript in the Kirkpatricks' house whenever the muse struck. The constraints of life at Gastons, where other people had to be taken into consideration, framed the direction that Jack's writing discipline began to take. It is a discipline that others noticed about him years later. George Watson, one of Lewis's last research pupils at Oxford, who became his colleague at Cambridge, wrote that "writing was Lewis's life."[53] Watson once asked Lewis if he ever found it difficult to write, to which Lewis replied, "Sometimes . . . when I come back in the evening after dinner, I tell myself I am too tired and shouldn't write anything. But I always do."[54] Decades after he began discussing the mechanics of writing in his letters to Arthur, Lewis loved to discuss the process of transforming thoughts into words on the page. He remarked to Watson, "I find I want to begin every paragraph with 'It would be difficult to exaggerate . . . ,' so to break myself of the habit I am going to start the next paragraph with 'It would be difficult to exaggerate, but I'm going to have a jolly good try.'"[55]

During the course of his stay at Gastons, Lewis developed a sense of rhythm to his writing while he worked at developing his craft, as he would explain to Arthur Greeves in his letters over the ensuing three-year stay in Surrey. Within the limitations of a house like Gastons with its internal domestic demands, Lewis learned how to find moments to write without the need for long blocks of uninterrupted time. He did not need to get back in the mood to write every time he returned to his pen and paper because he never got out of the mood to write. Tutorials with Kirk, tea with Mrs. Kirkpatrick, long walks through an ancient countryside, and all the other experiences of ordinary life provided him with the straw he needed to make literary bricks.

Music

Lewis loved music from an early age, and the gramophone had become a major form of entertainment for him and Warnie during their hours alone at Little Lea while their father was at work. At Gastons, however, Jack found new delight in music, for Mrs. Kirkpatrick was an accomplished pianist, which Jack considered one of the many great assets of life at Gastons.[56] She had a varied repertoire, and by the end of Jack's third week at Gastons, she had played for him Chopin's preludes and *Marche Funèbre*, Tchaikovsky's *Chanson Triste*, Beethoven's *Moonlight Sonata*, Grieg's *Peer Gynt Suite*, and several popular airs that made Lewis think of home in Ulster.[57] To these she soon added Chopin's mazurkas and Beethoven's *Sonata Pathétique*.[58] Over time, however, Jack gradually lost his appreciation of her skill. He confided to Arthur Greeves that while she may have played all the notes, she played with all the enthusiasm of one pouring tea.[59]

Mrs. Kirkpatrick took steps to broaden Jack's horizons in other ways regarding music. Soon after his arrival at Gastons, she took him and Miss MacMullen to the London Coliseum to see a Russian ballet company perform. Ever the loyal Ulsterman, Jack wrote to his father that the Russian ballet was very good, but the balance of the program was no better than an average show at the Hippodrome in Belfast.[60] The English clearly had nothing on the Irish.

He must have worked hard to present the Coliseum as less than the best. The magnificent building was only ten years old at the time. It was the largest theater in England, seating over 2,300 people, and the only theater in Europe with elevators to the upper balconies. Built in 1904, it represented the last word in Edwardian opulence in the last decade of the glory of the British Empire. The eclectic style of the building included overly lavish decorative motifs in a classical-cum-Byzantine combination of extravagance that, if not tasteful, looked expensive. It stands just off Trafalgar Square, conspicuously situated in the heart of London.[61] The

Hippodrome in Belfast could not touch it. But perhaps this was Jack's way of telling his father that he missed home. In his letter to Arthur Greeves which went into greater detail about the program, he had no such disparaging remark about the program in comparison with the Hippodrome in Belfast, except that the music hall sketches that filled out the program were as boring as music hall sketches everywhere.[62]

When Jack went home to Belfast for Christmas, however, his patriotic defense of the Hippodrome failed him in a letter to Warnie. Jack had gone to several operas at the Hippodrome. The performance of *Faust* was "perfectly glorious," but *Il Trovatore* was "villainously sung," and he did not want to hear it again.[63] Then, when he went with his cousins and the Greeveses to see *Samson and Delilah*, the management changed the performance at the last minute to a revival of Daniel Auber's comic opera *Fra Diavalo*, which Jack considered quite inferior. Never one to give quarter when criticizing music, or anything else for that matter, Jack went on to describe a performance of *The Messiah* that he had attended. He praised the singing of Carrie Tubb, the soprano, then noted that she was "as ugly as the day is long," before going on to criticize the music of Handel in general. Allowing that Handel wrote before composers realized that there could be any point to music, he disparaged the "prettiness" and the appalling tunes of Handel, "as for instance where he makes the chorus repeat some twenty times that they have all gone astray like sheep in the same tone of cheerful placidity that they'd use for saying it was a fine evening."[64]

Jack took advantage of the provincial musical offerings of Surrey from time to time. In October 1915, he went to a concert in Guildford given by Eugène Ysaÿe, a highly idiosyncratic Belgian conductor and violinist of the time. Whether Jack was drawn by the music or by the hope of seeing a certain pretty Belgian girl we cannot guess, though he did not care for the concert. He wondered if the concert was so bad or if he might be losing his musical taste and judgment. He feared he might be becoming like his brother Warnie, whom he thought had lost all proper sensibility.[65]

Finding Narnia

In *An Experiment in Criticism* (1961), C. S. Lewis wrote that all stories are constructions that an author makes from "the stuff of real life."[66] Good writing has a quality, not so much of realism as of authenticity about it. Thus, a long-held rule of thumb about storytelling is to write about what you know. Many first novels make the mistake of telling about the author instead of about what the author knows. The autobiographical novel rarely works. Ernest Hemingway's novels come perilously close to the line that separates interest from boredom, but he rescued his stories by allowing something to happen that never happened to him. Everything else is there: Paris in the 1920s, bullfights in Spain, the Great War in Italy, the Spanish Civil War, and deep-sea fishing in the West Indies.

Great chunks of The Chronicles of Narnia emerged from the stuff of the life of Jack Lewis when he lived with W. T. Kirkpatrick in Great Bookham. Years later, Lewis said that the Narnia stories began with a mental image he had, at the age of sixteen, of a fawn walking through the snow in the woods while carrying packages wrapped in brown paper and holding an umbrella.[67] Lewis turned sixteen his first year at Great Bookham with Kirkpatrick. Interestingly, Peter and Susan could not return to Narnia after this age, just as Wendy Darling could not return to Neverland once she got too old. We can almost pinpoint the week that the Narnian landscape began to form in the mind of Lewis long before he knew it was Narnia. In a letter to Arthur on November 17, 1914, just a few days before his sixteenth birthday, Jack described the recent snowfall:

> We have been deeply covered with it all week, and the pine wood near hear [sic], with the white masses on ground and trees, forms a beautiful sight. One almost expects a 'march of

dwarfs' to come dashing past! How I long to break away into a world where such things were true: this real, hard, dirty, Monday morning modern world stifles one.[68]

This was the landscape in which Jack Lewis first imagined a fawn with umbrella and packages. The landscape must have made a profound impression on the teenage boy, for when he returned to Belfast a few weeks later, he purchased a gramophone record of Edvard Grieg's "March of the Dwarfs" for his burgeoning record collection. Lewis would not have had the story of Narnia in mind at this age, but the landscape of Narnia and its inhabitants was slowly taking shape as another world. Young Lewis walked through the wild woods of Surrey almost every day during his afternoon explorations of the countryside in good weather and in bad. He was free to ramble every afternoon after lunch from 1:00 until tea at 4:30.[69] Normally, he took these afternoon walks by himself.[70]

We are perhaps tempted to think of C. S. Lewis as the old professor in *The Lion, the Witch and the Wardrobe*, because during World War II, Lewis and Warnie opened their home to refugee children from London like the Pevensie children. During the Second World War, however, Lewis hardly qualified as an old professor, for he was barely in his early forties. No doubt the company of Jill Flewett, whom Jack quickly nicknamed June and who lived at the Kilns from 1943 until 1945, sparked recollections of another child and another war. Perhaps more likely, W. T. Kirkpatrick, who was sixty-six in 1914, is the professor of *The Lion, the Witch and the Wardrobe*, and Lewis is the boy who came to live with him during the war. Only, it was not World War II; it was the Great War. A more obvious scrap of evidence is that Lewis named the man Professor Kirke.[71] For good measure, Lewis gave Digory Kirke a great uncle named Kirk. Whereas Jill Flewett spent her days in servitude to Mrs. Moore at the Kilns, Jack spent his afternoons roaming about as the Pevensie children did. C. S. Lewis did not know about children as a result of raising children; he knew about children by remembering.

The Kirkpatricks' house of Gastons in Great Bookham, though a most comfortable house, was not the great house that belonged to the professor in *The Lion, the Witch and the Wardrobe*. The professor's grand house was so famous that tourists came to see it, and Mrs. Macready constantly gave tours to the steady stream of the visiting public. She told the visitors about "the pictures and the armour, and the rare books in the library."[72] C. S. Lewis would have been familiar with life in a large house like Glenmachen, where his Ewart cousins lived, but Glenmachen was not a historic property that attracted tourists. It was a rather new house in an ancient land.

C. S. Lewis might have learned about life for children in a great historic house from his friend Lord David Cecil, who had become a part of Lewis's literary circle in Oxford during World War II. Lord David was the younger son of the fourth Marquess of Salisbury and the younger brother of the fifth marquess. His grandfather, the third marquess, served three terms as prime minister under Queen Victoria. Lord David grew up at Hatfield House, the family seat, which had previously been the royal palace where young Princess Elizabeth was kept in confinement by her older sister Queen Mary. Lord David's ancestor, Sir William Cecil, served as Queen Elizabeth's principal advisor. James I traded Hatfield House with Sir William's son, Robert Cecil, who served James as his father had served Elizabeth. Hatfield House is one of the greatest of great houses of England, full of pictures, armor, and rare books in the library. Lord David Cecil contributed a poem to *The Princess Elizabeth Book* (1935) that describes growing up in the big house where another Princess Elizabeth had once lived. It is most unlikely that the Inklings would not have heard something of Lord David's life at Hatfield.

The landscape of Narnia did not come exclusively from Surrey, but it appears to have come largely from the places Lewis loved as a boy. His description "The castle of Cair Paravel on its little hill towered above them; before them were the sands with rocks and little pools of salt water, and sea weed, and the smell of the sea, and long miles of bluish-green waves breaking forever and ever on the beach"[73] compares strikingly to Dunluce Castle, which stands by the sea on the Ulster coast near Lewis's home in Belfast.[74] Recalling the sound of the waves breaking along the Ulster coast in a letter to Arthur Greeves from Great Bookham, Lewis said, "Waves make one kind of music on rocks and another on sand, and I don't know which of the two I would rather have."[75] Dunluce was the castle where Flora Lewis had taken her boys to romp during the summer holiday at Castlerock. It was a castle of memories.

In its glory, Dunluce would have been the model of a kingly castle, but Lewis saw it in ruins, as the four Pevensie children saw Cair Paravel upon their return to Narnia in *Prince Caspian*. The kingship of Narnia under the children followed the ancient formula of Ireland long before the Norman invasion. Ireland had multiple kings and kingdoms, but one high king at Tara. Lewis also turned to the Ireland of his boyhood for the great stone table upon which Aslan was slain. Such a stone table, weathered with age, marked the burial place of St. Patrick himself.

Winter was Jack's favorite season, which is ironic, given the negative tone tied to winter in *The Lion, The Witch and the Wardrobe*, where Christmas never comes in the perpetual winter of the witch's spell.[76] To Arthur he exclaimed, "How I do love winter."[77] He particularly liked what he called a *real* winter like February 1917, when the temperature stood at seven degrees and his water jug froze solid, along with all the water pipes at Gastons.[78] It snowed in Great Bookham the last week of February 1916, and Jack wrote to Arthur about how much he liked to walk in the snow while it was still falling. He loved how snowflakes felt when they fell on his face. He loved to see the countryside through the haze of falling snow. He also loved the way the snow clung to every branch of every tree in the woods and arranged itself in fantastic shapes. To Jack, every snow-covered tree was "laden like a Christmas tree."[79] He would write this way some thirty-five years later when describing the snow in Narnia, but it was not merely a description he gave. With the snow of Narnia, he shared an experience. He exulted in winter and especially in a snow-covered landscape. He loved to see the snow piled high on the red tiles of the roofs in the village, and he rejoiced to see the red glow of the blacksmith's forge against the background of the snowy whiteness.[80]

A cold snap in June 1916 meant that fires were kindled again at Gastons, and Jack remarked on how homely and cozy the fire made things, for it was like having "a bit of the good old Winter back again."[81] Jack went up to London once with Mrs. Kirkpatrick to visit the Royal Academy of Art, which had mounted an exhibition. He had never been to such an exhibition, and he wanted Arthur to buy the catalog so that they could compare notes. Of special interest to Jack was a painting, the title of which he could not quite remember—"The Valley of Weugh," or Skugh or Feugh or something like that. What impressed him about the painting was "a glorious snow scene."[82]

The first week of October 1916, Jack found himself in one of his haunted woods when he walked with a party to the village of Friday Street some ten miles from Great Bookham. The group got lost on the way and found themselves at the same spot they had been an hour earlier. Jack was delighted! He could not describe his feelings to Arthur upon realizing that he was lost in the wild woods, wandering in circles, like Alice lost in Wonderland. Eventually they descended a hill and found the small village of very old, red-tiled cottages beside a small lake, all hemmed in by towering trees. Best of all, they came to the Stephen Langton Inn, where they had tea and were entertained by a jackdaw that ate crumbs around their feet and answered to the name Jack![83] The county of Surrey fed and reflected Jack's imagination as he was rereading Malory and reveling in the mystical parts that his journey through the lost woods only intensified. Children visiting Narnia many decades in the future would venture through such woods before finding a warm, cheerful hearth.[84]

The stories of Narnia took inspiration not only from the landscapes that Lewis loved as a boy, and to which he often returned on holiday as an adult, but also from the stories he read and re-read. He had delved deeply into Shakespeare by the time he went to Malvern, and the stories of Hamlet and of Richard III probably provided elements that reworked themselves in *Prince Caspian*. Caspian, like Hamlet and the poor princes who were murdered in the Tower of London, had an uncle who had usurped the throne. The imagination requires only the suggestion of an idea to create an entirely new story in an entirely new world out of the stuff we know.

At Great Bookham, Lewis read the classics of Homer and Virgil in Latin and Greek for Mr. Kirkpatrick, while he read Norse sagas for pleasure on his own. The wandering sea adventures of Odysseus and the voyages of the Vikings provided a possible framework for *The Voyage of the Dawn Treader*. Eustace was turned into a dragon, just as Circe turned the sailors of Odysseus into swine. The actual adventures of the children in *The Voyage of the Dawn Treader*, however, sprang from the imagination of Lewis.

In *The Silver Chair*, the children take a dangerous trip to the land below, like the trip of Orpheus to the underworld to rescue his wife from the clutches of Hades. The children go below to rescue Prince Rilian from the clutches of the Green Witch. Along the way, they come to the land of the giants and their giant bridge. In Ulster, close to Dunluce Castle, the unusual rock formation known as the Giant's Causeway captured Lewis's fancy as a boy. The landscape of castles and fantastic rock formations fed the romantic imagination of Lewis in his early adolescence, and he loved such places for the rest of his life. He did not inhabit a fairy land only in imagination. Rather, he inhabited a world sprinkled with the romantic remains of a medieval world that nurtured his imagination during a most impressionable period in his life.

In *The Horse and His Boy*, Lewis called upon the well-used motif of the twins who lived life apart from one another. The twins' story is another form of the doubling or doppelgänger plot. The story is as old as Jacob and Esau. The time frame and the age span vary, but it is the same essential plotline. Before he went up to Oxford, Lewis would have grown familiar with this plot from his pleasure reading while living in the village of Great Bookham, a name that bestows an exaggerated sense of its size and majesty. From Alexandre Dumas, Lewis would have known of the twins in *The Man in the Iron Mask*. From Mark Twain, he would have known of the doubles who could have been twins in *The Prince and the Pauper*. From Shakespeare, he would have known of the brother and sister twins in *Twelfth Night*. Great Bookham also added the opportunity for Lewis to get to know horses in a way he could not have learned at school. The neighborhood and countryside were still filled with the horses that pulled delivery wagons and plows in a world not yet completely dominated by the internal combustion engine.

In *The Magician's Nephew*, Lewis would draw upon the elements of classical mythology wed to the Bible's story of creation. The great winged horse would have appeared in his reading with W. T. Kirkpatrick. The walled garden, with its fruit, belongs to the tales of Hercules and to Freia of *Das Rheingold*. He would have encountered the story of creation at church, before he gave up church. With *The Magician's Nephew*, however, Lewis inserts an important piece of himself. Digory's mother is dying, and he cannot do anything about it, just like little Jacks, whose mother died when he was only nine years old.

In *The Last Battle*, a company of former children who had visited Narnia make their final trip to Narnia, or rather to Aslan's Country, but this time without the aid of magic rings, a huge wardrobe, or a Narnian picture. For their last trip, they are all killed in a colossal train wreck. Just such a wreck occurred at Watford, where Lewis had his first dreadful school experience. Being killed in a train wreck might have seemed a preferable experience to him. The catastrophe was reported with photographs of the carnage in the national papers and magazines, no doubt leaving young Lewis with memories of an ideal way to go if the plot requires the death of a number of people all at the same time. *The Last Battle* also draws on another image from what Lewis began reading at Malvern: *Siegfried and the Twilight of the Gods*. The end of the Norse gods comes with Valhalla consumed in flames as all the gods perish together. In *The Last Battle*, fire consumes the little stable that has become the last bastion of King Tirian.

The wreckage of the Watford trains, as shown in *The Illustrated London Times*, December 10, 1910

Another feature of *The Last Battle* comes from Jack's experience of the horrors of school and longing for the holiday that seems will never come. Yet, young Jack maintained hope that the end of term would come and all would be well. Simply thinking about the end of term helped him get through the terrors and the drab days as they slowly plodded by. Finally, the last day would come and he could go home. He talked about this longing for home and a better place in his letters to his father, and many years later, he wrote about the vivid memory of the experience in *Surprised by Joy*. He captured this idea at the conclusion of *The Last Battle* when Aslan announces, "The term is over: the holidays have begun."[85]

We often know things without remembering how we came to know them. In the course of life we pick up a vast storehouse of experience and knowledge that serves us well when we need it. C. S. Lewis probably did not sit down and intentionally collect memories of what he had read and seen and done as a teenage boy in order to integrate them into a well-fashioned series of children's books about the imaginary land of Narnia. When he began writing, however, he had at his immediate disposal the rich tapestry of literature he had read, which first came to him when he spent his free afternoons wandering a wild world not far from London.

The First Vacation from Gastons

The most notable event of Jack's Christmas break at the end of his first autumn with Kirk was his confirmation and first Communion as a Christian, even though he had only recently become a confirmed atheist. Albert Lewis made the decision as well as all the arrangements. Jack had attempted to negotiate a postponement till Easter, probably in hopes of yet another stay of execution, but it did not work.[86] He suggested that a return home early for confirmation would upset Kirk's schedule, which would be impolite and inconvenient for Kirk. He urged his father not to write to Kirk about changing the time for his Christmas break until he had given the matter more thought. He even resorted to deploring the additional expense that would be involved, though a lapse of logic on this account left a gaping hole as to why any extra expense would be involved. In the end, Jack returned to Belfast on November 28, underwent religious instruction for a week, and was confirmed on December 6, 1914.[87]

The confirmation, along with that of Jack's cousin Joey, took place at an evening service at St. Mark's Church. In a letter giving all the news about the confirmation, Albert took the occasion to remind Warnie that he, too, had been confirmed in Christ.[88] Albert also expressed the hope that Jack would not be converted to "some of the Gastons heresies." The confirmation was a failure, but the conversion to the Gastons heresies was a roaring success.[89] Finally, Albert was concerned about Jack's narrow chest. With Jack's long history of ill health, Albert regarded Jack's thin chest as a harbinger of bad things to come.[90] Albert was again expecting the worst.

C. S. Lewis regarded his confirmation as one of the worst acts of his life. In the complete absence of faith in Jesus Christ, Jack had submitted to his father's plans for his religious instruction, confirmation, and first Communion. Later, the middle-aged Lewis viewed the episode as an act of cowardice that led to hypocrisy that ended in blasphemy. Though he might not have appreciated the theological significance of his charade, he understood full well that he was living a lie. At the time, however, it seemed the easiest way to avoid an uproar with his father, who had no idea that Jack had assumed the mantle of atheism. Convenience argued for playing a part. Convictions had no place here. No need to disturb the peace on the home front.[91]

5

Reading for Kirkpatrick and for Pleasure

1914

During his time with W. T. Kirkpatrick, Jack Lewis not only learned a great deal about logic and the classics; he also learned how to teach. Most young men who went up to Oxford and Cambridge had spent their youth in public schools where education meant essentially what it would mean in an American high school. Students sit in rows, listen to lectures, take notes, answer when called upon, and receive the education given to them. An American university education does not differ in any significant way from how high school operates. The system of education at Oxford and Cambridge, often referred to as Oxbridge, involves something quite different. It centers on the tutorial.

Mastering the Tutorial

In a tutorial at Oxford or Cambridge, a pupil meets once a week for an hour with a tutor—what Americans would call a teacher. The tutor assigns a paper each week for the pupil to write. During the ensuing week, the pupil writes the paper of about three thousand to five thousand words and then returns the next week to read that paper to the tutor. It amounts to researching and writing a term paper each week for an eight-week term. Instead of depending upon listening to a lecture, the education depends upon the student ferreting out the information from the books that the tutor has "suggested" the pupil read in the course of research. As the pupil in an Oxbridge tutorial reads the resulting paper, the tutor interrupts and poses questions to correct, amplify, or elaborate what the pupil has said.

On one occasion, as I read a paper on Cromwell's administration to my tutor, Barrie White, who also held the post of principal of Regent's Park College, I made a throw-away remark about how Cromwell's toleration of religious diversity would make it impossible to ever have the kind of religious persecution that had gone on before the English Civil War. The words were scarcely out of my mouth when White erupted from his club chair, where he had seemed to all appearances to be on the verge of a long winter's nap, and sprang halfway across the room to his wall of books. In one quick motion, he pulled from the shelf a book that he thrust in front of my face and declared, "Read that!" The Oxbridge system afforded incisive correction. Which may be why White's nickname around the college was "the Surgeon."

Jack Lewis would have a tremendous advantage over all the other pupils at Oxford because he was being tutored by W. T. Kirkpatrick while all the chaps at Malvern were playing games and falling further and further behind. The tutorial method depends upon training individuals to learn on their own. It does not provide the great safety net of a classroom full of students. Even an overzealous teacher cannot ask every student every question during a class period. In a lecture-based class, students may be bored, but they are never called upon to compete in any significant way with the sound of the teacher's voice. From the moment Jack Lewis stepped from the train in Great Bookham until the time he left Great Bookham for good, however, he was in one long tutorial in which he was expected to answer questions, give reasons, explain his views, and demonstrate his mastery of the material under study.

During their lessons, Jack and Kirk sat side by side on the sofa in Kirk's upstairs study. Most language teachers spend a great deal of time drilling students on grammar before ever attempting translation. A small group of teachers, however, begin by reading the language aloud without any explanation of grammar or effort at translation. This approach instills in the student a sense of the rhythm and nature of the language itself. My Hebrew professor, John Joseph Owens, had us reading aloud from the Hebrew text of Jonah for two weeks before ever asking for a translation or saying a word about grammar. By the end of the semester, we could all sight-read the text. This seems to be the approach of Kirkpatrick, who began Jack's first lesson by reading aloud to him in Greek the opening twenty lines of the *Iliad* before translating a hundred lines. He then gave Jack a Greek lexicon and asked him to work through the text himself and translate as much as he could. He then left the room while Jack worked at a little table with his Greek text and lexicon.

At first, Jack fell far short of Kirk's hundred lines, but before long, he found that he could go far beyond Kirk's mark. Kirk was teaching Jack not merely to translate words but to think in Greek so that soon he was taking in whole phrases without having to think about what they meant. He simply understood them. Reflecting on the process many years later, Lewis explained that he was no longer thinking of what English word to substitute for a Greek word. Instead, the Greek word produced the picture in his mind of what was meant.[1]

One of the reasons for beginning with Homer's *Iliad* instead of Plato's *Republic* probably involved the nature of epic poetry. Greek epic poetry lends itself to learning Greek vocabulary and language in a way that Greek philosophy or drama does not. In fact, one of the modern criticisms of Greek epic poetry is the very thing that makes it conducive to learning: it is characterized by the continuing repetition of stock phrases. Lewis devoted a large section of *A Preface to Paradise Lost* to explain how the repetition of "stock phrases" works and why it is such an enormous strength of recitation of such long poetic works that were originally recited for an audience rather than read privately by an individual.[2] The modern reader of poetry may pause over a line of poetry and ponder it, but a listening audience has no such luxury. The words must strike the ear with a familiarity that carries the audience along. A line that requires reflection will only cause the listener to miss the next line and destroy the effect of the whole.

While this feature of primary epic poetry made the public recitation of Homer's *Iliad* possible, it also aids in making Homer's Greek accessible to the student. Apollo is never only Apollo; he is Apollo, *dear to Zeus*. Athena is never only Athena; she is *the bright-eyed goddess* Athena. Hera is never only Hera; she is *the white-armed goddess* Hera or *ox-eyed* Hera. The sea is never only the sea; it is the *wine-dark* sea. And so throughout the long epic, Homer repeats the stock phrases that also conjure up the background and unique attributes of the figures in his great story. Achilles is "swift-footed" or "the son of Peleus." Zeus is "aegis-bearing" or "cloud-gathering." Agamemnon is "the son of Atreus" or "the mighty." The Greeks sail not in ships but in *swift* ships. Just as Wagner identified each person in his operas with a musical theme, Homer gave a stock phrase to each person in his grand epic, as with Menelaus *of the mighty war cry*. As the epic develops, the stock phrases build up and alternate so that Agamemnon may be identified as "king of men."

In *A Preface to Paradise Lost*, Lewis discussed at length the advantage of repetition of stock phrases for the audience. Homer repeated not only short phrases but also lengthier passages. Lewis noted that in the famous farewell between Hector and Andromache, a passage he regarded as one of the peaks of European poetry, Homer used twenty-eight phrases or entire lines employed over and over again throughout the *Iliad*.[3] Oral poetry of this kind, meant as it was for the entire community to take part in together, belongs to the world of ritual and builds a degree of familiarity as it unfolds, thereby stirring a sense of anticipation that carries the audience along.

The advantage of starting young Lewis on this kind of literature as a young man who had been exposed to Greek at Malvern, but just barely, seems evident. Unlike Greek drama or philosophy, Homer's *Iliad* allowed Jack to build vocabulary quickly as it reinforced what he had already encountered a few lines earlier. This quality of repetition also allowed him to build a sense of confidence and accomplishment in reading the epic. A third advantage cannot be overstated—in Homer, something is always happening. Homer knew how to tell a tale and hold the attention of the audience. Unfortunately, many approaches to learning another language—or learning to read English, for that matter—involve insipid lines of words in which nothing interesting happens. Kirkpatrick understood schoolboys as well as he understood Homer. Shortly before he died, C. S. Lewis granted an interview in his rooms at Cambridge to Brian Aldiss and Kingsley Amis to discuss science fiction for *SFHorizons*, a new journal that Aldiss edited. Lewis observed that once a writer has created an exciting world, "something must happen."[4] The story provides its own incentive and reward for learning to read it.

At the end of his first week with Kirkpatrick, Jack wrote to his father about the contrast between what was expected at Malvern and what Kirk expected of him. Expectations often play a great part in performance, and Kirkpatrick had great expectations of what pupils could do if they only set themselves to it. Thus they began with mastering Greek by reading Homer's *Iliad*, the foundational story of Greek literature and the most influential story in Western culture alongside the Bible.[5]

Homer divided his story into twenty-four books, and Lewis marveled that Kirk had him reading a book each week. At Malvern, they had only read a book each term.[6] The term *book* can be misleading. With Homer and classical writers in general, a book is a division of a longer work corresponding to a modern chapter. Jack wrote somewhat pompously to Arthur Greeves that he must have heard of the *Iliad*, even if he could not read Greek and did not care for poetry. Lewis was entranced by the story itself, but also by the sound of the poetic language with its "fine, simple, euphonious lines, as they roll on with a roar like that of the ocean."[7] The young Greek scholar at once grasped that the ancient poem worked on the mind in a way different from modern stories, and this conception of how cultures have a way of expressing themselves and of thinking would grow in his mind to become the foundational element of his approach to literature in *The Allegory of Love* (1936), in which he explored how literature had changed as cultures changed from the time of the *Iliad* until the time of Shakespeare.

Lewis lived at the end of the age of the classical education, when an education meant reading the great Greek and Latin texts, but Kirkpatrick introduced him to a new way of reading Greek. The ancient Greek texts were largely lost to the Western world after the barbarian invasions of the fifth century, even though they remained well known in the Eastern Empire of Constantinople. A thousand years later, as Greek manuscripts began to be available in the West, scholars did not know how to pronounce the Greek words. Erasmus invented a system for pronouncing Greek that became the standard for Western scholars to the present day, but it had nothing to do with the Greek language. It was merely a convenient system that would sound like gibberish to a Greek. W. T. Kirkpatrick took a different course, and he would have been one of the earliest English-speaking scholars to take this course. He taught Jack the "new" or modern Greek pronunciation instead of relying on the Erasmian pronunciation.[8] Unlike English, a derivative language from many sources that has changed under the influence of German, French, and Latin sources, Greek has changed little since Roman times, and a growing body of scholars prefer to speak Greek with the modern pronunciation rather than the Erasmian.

Though more than twenty-five hundred years old, the *Iliad* was a story well known to all educated people. When women began to receive formal education, even they learned to read Homer in Greek, much to the horror of the more traditional set. Today, however, very few people know the story of the *Iliad* or why it continued to be foundational for the cultures of ancient Greece, the Hellenistic world, the Roman world, the medieval world, and into the modern world. Until the mid-twentieth century, writers of prose and poetry continued to ornament their work with the figures from the *Iliad*, just as their medieval forebears had done after the fall of the Western Roman Empire.

James Joyce named his great novel *Ulysses* for the Latin rendering of Odysseus, a central figure of the *Iliad* who conceived the deception of the wooden horse and around whom Homer's sequel, the *Odyssey*, is named. Edgar Allan Poe's poem "To Helen" is set in the context of Homer's epic as an analogy for the beauty of the woman who inspired Poe to write poetry:

> Helen, thy beauty is to me
> > Like those Nicéan barks of yore,
> That gently, o'er a perfumed sea,
> > The weary, way-worn wanderer bore
> > To his own native shore.

Without a knowledge of the literature of classical Greece, even modern literature is lost to readers in the twenty-first century. Before going on with the story of the formation of C. S. Lewis, we would do well to review the story that played such an important part in that formation.

The *Iliad*

The *Iliad* is the great epic poem of Greek culture. According to tradition, it was written around 800 BC by Homer. Most scholars would say that if such a person ever lived, he did not originate the story but compiled the strands of the great story into a single narrative that pays stringent attention to the demands of poetic construction. It takes hard work on the part of a poet to make the lines of a story conform to a set meter and rhythm. Even more so in that day, when the poem was recited publicly to the accompaniment of a lyre or some other musical instrument. How epic poetry achieves its effect would form a central section of Lewis's book *A Preface to Paradise Lost* (1942) as he explained to readers why the *Iliad* had such a stirring impact on him when he was young.[9] Scholars who grasp the difficulty of arriving at a cohesive epic like the *Iliad* by mere editorial work tend to agree that Homer actually lived and was a poetic genius.

The subject of the *Iliad* is the Trojan War, set approximately in 1200 BC, or some four hundred years before the time of Homer. The title of the poem comes from Ilium, another name for Troy. The excuse for the war is the abduction of Helen, the queen of Sparta, by Paris, the younger son of King Priam of Troy. Menelaus, the king of Sparta and husband of Helen, demands that all the cities of Greece join him in battle against the Trojans to retrieve his wife. Helen was almost the occasion for war earlier when all the great princes of Greece sought her hand in marriage because she was the most beautiful woman in the world. In the end, the suitors agreed that they would all support the man who won Helen's hand, because it seemed inevitable that someone would try to steal her away. Agamemnon, the brother of Menelaus and king of Mycenae, leads the Greek forces in their great armada of ships made famous by the line in Christopher Marlowe's play about the Trojan War "Was this the face that launched a thousand ships?"

At a deeper level, however, the story is not about Helen at all. It is not a love story. As Lewis explained in *The Allegory of Love*, the true love story did not come into being until the eleventh century among the troubadours of France with such tales as the triangle of King Arthur, Queen Guinevere, and Sir Lancelot. The *Iliad* is about jealousy, anger, revenge, arrogant pride, deception, vanity, greed, insolence, and cowardice, on the one hand, and courage, loyalty, honor, obedience, and religious piety, on the other. It is a story not of the rivalry of nations but of the behavior of individuals.

Though the Trojan War involves the ten-year siege of one of the great trading cities of the ancient world, the *Iliad* only involves the culmination of the siege while it relies on flashbacks to explain why such fierce and deadly rivalry has sprung up in the camp of the Greeks between King Agamemnon, the greatest Greek chieftain, and Achilles, the greatest Greek warrior. Agamemnon is forced by public pressure to give up his war prize, the daughter of the priest of Apollo, so in anger, he takes the woman that Achilles has taken as a prize of war. In response to this insult, Achilles and his warriors, the Myrmidons, withdraw from battle. Menelaus challenges Paris to single combat in order to settle the dispute without further war and completely overwhelms the young prince. Paris, however, escapes Menelaus at the last moment and the war resumes.

Patroclus, a kinsman of Achilles who has tired of waiting on the side as the other Greeks fight, dons the armor of Achilles and goes out to fight Hector, the elder son of King Priam and the hero of Troy. Hector slays Patroclus, believing he has slain Achilles. In fury, Achilles returns to the war and kills Hector in battle. Refusing to allow Hector the honor due a slain warrior, Achilles drags his body around the city walls of Troy in mockery of the one who killed his cousin. Finally, King Priam steals away to the tent of Achilles by night and humbles himself before the warrior as he begs for the body of his son in order to give him a proper funeral. The funeral of Hector marks the end of the *Iliad*, but not the end of the Greek telling of the story of the Trojan War.

Homer wrote a sequel to the *Iliad* in which the courage and strength in battle of Achilles in the first book are mirrored by the craft and sagacity of his friend Odysseus, king of Ithaca, in the second book, the *Odyssey*. This epic poem of twenty-four books tells of the ten-year wanderings of Odysseus and his men in their efforts to return home to Ithaca following the Trojan War. At the end of the war, Achilles is killed by an arrow that strikes his heel, his only vulnerable spot. After the war has gone on for ten years without either side gaining an advantage, the Greeks appear to have departed for home, leaving a great wooden horse behind. The Trojans bring the great horse into the city and celebrate the departure of the Greeks, but it is all a subterfuge conceived by Odysseus. Hidden within the horse is a body of Greek soldiers, who slip out of the horse after the city is asleep and open the gates, allowing the Greek army to enter and take the city.

Homer did not go into detail about the horse or the taking of the city, for the deception seemed a less honorable way to win a war to the Greeks of Homer's day. It fell to Virgil, the great Latin poet of Roman nationalism, to craft the more detailed version of the story in his *Aeneid* some eight hundred years after Homer, during the rise of imperial power in Augustan Rome.

Following the victory of the Greeks, Odysseus and his companions fall into one calamity after another, hindering their return journey. The epic poem is actually a collection of adventures like the twelve labors of Hercules. This nonlinear epic, which begins at the end of the ten-year journey, works its way backward and forward. Lewis adopted this structure of a collection of adventures for his third Narnia story, *The Voyage of the Dawn Treader* (1952). He was not alone in taking inspiration from the *Iliad* and the *Odyssey*. Throughout the golden age of Greek drama, the principal expression of Greek literature apart from the philosophical works that survive, the Greek dramatists fleshed out the stories of the participants in the Trojan War in plays such as the *Oresteia*, a trilogy of plays by Aeschylus that explore the family of Agamemnon and its ruin, and *Ajax* by Sophocles, which explores the ruin of the warrior Ajax, who thought he deserved the armor of the fallen Achilles. The *Oresteia*, usually known as "Fall of the House of Atreus," tells the story of the murder and mayhem within the family of Agamemnon, from his father Atreus through his children. C. S. Lewis used an element of this story in *Till We Have Faces* (1956). Agamemnon offers his daughter Iphigenia as a human sacrifice to the goddess Artemis to assure a safe journey for his Greek fleet to Troy. In *Till We Have Faces*, set about the same time period as the Trojan War, King Trom of Glome sacrifices his daughter Psyche to the god known as the Brute.

What these two brief summaries have not included is the part played by the gods in all these events that formed the identity of the Greeks. The gods, with their own petty jealousies and rivalries, are behind it all. The only reason that Paris manages to abduct Helen is that the goddesses Hera, Athena, and Aphrodite have a quarrel over which one is the fairest. The quarrel has been instigated by Eris, the goddess of strife, who has offered a golden apple as a prize for the fairest goddess. Paris agrees to judge the goddesses, all of whom offer him bribes to choose them. He accepts the bribe of Aphrodite, who has promised to give him the most beautiful woman in the world as his reward for choosing her. Of course, the most beautiful woman in the world is Helen, who is already married. Thus, the strife of Eris extends beyond its initial conception. Throughout the *Iliad*, the gods take sides in the battles, as when Aphrodite rescues Paris from being killed in battle by Menelaus. Throughout the *Iliad*, Homer weaves the natural and the supernatural together as a single fabric.

Though Jack Lewis had entered a period in his life when he thought of Greek gods and the Hebrew God as all make-believe, the stories had done their work, and he would never shake them. Though he believed that divine revelation was only fairy tales while he lived with W. T. Kirkpatrick, Jack would finally come to believe that fairy tales were corruptions of divine revelation maintaining elements of truth.

He Thought He Was Doing His English Prep

While classical study occupied the mornings at Gastons, the early evenings were devoted to English literature, or more precisely, the examination of literary theory. For the first book under examination, Kirkpatrick assigned the two-volume *History of the Civilization of England* by Henry Thomas Buckle, which ran to 1455 pages. A self-educated man, Buckle had the money and leisure to devote to his project of discovering the scientific laws responsible for the advance of civilization. He regarded metaphysics as a useless enterprise that had never led to any discoveries contributing to the storehouse of knowledge.

Buckle began his second volume with a summation of his four primary propositions discovered in the first 854 pages. He taught that progress depends upon scientific investigation, that scientific investigation requires the development of a spirit of skepticism, and that scientific investigation increases intellectual truth and diminishes the influence of moral truth, which does not increase. In addition to these three, Buckle concluded with a fourth proposition about the laws governing the development of civilization:

> That the great enemy of this movement, and therefore the great enemy of civilization, is the protective spirit; by which I mean the notion that society cannot prosper, unless the affairs of life are watched over and protected at nearly every turn by the state and the church; the state teaching men what they are to do, and the church teaching them what they are to believe.[10]

Buckle regarded Adam Smith's *The Wealth of Nations* as "the most important book which has ever been written" because of its doctrine of freedom that stands against church and state.[11] Buckle was drawn to Smith's interpretation of history with the conclusion that the church could not survive without the power of the state to prop it up.[12] Freed from the artificial moral restraints of the church, people are at liberty to pursue self-interest and embrace selfishness as a positive driving force in the development of civilization: "For human institutions are constantly stopping our advance, by thwarting our natural inclinations."[13] Buckle regretted that Smith had not lived to see the work of Thomas Malthus on population growth and misery, which Buckle took as an expansion of Smith's work. The third member of Buckle's trinity was David Hume, who had recognized that religious doctrines could be overcome only "by a spirit of fearless and unrestrained liberty."[14] Hume is perhaps best known for his argument that in an eternal universe, life would have eventually arisen as a chance occurrence.

Between the publication of Buckle's first volume in 1857 and the publication of his second in 1861, Charles Darwin had published *On the Origin of Species by Means of Natural Selection, or the Preservation of Favoured Races in the Struggle for Life* (1859). The two men shared the same assumptions and drew similar conclusions in their efforts to explain why the English were the most advanced people on earth and why peoples like the French and the Spanish were inferior. Such an attitude made the comic operas of Gilbert and Sullivan possible. It also made the British Empire of the nineteenth century possible. Both men firmly believed that self-interest would soon make warfare obsolete, and without this attitude, World War I might never have happened.

Buckle's massive work of philosophical speculation and conjecture—despite his professed aversion to metaphysics—formed the foundation for how Kirkpatrick set Lewis to thinking about literature and all of civilization and its accomplishments. Lewis pursued his studies with Kirkpatrick through a lens of naturalism that assumed religion is only a human construct and God a useful superstition for controlling the masses. Kirkpatrick had shown his hand for a moment in his letter to Albert on October 4, 1909. In one sentence commenting on the establishment of a Chair of Scholastic Philosophy at one of the new "red brick" universities in 1909, Kirkpatrick revealed his views on religion, materialism, and his own philosophy of science:

> In these days when a scientific anthropology is throwing so much light on the origin of man and the growth of his moral

and religious views, including Scholastic Philosophy itself, the
bare idea of training young minds, who ought to be brought
in contact with truth, so far as it can be known, in the rigid
Scholasticism of an age of superstition, binding them with the
fetters of an ignorant past, is really too absurd for criticism.[15]

Thus, Kirkpatrick explained why he had not planned for Jack
Lewis to read Plato and Aristotle with him until later. Plato and
Aristotle had dangerous ideas because they tended to discuss the re-
lationship between the physical world and a spiritual world, which
Kirkpatrick so abhorred. He would not confuse the mind of young
Clive Lewis with philosophy that took the spiritual world seriously.
The gods of Homer were easily dispensed with by literary criticism,
but the idea of spiritual reality was much more difficult to purge.

Years later, Lewis spoke and wrote about the problem of underlying philosophical presuppositions in textbooks when he gave
a series of lectures at Durham University during World War II
that were later published as *The Abolition of Man*. He discovered
that some of his pupils at Oxford had acquired the notion that
all statements of value were only expressions of the emotional
states of the speakers. The pupils had absorbed this view from
an English textbook, *The Control of Language* (1940), by Alex
King and Martin Ketley.[16] Lewis addressed his subject with an
emotional bite not usually found in his work, and his discussion
of the subject suggests that he knew exactly what he was talking about from his own experience. He was concerned that the
authors were dealing with schoolboys, never mind the girls who
might read it. The authors were targeting someone who "thinks
he is doing his 'English prep' and has no notion that ethics, theology, and politics are all at stake."[17] Lewis explained, "It is not a
theory they put into his mind, but an assumption, which ten years
hence, its origin forgotten and its presence unconscious, will condition him to take one side in a controversy which he has never
recognized as a controversy at all."[18] While Jack Lewis thought he

was doing his English prep, he was actually constructing a coherent and closed naturalistic universe that it would take him many years to reconsider.

Beyond Homer

By June 1915, Jack had finished reading Homer and Virgil, and he was prepared to deliver the verdict that Homer was better than Virgil, an opinion he would hold and defend for the rest of his life.[19] In *Surprised by Joy*, Lewis confessed that he never developed a taste for Virgil.[20] He regarded Virgil's *Aeneid* in many ways as a reproduction or derivative work of Homer's *Iliad*. In his *A Preface to Paradise Lost* (1942), C. S. Lewis devoted considerable attention to a comparison of the *Iliad* as primary epic and the *Aeneid* as secondary epic. In this way, Kirk prepared Jack to think about English literature through ancient Greek and Roman literature. Unfortunately, Kirk insisted that Jack read more than a couple of old adventure stories.

Inevitably, Jack had to read Cicero and Demosthenes, whom the mature Lewis referred to as the "Two Great Bores."[21] Jack wrote to his father that he cared nothing for oratory in any language, so he refused to provide an opinion about "our friend with the mouth full of pebbles," thereby providing his father with his opinion of Demosthenes. However, Jack thought that Demosthenes, unlike Cicero, at least had something to say. Even if they had nothing to say except on subjects of ancient politics, about which Jack cared nothing, as the greatest orators of their ages they provided Jack with some of the clearest examples of Greek and Latin prose. They helped him refine his understanding of classical grammar, even if they bored him to tears in the process. In the end, they contributed to his fluency in the classical languages, for which he would be known, so that C. S. Lewis could crack jokes and make quips in Greek or Latin with ease.

After Homer, Lewis gloried most in Lucretius, Catullus, Tacitus, and Herodotus. Of the Greek playwrights, Jack read the plays of Euripides, Sophocles, and Aeschylus. Kirk did not assign any of Julius Caesar, nor was C. S. Lewis ever tempted to read him, which he appears to have regarded as a major achievement.[22]

William Morris and His Ilk

Though Jack thrilled in his time with Kirkpatrick each day and their journeys into the ancient past, the evenings belonged to him, when he could journey into the world of imagination through his novels. He devoured fiction rapaciously, and each new book only increased his appetite for more. Kirkpatrick was not a great one for reading fiction. He was concerned with facts. Jack, however, managed to lead a double life—materialist by day and romantic by night.

In March 1939, C. S. Lewis published a collection of essays entitled *Rehabilitations*. Included was an essay on William Morris, who had passed out of fashion among the literary effete of England. Despite the prevailing opinion of literary critics at the time, Lewis argued that Morris still had his admirers among ordinary people. Perhaps with tongue in cheek, Lewis remarked that those who read Morris "read humbly for the sake of pleasure."[23] He added that this group was hardly in a position to give a critical explanation for why they liked Morris or continued to read and reread him twenty or more years after their first reading. They were not equipped for the intellectual warfare that is literary criticism. Lewis added that he knew one person who could only give the simple explanation "It's the Northernness—the Northernness."[24]

Of course, Lewis was speaking of Arthur Greeves, with whom Jack Lewis had carried on a perpetual discussion of Morris through the post from England to Ireland while he was living and studying with W. T. Kirkpatrick. Morris first arose in their correspondence in a letter that Jack wrote on November 10, 1914. The letter assumes a background discussion between the two boys that probably went back as far as their first meeting when "northernness" became the bond between them. William Morris was a Victorian writer who captured the notion of northernness in his stories. Lewis had first encountered his name in books about Norse mythology, and then he read Morris's *Sigurd the Volsung*, Morris's effort at retelling the Siegfried story. Jack did not care for this book as much as he had hoped he would, and the mature Lewis speculated that the problem was with the meter of the poem, which did not suit his ear. The verse simply did not sound right.

Though he came to love Morris in general, Lewis particularly loved *The Well at the World's End*. He first came across it in a book case at Arthur Greeves' house, probably during the summer vacation of 1914. In his letter to Arthur on November 10, 1914, Jack mentioned that he had ordered a copy of *Sigurd the Volsung* from the same publisher and series as Arthur's copy of *The Wood at the World's End*.[25] Lewis had absentmindedly conflated two of Morris's titles: *The Wood beyond the World* (1894) and *The Well at the World's End* (1896). In his footnote to this letter, Walter Hooper opted for *The Well at the World's End* as the book that Lewis intended.[26] Hooper is almost certainly correct in his judgment, for in his next letter, Jack responds to Arthur's critique of *The Well at the World's End*. The reference to Arthur's copy would also agree with Lewis's comment in *Surprised by Joy* that he had first become aware of *The Well at the World's End* while looking at Arthur's books. Not only did Jack talk about this Morris book in letters to Arthur throughout his time at Gastons, but he continued reading it and talking about it to others throughout his life. He wrote about it in his essay "On Stories," which was his contribution to *Essays Presented to Charles Williams*. Alastair Fowler related how Lewis persuaded him to read the book many decades later when he was the pupil of Lewis.[27]

The occasion for mentioning Morris came from a trip to nearby Guildford where Lewis had purchased a copy of Morris's lyric poems in the same series as Arthur's copy of *The Well at the World's End*. In later life, Lewis cared nothing for material things, whether furniture, clothes, or any of the other accessories of life.

As a teenager, however, he loved beautiful bindings for books. He wanted the best editions and held cheap editions beneath contempt. His letters are full of discussions of the quality of different editions of books and betray how, in his later years, his devotional writings could have such a well-informed understanding of lust, greed, and covetousness. In short, he was a typical teenager in many ways. As such, he told Arthur that he had ordered the superior edition of Morris's *Sigurd the Volsung* for his collection. This book is a narrative poem that retells the story of Siegfried and Brünnhilde first published in 1876, the same year that Wagner first produced his *Ring* cycle at Bayreuth.

William Morris nurtured the romantic impulse within Lewis. Born into a prosperous middle-class family, Morris went up to Oxford as a member of Exeter College, where Lewis's friends Nevill Coghill, Hugo Dyson, and Ronald Tolkien would be members over half a century later. At Oxford, he fell under the spell of the medieval world that he found at every turn. The Gothic Revival had grown out of the popularity of the works of Sir Walter Scott, and Gothic motifs ornamented the architecture of mid-Victorian England, the most prominent example of which is the massive Westminster Palace, where the houses of Parliament meet. This Gothic Revival masterpiece was built when Morris was up at Oxford during the 1850s, following the great fire that destroyed the original palace in 1834. Yet Morris did not care for Gothic Revival; he preferred the original forms of Gothic architecture and would devote the rest of his life to reviving the arts and craft skills of the medieval world. Inspired by John Ruskin's thought on Gothic architecture and the world that produced it, Morris set about to revive the cottage crafts that the industrial revolution had obliterated.

Morris was drawn to the Pre-Raphaelite Brotherhood, a group of artists whose work depicted the romantic interpretation of medieval legends and stories, such as the King Arthur legends that began to captivate Morris. Morris became close friends with

160

Dante Gabriel Rossetti, the leading figure of the Pre-Raphaelites. He tried his hand at painting, but soon turned to the establishment of a workshop that produced handcrafted textiles, stained glass windows, wallpaper, furniture, and tiles in the medieval style. His work soon became the rage and a hallmark of the late Victorian age. With the burden of success, Morris withdrew from London to Kelmscott Manor in Oxfordshire, where he turned his attention to writing poetry that retold the old stories he loved. He soon fell in love with Iceland and the Old Icelandic sagas that would captivate young C. S. Lewis. In the last years of his life, he founded the Kelmscott Press, which he devoted to the publication of exquisite books with elaborate illuminated print and illustrations that reflected his love of the Romantic and medieval. In addition to publishing his own books, Morris published works by Keats, Shelley, Swinburne, Ruskin, and his favorite medieval texts.

The Well at the World's End

The work of Morris that had its greatest effect on C. S. Lewis was *The Well at the World's End*. As might be expected, it is a story set in the ahistorical medieval world where the four sons of King Peter of Upmeads set out to explore the world. The story follows the adventures of the youngest son, Ralph. Early in his journey, Ralph rescues a maiden from two villains who have captured her. He travels on to find shelter in the castle of the Lady of Abundance, whom he does not meet. The household tells of the lady's beauty and virtue, which stirs a longing for this lady he has not seen. Images of the lady that Ralph sees in the castle and descriptions of her in a book he reads only inflame his desire to meet her all the more. He lingers at the castle for some time in hopes of meeting the lady, but finally, he continues his journey, only to meet the lady on his way. She turns out to be the very lady he rescued at the beginning.

The lady's life is complicated by two knights who fight over her, and one knight kills the other. The victor almost kills Ralph, but the lady agrees to become the knight's lover if he will spare Ralph.

During the night, however, the Lady of Abundance leads Ralph in an escape. As they flee the murderous knight, the lady tells Ralph that she is of a great age and has been to the world's end where she has drunk from the well that supplies her with perpetual youth. She also tells Ralph of a Lady Ursula, who is ideally suited to him. While Ralph is out hunting, their pursuer kills the lady and attacks Ralph, but Ralph shoots an arrow into his head and kills him. Ralph then sets off to find the well at the world's end.

Ralph meets his older brother Blaise, whose attendant, Richard, has heard of the well in the town of Swevenham. On the way to Swevenham, Ralph joins company with traveling merchants and learns of Lady Ursula, who has been sold into slavery to the evil King Gandolf of Utterbol. Morfinn the minstrel agrees to lead Ralph to Utterbol, but Morfinn betrays him to Gandolf. Eventually, however, both Ursula and Ralph escape independently from Gandolf, only to meet in a deep wood where they join together to find the well at the world's end. Along the way they fall in love before drinking the water that provides youth. The tale continues as the couple make their way back to Upmeads and endure many trials before they become the new king and queen of Upmeads.

The story seems to stall after reaching the well, for the well is the prize, the goal, the point of the story. Arthur Greeves appears to have pointed out this defect, for Lewis quickly responded to Arthur with a defense of what Morris had done:

> I quite see your point, and, of course, agree that the interests of the tale reach their climax in the great scene at the World's End: my reply is that the interest of the journey home is of quite a different nature. It is pleasant to pick up all the familiar places and characters and see the same circumstances applied to the heroe's [sic] new role of 'Friend of the Well'.[28]

Perhaps Jack really believed that the journey home was interesting, or perhaps he could not let Arthur have the last word. What we do know is that nearly twenty years later, while spending a fortnight with Arthur in Ireland after the death of Albert and his own reluctant conversion to Christianity, Lewis wrote his own retelling of this tale as *The Pilgrim's Regress*. A critical aspect of *The Pilgrim's Regress*, in contrast to Bunyan's *The Pilgrim's Progress*, is that Bunyan ends his story with heaven as the goal, while the story of Lewis has salvation as the goal in the midst of the story, with his pilgrim then making his journey back through the life he had lived. Lewis modeled *The Pilgrim's Regress* on *The Well at the World's End*.

With *The Well at the World's End*, Lewis was struck by that sense of longing and desire for something ineffable that he had experienced several times since his childhood. The first half of the story focuses on this longing and the journey necessary to satisfy it. In his preface to the third edition of *The Pilgrim's Regress*, Lewis explained this experience of desperate longing and desire that nothing in ordinary experience can satisfy and specifically referenced Morris and *The Well at the World's End*.[29] The full title for Lewis's first book that he wrote as a Christian, an allegorical spiritual autobiography, is *The Pilgrim's Regress: An Apology for Christianity, Reason, and Romanticism*. The point of his preface to the third edition in 1943 was to explain that his use of the word "romanticism" in the title had been a mistake because of the many uses of the term, none of which quite got at what he meant by his experience of longing and desire. When he wrote his prose version of *The Pilgrim's Regress* a little over a decade later, he appears to have borrowed J. R. R. Tolkien's term "joy" to represent this longing and desire. At the end of his long essay "On Fairy-Stories," originally presented as the Andrew Lang Lecture at the University of St Andrews in 1938 and later included as his contribution to *Essays Presented to Charles Williams*, Tolkien explained the stab of longing as Joy:

> The consolation of fairy-stories, the joy of the happy ending: or more correctly of the good catastrophe, the sudden joyous

"turn" (for there is no true end to any fairy-tale): this joy, which is one of the things which fairy-stories can produce supremely well, is not essentially "escapist," nor "fugitive." In its fairy-tale—or otherworld—setting, it is a sudden and miraculous grace: never to be counted on to recur. It does not deny the existence of *dyscatastrophe*, of sorrow and failure: the possibility of these is necessary to the joy of deliverance; it denies (in the face of much evidence, if you will) universal final defeat and in so far is *evangelium*, giving a fleeting glimpse of Joy, Joy beyond the walls of the world, poignant as grief.[30]

In fact, Lewis had been referring to his experience of deep longing as Joy for years before he met Tolkien. It is more likely that Tolkien developed this idea under the influence of Lewis.[31] For Lewis, the very title of *The Well at the World's End* captured this idea of Joy and impressed it upon him as a young reader.

Le Morte d'Arthur

While Lewis read his novels for fun, Kirk had put him to reading English literary criticism as part of his course of study. Reading Buckle's *History of Civilization in England* during the fall of 1914 probably first sparked in Lewis the idea of reading Sir Thomas Malory's *Le Morte d'Arthur* (1485). On the morning of November 17, 1914, Lewis woke up wondering why he had never bought a copy of the book and immediately ordered it from Dent's catalog in the Everyman edition for two shillings![32]

While this book would open to Lewis the marvelous world of King Arthur and his knights, it would also provide the foundation for his career as a fellow and then professor of medieval and Renaissance literature until his death. Malory's late retelling and embellishment of the Arthur legends came at the end of the medieval period after a number of others had composed their versions of Arthur over the previous four centuries in France, as well as England. The poetry that dealt with Arthur, Lancelot, Merlin,

Guinevere, Galahad, and all the other figures that populated the legends of old Britain would form the core of Lewis's first important academic book, *The Allegory of Love* (1936). Had he written nothing else, this book alone would have guaranteed his reputation among twentieth-century English literary critics.

Though Malory's *Le Morte d'Arthur* is the most famous of the medieval treatments of Arthur, it is not the best or the first. Malory added to a tradition that had grown and changed for nearly a thousand years by the time he took up his pen. When the grown Lewis wrote *The Allegory of Love*, he began his discussion of Arthurian poetry with Chrétien de Troyes, a twelfth-century poet of northern France in the court of the countess of Champagne (the daughter of Eleanor of Aquitaine by her first husband, King Louis VII of France).[33] Chrétien introduced the adulterous love affair between Lancelot and Queen Guinevere in his allegorical poem *Lancelot*. In his last great critical work, *The Discarded Image* (1964), published just after his death, Lewis again found that he could not treat his subject without mentioning Malory, who had opened the world of medieval English literature to him. In the end, however, Lewis did not think Malory the best or the most important, as he remarked:

> Many generations, each in its own spirit and its own style, have contributed to the story of Arthur. It is misleading to think of Malory as an author in our modern sense and throw all the earlier work into the category of 'sources'. He is merely the last builder, doing a few demolitions here and adding a few features there.[34]

For a boy on the verge of his sixteenth birthday in war-threatened England who had been drinking deeply of romance and antiquity, however, Malory was the cat's meow. Jack now believed that Malory was the master, and Morris merely the copyist.[35]

Jack was still reading Malory when he returned to Gastons after the 1914 Christmas break. Having almost completed *Le*

Morte d'Arthur, he now confided to Arthur Greeves that he did not think Malory a great author, but that two gifts set Malory apart. He wrote a strong narrative, and he developed the characters over the course of the narrative. Unlike modern writers who might describe a character in depth at first introduction, Malory revealed more and more of the personality of a character in the course of the unfolding of the story. Lewis also liked the way Malory enticed a reader by the titles of the chapters, such as "How Launcelot in the Chapel Perilous gat a cloth from a Dead corpse."[36]

The Faerie Queene

Jack first mentioned reading Edmund Spenser's *The Faerie Queene* in a letter to his father in February 1915 when he quoted a line he comically referenced as "about the thousandth canto of his poem." He cited the quotation "Oh, what an endlesse work I have in hand" not in order to discuss Spenser but to beg the favor of sending his copy of Euripides's *Helena*, which he had left behind in the little end room at home.[37] We do not know if Lewis was reading *The Faerie Queene* for the first time, if he was merely quoting from one of his history-of-English-literature books, or if he had only read an abridged edition found in the library at home.[38] We do know, however, that he began reading it in earnest during the summer break of 1915, when he went home to Ireland, and he was still hard at it when he wrote to Arthur on October 5 to say that he was halfway through volume 2.[39] His letters during this period complain of a particularly wet season, but years later, he still remembered how it felt to read *The Faerie Queene* for the first time:

> Beyond all doubt it is best to have made one's first acquaintance with Spenser in a very large—and, preferably, illustrated—edition of the *Faerie Queene*, on a wet day, between the ages of twelve and sixteen; and if, even at that age, certain of the names aroused unidentified memories of some still ear-

lier, some almost prehistoric, commerce with a selection of 'Stories from Spenser', heard before we could read, so much the better.[40]

Lewis tells us that this reader who discovered Spenser early would never abandon him. Instead, he would grow up with the book and grow to appreciate new things about it from youth's attraction to it as a wonder-tale, to a critically sensuous pleasure in its melodious lines, to an understanding of its place in the development of English literature, to a growing recognition of its wisdom. In short, Lewis describes how this poem affected him from early adolescence until the beginning of World War II.

In an essay on Spenser included in an American anthology in 1954, Lewis declared that *The Faerie Queene* had been "everyone's poem" until 1914 and was the means by which many people first discovered that they liked poetry, for it appeals to "the most naïve and innocent of tastes."[41] Speaking with the authority of one who knows from his own experience, Lewis explained that "it demands of us a child's love of marvels and dread of bogies, a boy's thirst for adventures, a young man's passion for physical beauty."[42] Not all the commentaries and scholarly essays in the world can provide these if the reader does not possess them. With these words, the mature C. S Lewis explained why *The Faerie Queene* had appealed to him at an early age and why it continued to appeal to him in later life.

To a certain degree, *The Faerie Queene* was the making of C. S. Lewis. His examination of *The Faerie Queene* forms the culmination and point toward which *The Allegory of Love* (1936) drives. *The Allegory of Love* established the reputation of C. S. Lewis as a formidable literary scholar who had to be noticed. This first monumental scholarly work by Lewis led to the invitation to write the volume on the sixteenth century for the Oxford History of English Literature series (OHEL, an acronym he found suggestive of the punishing assignment before him). Published as *English*

Literature in the Sixteenth Century, Excluding Drama, it would not see the light of day until almost twenty years later, after the interruptions of a world war and the declining health of Mrs. Janie Moore, for whom Lewis cared.

In *The Allegory of Love*, Lewis explored what might be called the anthropological problem of marriage for love. Throughout the world since prehistoric times, marriage has constituted a business transaction in which goods change hands. Chickens, goats, rugs, land, and daughters are traded. A man is paid by a girl's family to take her off the hands of the father, brother, or next of kin. We find this business transaction in the earliest pages of the Bible, and it still continues today in Asia, Africa, and South America. The anthropological problem for Western culture is why it would have been given up in favor of marriage for love. In *The Allegory of Love*, Lewis traced the courtly love tradition as expressed in allegorical poetry from eleventh-century France through to Spenser in the last decade of the sixteenth century, when the tradition ends with *The Faerie Queene* and its exaltation of marriage rooted in love. Courtly love was rooted in adultery and an almost blasphemous adulation of the mistress, reinforced by the church's condemnation of sexual relations as sin, whether within marriage or not, and the view that marriage was a business transaction. Lewis began his final chapter of *The Allegory of Love* with the explanation that "the last phase of that story—the final defeat of courtly love by the romantic conception of marriage—occupies the third book of *The Faerie Queene* and much of the fourth."[43]

The Faerie Queene not only opened the scholarly career of Lewis; it also closed it. After Lewis's death, noted scholar of Renaissance literature and former Lewis pupil Alastair Fowler edited Lewis's lecture notes on Spenser for publication as *Spenser's Images of Life*.[44] Lewis began his introductory lecture by commenting: "*The Faerie Queene* is perhaps the most difficult poem in English. Quite how difficult, I am only now beginning to realize after forty years of reading it."[45] The holograph image of his actual notes reveals that Lewis had struck through the number of years he had read the poem on two occasions. Originally, the notes gave fifteen years and then thirty years before the last revision to forty years. That date should have been revised again, for it had been over fifty years since his first reading of *The Faerie Queene*. At the end of his lectures on *The Faerie Queene*, Lewis returned to his first reading: "It is, if you like, Spenser's Hymn to Life. Perhaps this is why *The Faerie Queene* never loses a reader it has once gained. (For that is one of the first critical facts about the poem.) Once you have become an inhabitant of its world, being tired of it is like being tired of London, or of life."[46] By reading *The Faerie Queene* as a young teenager, Jack Lewis had set himself on a most dangerous path that he had no idea he had begun.

Though C. S. Lewis, the illustrious scholar of medieval literature, called *The Faerie Queene* the most difficult poem in English literature, it is also accessible to the boy who likes marvels and monsters or the youth who likes adventure. It operates on many levels. Written as an allegory in which everything means something else on another level, it points to the story of Christ and, at the same time, toward the world of Platonic ideals. Jack Lewis would not have been bothered with the veiled meanings. The story itself grabbed him. He identified with it to the extent that he alluded to it in the preface to the third edition of *The Pilgrim's Regress* when he remarked, "To have embraced so many false Florimels is no matter for boasting: it is fools, they say, who learn from experience."[47] The allusion is an apt one, for in *The Faerie Queene*, Florimel is a virtuous lady, but a witch fashions a false Florimel from snow as a deception.

For the benefit of those who have never read *The Faerie Queene*, a brief summary will be necessary in order to appreciate fully what part this story and others like it would play in the life journey of Jack Lewis. The story involves several figures whose stories intertwine, diverge, and reconnect in the course of the grand narrative. Characters leave the main storyline for lengthy passages, only to reappear at a critical moment to rescue or imperil someone else. The story opens with the picture of a knight and his lady traveling across a countryside. The knight bears a shield of silver emblazoned with a red cross. The lady leads a lamb. Spenser's readers would have known at once that they have entered the pageant of St. George, the patron saint of England whose red cross on a whole field is the flag of England. In the medieval pageant, St. George is accompanied by a lady leading a lamb.[48] The Elizabethan reader already knew that a dragon would be slain, but Jack Lewis would not have known all of that. He would have to wait to find out what would happen.

6

War and Romance

1915

In January 1915, Kirkpatrick suggested to Albert that Jack had
the potential to win a classical scholarship to Oxford, but that
his exceptional intellectual abilities might hinder him. His literary
judgments and his unerring instinct for literary quality marked his
advanced mind, but the examiners for the scholarships looked more
for strong memory work, attention to grammatical norms, and re-
ceptivity to instruction. Jack's critical and original mind could be
his greatest handicap in preparing for a scholarship examination,
and Kirk wanted Albert to realize that the task of preparing Clive
would be a challenge.[1] Kirkpatrick did not want Jack wasting time
with the study of French and German. Jack's greatest strengths lay
in his proficiency in Greek and Latin; therefore, his greatest opportunity for a scholarship lay with the *literae humaniores* or ancient
classics. He would read French with Mrs. Kirkpatrick more to give
him exposure to the language than as a serious subject of study. He
could do the same with German as time allowed, but not in a way
that would take away from his real study.[2]

The Realities of War

Jack had delayed returning to Gastons at the end of the 1914 Christmas break because his father feared a German invasion of England.[3] Kirk had nothing but contempt for the near panic over fear of invasion. He reasoned that an invasion by the Germans would require a confrontation with the British fleet, which would quickly put an end to German aspirations. The last thing the Germans would want was a massive encounter of their navy with the might of Britain.[4] The war had taken on a grimmer tone since Jack had arrived at Gastons the previous September. One of the first people he met upon his first arrival at Gastons had been Oswald Smythe, a former pupil of Kirk who had come for a weeklong visit. Smythe returned in January 1915 with the news that his brother, who had lost an arm in combat, would soon return to France. The use of severely wounded and crippled men suggested to Jack that matters might be worse than previously imagined. Smythe also contradicted the reports of the splendid performance of troops from India, whom he criticized as "worthless, and absolutely unfitted for trench fighting," and to make matters worse, in the habit of not burying their dead.[5] This report seems odd, since both Hindus and Sikhs cremate their dead. The story suggests the extent of the power of rumor during war. Relating this report to his father, Jack allowed that it was only one man's story and that as the war went on, everyone would grow less credulous.

Mr. Kirkpatrick, in contrast to Smythe, continued to make humorous comments on the course of the war at home as well as on conditions at the front. Kirkpatrick appears to have enjoyed performing for an audience, especially when he had a foil. The best of all foils was the local curate. Normally, Kirk did not take tea, but he made an exception when the curate came. Rather than a demonstration of respect for the curate's clerical dignity, Kirk's attendance at tea possibly provided him with an opportunity to put God's representative in a bad light. Jack reported with some glee:

> Kirk has many amusing reflections, as usual, on the present
> crisis, especially when the curate came yesterday at afternoon
> tea and told a number of patriotic lies about Germany and
> the Germans. Kirk then proceeded with great deliberation to
> prove step by step that his statements were fallacious, impos-
> sible, and ridiculous. The rest of the party, including Mrs. K.,
> Louis, and myself enjoyed it hugeously.[6]

Kirkpatrick's wife and his son, Louis, had known this kind of
afternoon's entertainment for years, but this sort of behavior at
tea was all new to Jack, who hated the usual polite conversation
one expected at tea.

What kind of patriotic lies might the curate have been telling
about Germany and the Germans in January 1915? If it is true that
the truth is the first casualty of war, then it is difficult to take sides
in this debate over tea. The German army did commit atrocities
against the civilians of Belgium and France during their invasion in
August and the fall of 1914. The "rape of Belgium" involved the
mass execution of hundreds of civilians at a time in multiple loca-
tions. The British propaganda machine took advantage of what
was already a horrific war crime and magnified it to a level that
people like W. T. Kirkpatrick would only ridicule as a fabrication.
In the end, Jack Lewis was left feeling quite complacent about the
war and not inclined to believe how bad things were supposed to
be. If Kirk could make amusing remarks about the war, then Jack
could follow in his train and be amused. If, in the process, the
clergy looked ridiculous, all the better.

The Threat from Sea and Air

For the most part, Jack thought of the war only in terms of its
inconvenience to him. He had not received the usual letter from
his father by early February, and he wondered if his father were
ill or if the "submarine nonsense" had interrupted the mails. War
would cease being amusing if the submarines meant that he would

have to spend his Easter holiday in England rather than Ulster. Albert Lewis continued to fret, and this fretting only grew more intense when the Germans sank the cargo ship *Kilcoan*, designed by Albert's brother Joseph, in a raid near Fleetwood on January 30, 1915.[7] Fleetwood, a small port in northwest Lancashire at the mouth of the river Wyre, was one of the ferry routes to Larne in Northern Ireland that Jack often took to cross the Irish Sea. In a letter to his father the next week, Jack dismissed the submarine danger as only a scare tactic of the Germans to disrupt commerce. He seemed to suggest that the tactic had worked on gullible people like his father.[8]

In February 1915, Warnie obtained a rare leave to go home. He swooped into Bookham unannounced and declared his intention to take Jack home with him to Belfast. Kirkpatrick wrote to Albert that "when a man appears suddenly and unexpectedly from the battle field, we don't feel able to refuse him anything," even though Kirk opposed the idea. In keeping with his pattern, Warnie borrowed the money from Kirk for the two brothers to make the trip to Ireland with the assurance that Albert would make it good.[9]

By March, Jack feared that his father would not even consider allowing a trip home for Easter break. Jack reasoned that he would not mind waiting until summer to come home if he had any reason to believe that the submarine threat would subside, but it would make no sense to stay in England at Easter because of the submarine scare, only to come home in summer in spite of the same submarines. Jack seemed to think that his father's fear of submarines could keep him away from home for two, five, or six years. In all likelihood, it was not the fear of being kept from his father that concerned Jack.[10] More likely, he did not like the prospect of being separated from his only friend. At this independent stage of adolescence, Jack had learned to practice the art of not spending time with his father even when they were in the same house.

On April 7, 1915, Warnie arrived once more at Gastons, on leave, prepared to whisk Jack off to Belfast, but this time he found that Kirk had mustered the moral fortitude to deny a man straight from the battlefield whatever he wanted. Warnie wired Albert with a plea to intercede with Kirk. Kirk took the position that Warnie could visit his father in Belfast and then return to visit Jack at Gastons, but Warnie would not have it. He wanted to be with both Jack and his father for the full time of his leave, and Kirk relented.[11] Jack and Warnie clearly did not share their father's fear of submarines. They meant to cross the Irish Sea, and they would not be hindered by a small thing like war.

If underwater boats posed a threat to shipping, the great German airships posed a threat to the cities, a threat also dismissed by Jack as overrated. Of the zeppelin threat, Jack thought it would be a "childish folly" for the Germans to put so much time, effort, and money into killing a few babies and knocking over a few chimneys.[12] The remark betrays a childish disconnection between Jack and the realities of total war as it had begun to affect people in the cities of the British Isles. It also betrays a continuing immature callousness with regard to the pain and suffering that would mount into tens of millions of deaths by the war's end. Jack was still a boy who thought and acted like a boy despite having a well-functioning brain.

The zeppelin threat was real. In January 1915, the UK Home Office issued orders for all lights visible from outside to be extinguished between 5:00 p.m. and 7:30 a.m., as well as headlights on motor cars.[13] The previous century's advances in public lighting and electrification of homes suddenly disappeared, and the small villages of England, like Great Bookham, found themselves returned to a bygone era. A few days later, however, the blackout regulations were revoked. As the year progressed, the authorities wavered on what measures should be taken to guard against the threat of air raids by German zeppelins loaded with bombs. As imagined fears turned to harsh reality once the zeppelins began to make their raids on England, new orders were issued and strictly enforced. Private homes were required to cover their windows so that no internal light could be seen from outside. Homes, churches, shops, factories, and all other establishments of any kind had to shield all sources of light during the night hours. In Guildford, the time for Evensong was moved forward on Sundays so that people could get home before dark.[14]

During the course of the war, German zeppelins raided England fifty-one times while German airplanes mounted fifty-two raids. These raiders dropped approximately nine thousand bombs, which killed 1,413 people and injured 3,408 more. Approximately half of the casualties were in London.[15] Great Bookham's name belies the fact that it was not a great city or town. Kirk wrote to Albert to assure him that Great Bookham was completely outside the range of the German zeppelins; Surrey lay in total darkness at night and had nothing to fear from zeppelin attack.[16] As it turned out, Kirk was mistaken in his logic. The Germans did not drop bombs on Great Bookham, but they did attack nearby Guildford, where Jack often visited. The attack came on October 13, 1915. Zeppelin L.13, commanded by Kapitanleutnant Heinrich Mathy, circled the perimeter of London by St. Albans, Watford, Uxbridge, and Staines before coming to Guildford. From Guildford, the airship cruised on to Redhill, Bromley, and Woolwich.[17]

Given Albert Lewis's tendency to expect the worst from the war, news of the zeppelin raid near Great Bookham might be expected to have driven him to extreme solicitousness for his son's safety. By a happy coincidence for Jack, the government's Press Bureau acted as though in conspiracy with him. It exercised strict censorship over the publication of any details related to air attacks in England. The newspapers could not even publish the location of raids without permission of the Press Bureau. No report of zeppelin attacks that could possibly fall into the hands of the Germans and provide them with information about their bombing effectiveness could be produced. The local Guildford newspapers did not even report to its readers any news of the attack they had experienced.[18] The official report of the raid issued on October 14 made no mention of Guildford and only stated that the enemy airships had "visited the Eastern Counties and a portion of the London area."[19] Albert Lewis would have had no reason to suspect that the war had come so close to Jack unless Jack volunteered the information. Adolescent boys out to establish their independence do not volunteer information to their parents. As a result, Albert did not create a stir as he had done over the submarines that might have blown up Jack's ferry crossing the Irish Sea. Jack, never wanting to provide his father with any reason to exert his parental authority, continued to treat the war as a joke.

On October 22, perhaps to head off any interrogations about the zeppelin attack in case Albert learned of it, Jack wrote to his father that zeppelins were the principal amusement at Gastons.[20] He then created a subterfuge by distracting his father's prying eye away from Great Bookham to London. Without mentioning the nearby raid on Guildford, Jack reported that they had seen the glare from the attack on Waterloo Station in London, but of course, it was so far away that they really only saw a few flashes and could not hear a sound. He was very safe. He was very far away from danger. His father need have no fears. He then turned to ridicule and suggested that zeppelin hysteria had caused people to imagine that they heard zeppelins overhead, but it usually turned out to be only a "motor byke [*sic*] in the distance."[21] Then he covered himself by mentioning, "Once we heard the noise of the thump of a hammer at Guildford, and people say that was the dropping of bombs, but I have my doubts."[22]

The Belgian Hope

For Jack, the only real reason to even notice the war arose because of the Belgian refugees who had settled in the vicinity. In the wake of the German invasion, an estimated quarter of a million Belgians fled their homes and sought sanctuary in England.[23] Nearby Guildford, where Jack regularly spent his free time, found a place for between two thousand and three thousand refugees. Small villages all over England like Great Bookham provided refuge for the Belgians for the duration of the war. The Belgians fled with little more than the clothes on their backs. They needed homes, furniture, clothes, food, and jobs. While the government waged war, local committees sprang up across the kingdom to care for the refugees. Jack had made fun of the "typical fussy 'Parishional' way" of providing help to the needy when the Belgian refugee crisis had first come to Great Bookham, but apart from the sense of Christian compassion and responsibility felt by people in the churches, the local committees would not have sprung up.[24] During his most smug, cynical period of atheism, Jack acknowledged through his ridicule that it was the local parish that showed hospitality to the homeless. The War Distress Committee in Guildford, for instance, was led by the Reverend E. C. Kirwan, Rector of Holy Trinity Church (Church of England); the Reverend Alex Cowe, Congregational minister; and Father J. J. Higgins, priest at St. Joseph's Catholic Church.[25]

In most places, the Belgian children enrolled in the local village schools with instruction in English. Belgians might have found themselves in great country houses left vacant by their absentee owners, who made them available for the war effort. Others found themselves in deserted farm cottages left vacant by farm laborers serving in the trenches of France. Once-prosperous Belgians found themselves wearing the old, discarded clothes that English neighbors had donated to the local committee. They relied on the parcels of food that the local parishioners delivered to them each week. Jack accompanied Mrs. Kirkpatrick when the responsibility fell to her, and he observed the concrete expression of faith. We have no reason to believe that this experience touched him in any way at the time. While the parishioners busied themselves in well-doing, Jack was reading enlightened views encouraged by Kirk that suggested that war served a useful purpose by thinning out the weaker elements of the population.

It was not Jack's deep compassion for the poor souls who had been driven from their homes by the invading, rapacious Germans that stirred him. Instead, he had inadvertently developed a crush on one of the young Belgian girls. He had told Arthur of his unrequited love while in Belfast during the Christmas holiday. By the beginning of February, Jack had managed to circumvent the language barrier enough to convince the object of his devotion to rendezvous with him. He did not elaborate in his letter to Arthur what he had in mind for this first private meeting, but the cryptic wording suggests that he and Arthur had already discussed what Jack intended. Apparently, Jack's beloved had been sick, but she had improved enough to fix a date. Jack was in absolute rapture over his anticipation of their date.[26]

When Jack wrote to Arthur two weeks later, however, his hopes had been dashed. The rendezvous had not come off, and, worst of all, his beloved was not speaking to him. For some reason, Jack did not show up for the date. He did not explain to Arthur why he did not show up, but from calling his great love "an awfully decent sort" in his earlier letter, he had come to remark that "like all the rest of her sex she is incapable of seeing anything fair."[27] Whatever the reason that Jack could not keep the appointment, the young lady was disturbed, and before Jack could make things right, she left with her mother to visit friends in Birmingham.[28] Six weeks later, however, Jack could report that he had received a letter from "Her," and all was well again.[29] The exchange suggests that Jack gave Arthur to believe that he had negotiated the loss of his virginity. The truth appears to be less romantic.

In 1931, Warren Lewis was busy typing up all the Lewis family papers he could find. Apparently, he asked Jack to obtain all the letters that Jack had written to Arthur so that he could properly document Jack's life. A few weeks after Jack's famous talk with J. R. R. Tolkien and Hugo Dyson on Addison's Walk, he wrote to Arthur suggesting that they suppress the letters in which they discussed sex, especially the correspondence that discusses Jack's "pretended assignation with the Belgian."[30] As teenage boys are prone to do with their friends about their sexual conquests, Jack had been lying or, at least, he claimed to have lied. Yet, it was an odd lie for a boy to tell another boy. He did not claim to have had sex. Instead, he claimed that he had failed to score with a girl who seemed eager to please. Confusion, on the other hand, is a frame of mind perfectly consistent with teenage boys who have begun to develop an interest in sex.

A Future for Jack

By April 22, 1915, Kirkpatrick advised Albert that Jack continued to exhibit the kind of performance that should win him a classical scholarship to Oxford, which would mean approximately eighty to a hundred pounds per year, or about half his university expenses. While a scholarship could mean the possibility of an academic life, Kirkpatrick noted that such a life soon degenerates into a dull, monotonous routine for many others, which Jack would find tedious. Conversely, Kirkpatrick thought Jack would excel at the bar. He had the mind for it, but whether he could handle the oratorical aspect was still an open question. As they were about to embark on reading Demosthenes, the greatest orator of antiquity, Kirk thought it would soon be evident if his young charge had the makings of a barrister.[31]

Albert liked the idea that his second son would follow him in his profession. Consequently, he began planning a career at the bar for Jack and wrote to secure Kirkpatrick's agreement to this plan. Kirkpatrick, however, suggested as diplomatically as possible that Albert could not plan Jack's career for him. In his "on the one hand, on the other hand" manner, Kirkpatrick pointed out that Oxford men often went to the bar or became fellows of their colleges, only to be unhappy in both professions. Ignoring his own observations, Kirk then declared that owing to Clive's "sensitive nature" and love of books, the academic life would suit him better than the bar. Kirk recognized what animated Jack: "He has singularly little desire to mingle with mankind, or study human nature. His interests lie in a totally different direction— in the past, in the realm of creative imagination, in the world which the common mind would call the unreal, but which is to him the only real one." Kirk would not predict whether these inclinations would continue into adulthood, but he considered it a mistake to attempt to force Jack into a different direction, which would only end in failure.[32] In fact, Kirkpatrick had Jack pegged to his dying day.

Kirk always regarded Jack as an exceptional student, far beyond the kind of boy he had normally taught. Kirk had had his eye on Jack since he won the classics scholarship to Malvern. Albert had sent Kirk a copy of Jack's winning essay, and Kirk pronounced it "an amazing performance for a boy of [Jack's] age"—or a boy of any age, for that matter.[33] His translations from Greek and Latin were remarkable in their literary skill, phrasing, and appreciation of the original text. On the other hand, his efforts at Greek and Latin composition fell short of the mark. It seemed odd to Kirk, because composition only involved basic memory work and imitation. The ordinariness of the work suggested to Kirk that it was too dull a task for someone with so active a mind.[34]

By August 1915, Kirk no longer regarded Jack as one of the best students of his age. Instead, he was "the most brilliant translator of Greek plays" that Kirk had ever met.[35] At the end of 1915, while sorting out the details of Jack's departure with Warnie for an extended Christmas holiday owing to the dates of Warnie's leave, Kirkpatrick declared to Albert that he had finally come to the conviction that Jack was ill-suited to any profession but a literary study. If he had to fight for survival like poor Belgium, he would probably fall into line and do what was necessary along with everyone else. Otherwise, he would be good for nothing else. Kirk no longer regarded the bar as a viable option.[36]

The Roots of the Mountain

During May 1915, after a month-long stay at home during the Easter holiday, Jack ordered the Longman's pocket edition of William Morris's novel *The Roots of the Mountain*. He dived into the book immediately upon its arrival, to the neglect of other matters, such as his weekly letter to Arthur Greeves. In a letter of contrition to Arthur on May 25, 1915, Jack blamed the book for his failure to write earlier.

Before we explore Jack's opinion of the second book he had read by his new hero William Morris, this would be a good point to take note of Jack's writing style in 1915. He had grown more flowery and extravagant in his imagery as he beat around the bush before getting out his point:

> B-r-r-r! Behold me coming with locusts & wild honey about my loins (or is it sackcloth & ashes) to kneel and tremble and apologise [*sic*] for my letterless week. However, qui s'excuse, s'accuse, as the French say, and if you want to seek the real author of the mischief you must go up to heaven, and find the four and twenty elders sitting in a row, as St John says, falling on their faces on the sea of glass (which must hurt rather but apparently is the 'thing' up yonder), and William Morris in white raiment with a halo.[37]

Jack Lewis at the age of sixteen could have won the Scripture knowledge prize at most English schools, but the Bible had become for him a literary source for clever quips. William Morris had taken the place of Jesus in his mind. From the perspective of Jack Lewis, William Morris was the only person truly worthy to receive glory, honor, and praise. Morris's only possible rival might be Arthur Greeves, whom Jack began addressing and would continue addressing as Galahad, beginning with this first letter after the Easter break of 1915.

As for *The Roots of the Mountain*, Jack thought it did a better job of sustaining his interest throughout than Morris had done with *The Well at the World's End*, but he did not think it was as good a novel. The great defect of the novel for Jack tells us that he had grown intensely aware of what he had long looked for in a story. While *The Well at the World's End* was full of the supernatural, the faerie, and the unearthly, *The Roots of the Mountains* had nothing of this sort. It did not differ significantly from just an ordinary novel. Jack enjoyed ordinary novels and devoured them, but he wanted more from William Morris. He wanted more of what he had found in *The Well at the World's End*.[38] The confirmed young materialist, after the mold of W. T. Kirkpatrick, wanted to experience the supernatural, the faerie, and the unearthly. Without knowing it at the time, Jack found himself in the midst of what we now call "cognitive dissonance." It was not merely a matter of trying to hold on to two mutually exclusive ideas. He wanted to have two mutually exclusive modes of being.

Of this period in his adolescence, Lewis wrote in *Surprised by Joy*, "Nearly all I loved I believed to be imaginary; nearly all that I believed to be real I thought grim and meaningless."[39] With his pleasure reading, he journeyed deeper into the world of Norse mythology, the King Arthur stories, and the world of fantasy. In his studies with Kirkpatrick, he drank deeply of the philosophy of brute materialism. Out of the world of imagination, Lewis appropriated a value system that had held civilization together for thousands of years. In the philosophy that he read with Kirkpatrick or heard from his master's lips, however, he found no basis for any system of values at all. He does not appear to have reflected on this conflict while he was living through it at Gastons. Few boys his age would have. Nonetheless, the conflict was by then a part of him, and it would come out. What he most loved and cherished had no logical place in the universe he had come to accept, and this realization would eventually become the basis for his primary argument for the existence of God. If the values he cared about do not emerge from a brute universe of mere matter, then where do they come from?

In a brute universe that consisted of "a meaningless dance of atoms," then no values exist.[40] Nothing is good or bad, beautiful or ugly, just or unjust; things merely exist. The materialist universe has no place for courage, loyalty, friendship, or any of the qualities that Jack most loved about the old stories. Of course, a reliable materialist like George Bernard Shaw could be relied upon to make fun of such ideas, and Jack liked Shaw.

To relegate to the world of imagination the experience of longing that crept upon Jack from time to time, instead of reconciling it to the real world, held one major advantage to Jack: his materialistic universe held "limited liabilities."[41] Without God, he might not look forward to eternal happiness, but he need have no fear of eternal punishment either. Jack had taught himself to avoid pain even if it meant limiting the possibilities of happiness. With death, everything would simply stop, and it would not be so bad because dead people do not know they are dead. They no longer exist to worry about such things. Such a mind-set encouraged the flippancy that Jack affected during this period of his life.

Lewis would also learn to take the imagination much more seriously. In fact, it would become one of the greatest concerns of his intellectual life. He would learn that it deals with much more than children's make-believe. He was not yet reflecting on the power of imagination in his letters to Arthur Greeves, but the mature C. S. Lewis recognized that his misunderstanding of the faculty of imagination had retarded his spiritual development as a teenager. He could be dismissive of imagination as a teenager because he thought the world of imagination was not real. Thus, he practiced the art of compartmentalizing his life. Though he regularly quoted Kirk on almost every subject, Jack never mentioned in his letters any discussion he might have had with Kirkpatrick about his love of mythology, northernness, the world of fantasy, dwarfs, or magic. He kept part of himself back from Kirk, just as he had learned to do with his father. He did not want Kirk to know the extent to which he loved a kind of story that to Kirk would have been rubbish, any more than he wanted his father to know that his confirmation into the Church of Ireland had been a sham.

The greatest urge of middle adolescence is independence. Establishing one's independence is a critical aspect of growing up. Otherwise, a person goes into life as "Daddy's little girl" or as a perpetual boy "tied to his mother's apron strings." The primary aim of independence involves the achievement of autonomy from the plans and control of parents. Jack had been pushing back from his father for some time. Rejecting his father's religious faith played a role in Jack's quest for independence, not as a passive-aggressive action to reject God because his father believed in God, but because he made the decision on his own for his own reasons. He found it easier and easier to dismiss his father's opinions as the ravings of a crazy old man, the way most boys his age over countless generations have done.

Reflecting on this period of his life from the vantage point of forty years' experience, C. S. Lewis observed that his rejection of Christianity had a strong connection with his pursuit of independence. During his time at Malvern College and following, he realized that "what mattered most of all was my deep-seated hatred of authority, my monstrous individualism, my lawlessness."[42] In this sense, his hatred of the prefect system and all that went with it at Malvern was as big an element—if not bigger at the time—in his drive toward independence as his father, who was already a distant figure with whom he only had to deal during holidays. One of the reasons he loved his life at Gastons so much was that he had become a free man. He had given his mind over to Kirk to be formed without his awareness, but Kirk did not interrogate him with an endless stream of questions and commentaries on life the way his father did, even though he interrogated him about how his mind worked. At this time in his life, the last thing Jack wanted was an interfering God, from whom one could never escape. Jack most wanted "some area, however small, of which I could only say to all other beings, 'This is my business and mine only.'"[43]

Romping the Neighborhood of Imagination

Jack roamed Surrey between Guildford and Leatherhead and beyond on long walks by himself. The scope of these walks could be far ranging and suggests that Jack walked briskly in order to cover the territory and return to Gastons in time for the next meal and lesson with Kirk. The major villages where Jack routinely walked were far enough by the main road, but he often took many of the footpaths that crisscross the county, so the walks would have been farther:

Guildford—9.5 miles from Great Bookham
Compton—14.3 miles from Great Bookham
Leatherhead—2.8 miles from Great Bookham
Friday Street—9.2 miles from Great Bookham

Mr. and Mrs. William Kirkpatrick, October 10, 1920. Used by permission of the Marion E. Wade Center, Wheaton College, Wheaton, IL.

In addition to his solitary walks, he also went with Mrs. Kirkpatrick on many of her jaunts. He rarely mentioned to Arthur or his father the purpose of the trips, but he regularly mentioned the villages he visited and what he saw there that warranted comment. In May, just after diving into Morris's *The Roots of the Mountains*, Jack went with Mrs. Kirkpatrick to the village of Compton, which lies to the southwest of Guildford. In the small, out-of-the-way village, Jack found a pottery workshop founded by his hero William Morris. It produced the elaborate fired and glazed tiles that adorned the great Victorian and Edwardian houses as aspects of the arts and crafts movement that Morris helped to foster. Morris's wallpaper designs covered the fashionable drawing rooms of the British Empire, and his tiles surrounded the fireplaces.

In the same village, Jack visited a small art gallery devoted to the paintings of George Frederic Watts (1817–1904), who had lived in Compton and designed the little gallery that contained 132 of his paintings. Jack was astonished to find paintings by Watts that he knew—*Orpheus and Eurydice*, *Endymion*, *Paolo and Francesco*, *Found Drowned*, and *Sir Galahad*.[44] The subjects of Watts's paintings paralleled Jack's tastes in literature. Watts brought to canvass the stories of classical Greece and of Malory, to Jack's pure delight. It never occurred to Jack that famous paintings would be in a small village instead of at the Louvre in Paris or the Tate Gallery in London. The subject matter Watts chose had fallen out of fashion by the early twentieth century, left behind by the Impressionist movement, which was itself quickly being left behind. Watts's paintings show the influence of the Impressionists with his blurred treatment of his canvasses. One thing Watts had in common with Arthur Rackham in his illustrations of the *Ring* operas of Wagner was an abundance of nude figures. Before the common availability of pornography, this sort of imagery would have been startling to an adolescent boy whose interest in sex was just beginning to ripen. Watts, however, did not deal in smut, and he received positive reviews from one who would play an important part in Jack's conversion several years later: G. K. Chesterton.[45]

Jack wrote similar accounts of his first trip to Compton to both Arthur and his father. Surprisingly, he did not mention the pottery workshop of William Morris to Arthur, with whom he had shared so many discussions of Morris. Instead, he told his father in such a familiar way (he referred to Morris as "my friend William") that one suspects he had talked to his father about Morris during his holiday at home.[46] Despite his efforts at independence, Jack still shared an interest in literature with his father, who had always encouraged his reading interests and funded his bibliographic vice. In fact, Jack quoted a passage from Morris in his next letter to his father to prompt him out of his tendency to fret over the deplorable state of the world and wilt into melancholy.[47]

Summer in Belfast

In this stimulating environment, it is not surprising that Jack was inspired to work more at his own compositions. On April 1, 1915, Jack returned to Belfast for his Easter holiday, which Kirkpatrick said he had earned.[48] Jack took advantage of this break from his study routine to write poetry. Between Easter 1915 and Easter 1917, he wrote fifty-two poems that he included in a notebook he named "The Metrical Meditations of a Cod." Throughout his letters during his adolescence, Jack used the term *kodotta*, a word he invented based on the Ulster colloquial word *cod*. A cod is a "silly troublesome fellow," and its verbal form means "to humbug or quiz a person; to hoax; to idle about." In explaining Jack's use of this expression in his collection of the Lewis family papers, Warnie said that the word could also be used for humorous self-deprecation. Jack used the word in this way in the title of his poetry collection.[49]

His times at home in Belfast gave Jack his greatest opportunities for adding to his body of poetry. His free time for writing at Gastons was limited. During his long vacation during the summer of 1915, Jack wrote six more poems to add to his growing collection of verse.[50] Exactly how he would spend his long vacation, however, became a matter of contention between Jack and Arthur. Arthur wanted Jack to go on holiday with him to the sea. Jack knew that he had already been destined to spend a week with his aunt at Larne, and he told Arthur that he did not think it would be very decent of him to leave his father alone for any longer when his vacation time was limited. He did not want Arthur to give up his own plans for going on holiday somewhere without him. Alternatively, Arthur could visit Jack by the sea at Larne, though he might be bored with Jack's relatives.

In this instance, Jack displayed unusual sensitivity to the feelings of his father—something we have little evidence of him doing otherwise during this period of his adolescence. It is such an unusual case of sensitivity to the older Lewis, who normally came in for all manner of neglect and contempt, that Jack may have had other motives for not wanting to go on holiday with Arthur at just this time. Concern for Albert was a good excuse, but it may have been a way of declining an invitation that made Jack uneasy.

While Jack had been developing a keen interest in the opposite sex, Arthur had been developing an interest, whether keen or not, in the same sex. C. S. Lewis made a strong statement about his unease with the young male sexual activity going on at Malvern when he wrote *Surprised by Joy*. Though he was devoted to his friend Arthur, he may not have wanted to place himself in an awkward position until all had been made clear between the two friends.

Apparently, they had their talk about the facts of life during the vacation time in Belfast, where each went back to his own home at night, for no strain or discomfort appears in their correspondence from this time forward over their different sexual orientations. Jack was to write freely to Arthur about his own sexual proclivities, and Jack appears to be aware of Arthur's preferences as suggested in his letters. This possibility for why Jack would have declined an otherwise grand invitation for a week by the sea has added credence when we note that the next subject that Jack responded to in his letter of June 1, 1915, was Arthur's discussion of sensuality. Jack stopped him cold.[51]

Arthur did not like Jack's refusal of a holiday together. Jack replied lightheartedly in his letter of June 8, 1915, with the observation that Arthur must have some serious grievance against him, otherwise the grammar of his letter would not have been so good. He repeated his reasons for declining: he was already booked for a week with an aunt and was concerned about taking time away from his father. Still, Arthur would not let the matter drop.[52] Jack's letter of June 29 once again took up his reasons for declining the "infernal holyday."[53] He then listed in formal logical progression his position on the vacation, but with a sarcastic, patronizing flare. This third effort appears to have ended the matter, or Jack may have put it to rest with an unplanned and unexpected face-to-face with Arthur in early July—weeks before his planned long vacation. Warnie breezed into Great Bookham unannounced on July 4 with the intention of taking Jack with him to Belfast for a four-day leave. Kirk resisted, but finally gave in, as usual, so Jack found himself at home again for a few days.[54]

In the midst of the correspondence over how Jack would spend his summer vacation, he made a special point of telling Arthur that he had met the prettiest girl he had ever seen in his life. She was eighteen years old—an older woman to Jack's sixteen years. Sadly for Jack, she was off to Dover to help with the war effort as a nurse, "or something like that."[55] He assured Arthur that he would not have to listen to another of Jack's love affairs, but in making the assurance, he reminded his friend that he regularly fell in love with pretty girls who crossed his path. There was no ambiguity to his sexual identity.

In *Surprised by Joy*, the mature C. S. Lewis remarked on this period in his life that he had come to know by experience that the longing and yearning that had stabbed him in his earlier encounters with Wagner's *Ring* and northernness were not simply repressed sexual desire in disguise.[56] It is evident from his free discussions with Arthur that Jack Lewis did not suppress his sexual desire as a teenager. To the contrary, he embraced it and sought opportunities for its expression, however successful and to whatever degree those efforts might have been. He had left the constraints of religious morality far behind and felt no transcendent urge to control himself. He now resided on the well-known ground of teenage boys who sneak so as not to get caught.

The First Crack in Jack's Materialism

The discussion of the pretty girl, however, sparked a thought in Lewis that would have disturbed Kirk if he had known about it. Jack told Arthur that the pretty girl was just like the grave movement in one of Liszt's Hungarian Rhapsodies. He then went on to speculate on how everyone he knew could be understood as like a piece of music. Gordon Ewart was like "The Pilgrims' Chorus" from Wagner's *Tannhäuser*. Kelsie Ewart was like Wagner's "The Ride of the Valkyries" from *Die Walküre*, but not so loud. Gundreda Ewart was like the dance movement in *Danse Macabre*. Poor Bob Ewart, the brunt of many a joking remark by Jack and who later succeeded his father as baronet, was like a Salvation Army hymn. Arthur was like a Chopin mazurka—wild, plaintiff, and disjointed. Finally, he said that Lily Greeves, Arthur's older sister, was like Grieg's "The Watchman's Song."[57] This last comment may tell us more about young Jack's state of mind with respect to Lily Greeves than it tells us about her. It is a stately and majestic composition that suggests a rare and unapproachable fairy queen.

The only reason that Jack's musings on the fit between people and music deserve attention is that in his next letter, in response to an apparent rebuttal from Arthur, Jack insisted that a relationship exists between one's character and one's physical appearance. He declared that a person's outward appearance is the direct consequence of his or her "soul, ego, [psyche], intellect—call it what you will."[58] What then followed was an unspeakable heresy for a devout materialist, a heresy that Kirk would have found deplorable. Jack expounded the necessary relationship between the body and the soul, and insisted that the idealistic side of him must have a corresponding outlet in his body.[59]

Materialists do not speak of people having souls. They do not speak of people having a physical side and something else. For the materialist, people are only physical. The universe is only physical. Nothing exists that is not physical. Anything that a person might call a soul, ego, psyche, or intellect is simply a chemical reaction within the cells of the brain. By this point in his studies with Kirkpatrick, Jack Lewis knew full well the doctrines of materialism, yet in an unguarded moment while debating with Arthur, he let slip an idea diametrically opposed to sound materialist thought. What might be happening?

If we look at what Jack had been reading steadily for years, we find that he most loved stories that dealt with character and those values that he most admired. Jack the literary man was at odds with Jack the philosopher. For some time he had taken the view that what was imaginary was not true and that only the physical was real. In this exchange, however, we begin to see that the materialist framework he had adopted as his point of view was beginning to fail him. At some level, he knew that there was more to life than meets the eye, but it would be many years before he worked it all out.

We need look no further than the next section of the letter in which he explained to Arthur how the soul is reflected in the body to see what kind of story was having an impact on how Jack thought, felt, and embraced the world. He mentioned reading a passage from Maurice Hewlett's *Pan and the Young Shepherd*. This story is yet another version of the same kind of story he had been devouring for months on end. It was a kind of story that he gravitated toward, and he could not get his fill of it. This is the kind of story in which someone goes off on a quest to attain something of immeasurable value against all odds. Inevitably, a beautiful lady is involved and somehow associated with the quest. The pilgrim will dare all and do all for the sake of the lady, and somehow honoring the lady advances the quest rather than diverting from it. This plot is the one that young Jack Lewis most loved. For this plot to work, however, there must be more to life than the mere physical. Jack had the logic of materialism arguing against spiritual reality, but he had his own experience arguing for it.

Years later, when he agreed to address the nation on the BBC during the next great war, C. S. Lewis built his entire argument for the existence of God not by logical argument but by appealing to the common experience of his audience. Philosophers have faulted *Mere Christianity* as a rather facile piece of amateur philosophy that does not rise above the mediocre. Lewis would probably say, "Fair enough." What the philosophical critics do not grasp is that Lewis is not doing philosophy as such in *Mere Christianity*; he is doing apologetics. A music critic might argue that *Mere Christianity* is a very poor sonata. Again, Lewis might humbly agree. Of course it is no more a sonata than it is philosophy. Perhaps those who critique it as philosophy are simply confusing it with philosophical logic because it follows the grammatical pattern of well-ordered English prose that one would hope to find in any good narrative. We may refer to this narrative as logic, but we miss the point of what Lewis achieved with his radio broadcasts. He was not relying on the power of his logic to convince an audience of something they did not believe, as he always failed to accomplish with Arthur Greeves. Instead, he was appealing to his audience to examine their own experience of life to see if they might not find what he had found in his own experience. The boy of sixteen, however, had not yet gone that far. His experience was still forming within him, but it lay unexamined.

An Unwanted Companion

Following his long vacation in August and September back home at Leeborough (née Little Lea), Jack returned to Gastons to discover that Kirk had taken on another live-in pupil. His name was Terence Forde, and he was the nephew of Mrs. Howard Ferguson from Ireland, whose husband was a friend of Albert Lewis from his school days at Lurgan. Terry had attended Campbell College, though Jack had not known him. To his father, Jack had nothing but nice things to say about the boy and how happy he was to have a new friend living at Gastons.[60] By now, Jack was worldly-wise enough to tell Albert what Albert wanted to hear. Ever the sentimentalist, Albert would be certain that this young man, with such a strong connection to his old school chum, would be perfect company for Jack.

To Arthur, however, Jack held forth on the demerits of the boy. He complained that he had not fled Malvern and its company for the wilds of Surrey only to be shackled with another pupil his own age. Perhaps to remind Arthur of his broadening interests, he did not leave the complaint at merely another pupil his own age, but added another pupil his own age *and* sex. Presumably, he was prepared to make the sacrifice for the company of a girl his age.[61] Jack judged poor Terry Forde hopeless with no interest in any of the things that really matter. As it was, however, Terry would spend most of his time in Leatherhead taking special classes in the sciences, Kirk providing little more than a roof over his head. Jack would not have Terry under foot most of the time.

A year after Jack's arrival at Gastons, his daily routine remained largely what it had been in 1914, except now he described it to Arthur in terms of relationships within the house rather than by reference to the clock. He woke up when he heard Kirk splashing in his bath, but he luxuriated in his bed another twenty minutes before getting up and going down to breakfast. After breakfast and a short walk, he and Kirk worked on Thucydides, whom he deplored, and Homer, whom he adored. Kirk allowed him a fifteen-minute break before going on to Tacitus, which ended at 1:00, when they ate lunch. After lunch, Jack was free to take his long walks across the countryside until 4:30, when Mrs. Kirkpatrick had tea. He loved the days when she was away having tea with one of her friends, because it meant he could lounge in a big chair beside the fire and read while he enjoyed his meal. (In England and Ireland, tea is not a drink but a small meal between lunch and supper.). After tea, generally around 5:00, Jack and Kirk worked on Plato and Horace until supper at 7:30. After supper, Jack spent time with Mrs. Kirkpatrick working on his French and German until 9:00. Then he was free again until bedtime, which for him was usually around 10:30. At the end of the day, he usually wrote in his diary and then worked on his poetry.

This kind of routine would follow him for most of the rest of his life. At Gastons he learned to manage the various demands on his time and the responsibilities that he undertook regardless of how he felt. From Kirk he learned the daily discipline necessary to do the grueling work of a fellow at Magdalen College. From Mrs. Kirkpatrick he learned the patience and grace needed to participate in the domestic life that Mrs. Moore would establish at the Kilns many years later. He could never have learned these lessons from his father or at an English public school. Had he not learned them, he could not have found the time to do the writing he did in the 1930s and 1940s. The Kirkpatricks were not merely preparing Jack for the entrance exams to Oxford. They were preparing him for the routine of life.

Living with a Contradiction

As 1915 came to a close, Kirk had set Jack to reading Arthur Schopenhauer's *The World as Will and Idea*.[62] Kirk thrived on Schopenhauer, a German philosopher in the tradition of Kant who held that spiritual or religious knowledge was not possible because the nonphysical world was not available to scientific examination. Thus, Schopenhauer viewed metaphysical philosophy as worthless. Though Jack regarded Schopenhauer as depressing, he valued his views on music and poetry, and his ideas saturated Kirk's conversation, which Jack swallowed whole. While he absorbed the philosophy of Schopenhauer, he had also begun to reread *The Well at the World's End* and to revel in a world that was diametrically opposed to everything Schopenhauer believed. Jack was consistently and persistently creating a contradiction within himself that he managed to ignore and would not face for years to come.

Jack ended 1915 at home at Little Lea from December 21 until January 21, 1916. Warnie had leave for Christmas, and Albert Lewis had both his sons home with him again.[63]

7

A Conflicted Soul

1916

By the end of January 1916, Jack was back at Gastons, where he had settled into the routine of life there. For six years, he had experienced the rhythm of shifting abruptly from life at Little Lea to life at school or with Kirkpatrick, which involved a radical adjustment to a different way of doing things and of relating to people. Remarkably, Jack made the adjustment well in spite of his rebellious and contrary temperament. In fact, he made the adjustment so well that one might accuse him of becoming well-adjusted.

Perhaps the continual shift from one place to another helped to modify the antisocial tendency in his character, enabling him to "put up" with people who needed only to be endured for a short time. In any event, he wrote to his father that the continual change had developed in him the ability to settle down quickly when a change in his environment came. As soon as he arrived in Great Bookham, he felt as though he had been there for some time. It helped that everything in the Kirkpatrick household was as it had always been, and he might have said the same about the situation at Little Lea.[1]

To his sentimental father, however, the urbane Jack could present a passable sentimental side, even though he always claimed to abominate sentimentality. On the last Saturday in January 1916, ordinarily a cold day—but this had been an unusually warm January—Jack took one of his long walks to the village of Dorking and wrote about it in a letter to his father.[2] He had grown fond of the old villages of Surrey, and in Dorking he found a setting that stoked his romantic nature. One old house in particular caught his attention with its multilevel construction, the date 1666 on its facade, and its ornamentation of dragons and monsters on its roof. To top it off, the town had an old inn where he could take tea in a parlor that dated back to "coaching days."[3]

By the age of seventeen, Jack Lewis had developed his own share of quirks that would follow him all his life and cause no end of confusion for his biographers. He was bad at math, but he was also bad at dates. When he was seventeen, Jack still saved letters. He kept all of Arthur's letters, stuck together on a pin, in their proper order so that he could flip through them as through a reference book and read over passages again. Arthur had the same habit of saving letters from Jack, which is why we know what he thought, how he felt, and what he did at a time of life when his letters to his father were less reliable as to the true state of affairs. In time, however, C. S. Lewis cleaned house and discarded his past, but that Lewis belongs to a later time of life. When Jack reread the letters from Arthur, he thought of them in terms of stages of their friendship and not by date. This self-understanding by the young Lewis goes a long way toward explaining a lifelong problem Lewis had with dates. He acknowledged the problem, and his brother concurred. He was not so concerned with when something happened as with how the event stood in relation to the whole. He was not so concerned that a letter was written in September 1914 as he was that it was written when he and Arthur were talking about Loki.[4]

Jack did not like the idea of sharing Kirkpatrick and Gastons with Terry Forde. Kirkpatrick's new pupil continued to offend Jack by his very being. While Jack sat writing to Arthur, his mood grew ever fouler as the "bloody little beast" sneaked upstairs and proceeded to use all the hot water for his bath. Jack loved to luxuriate in water, whether swimming or lounging in a hot bath. He sarcastically noted that he would have to take his bath without hot water since the Kirkpatricks only went to the expense of heating the water "about once a month."[5] An influenza outbreak at St. John's school in Leatherhead forced the closing of the school for the winter term, and Jack lamented that his counterpart would be ever present at Gastons for the foreseeable future.[6] Jack entertained himself through the summer by stealing pages from Forde's exercise books to write his letters to Arthur.[7]

Toward an Academic Career

By January of 1916, Albert and Kirkpatrick were hard at work planning Jack's academic career at Oxford. The Oxford admissions process, then as now, was quite different from applying to a college or university in the United States. If you visit the city of Oxford and ask directions to the university campus, you will be met with quizzical glances. The University of Oxford owns several buildings, notably the Bodleian Library complex, the Clarendon Building, the Examination Schools building, and a few other jointly held properties, but the university is not a campus but a confederacy of independent colleges that collectively maintain a library and administer examinations. Floating within this amorphous relationship of colleges are the various faculties for the various disciplines offered collectively by the university. The English faculty comprises those fellows of the various colleges who offer tutorials and lectures in English.

When Jack Lewis began to make preparations to enter Oxford, he had to be accepted by a college as well as by the university. It was possible to be accepted to the university without having a college. Likewise, one might have a college but not gain admission to the university. Kirk advised Albert that "Clive can put down his name for a number of Colleges in the order of preference, and if he gains an exhibition he will have to take whatever college will elect him."[8]

Jack's greatest academic weakness continued to be in composing essays in Greek. His tendency to originality posed a danger, since the examiners at Oxford did not want originality. They wanted simple memory work and imitation, and Kirk declared that Clive had a "temperamental disability" at such performance.[9] The adolescent Jack was well on the way to establishing an independence of mind that approached stubbornness. He would do things his way, and Kirk realized it. Increasingly, Kirk came to the view that Jack's skill at Greek composition no longer mattered, because the universities no longer placed stress on it. They had shifted attention to knowledge of classics, philosophy, literature, and history, all of which played to Jack's strengths.[10]

In January 1916, Kirk expected that Jack would enter Oxford in the fall of that year.[11] The great fly in the ointment that began to raise its head was the prospect that Jack might be drafted into military service before he could go up to Oxford. Kirk, ever the realist, proposed this possibility to Albert, ever the romantic. As the year proceeded, the deliberations between Albert and Kirk turned more to Jack's liability for military service. Kirk advised that conscription had become the norm for university students in 1916, but the possibility of avoiding the draft would come if Jack entered Trinity College, Dublin, instead of an English university.[12] Warnie took the view that Jack should stand for an Oxford scholarship during the war, while the competition was low. Even if he had to go down from university to discharge his military obligations, he could then return to Oxford after the war with his scholarship safely in hand. As was often the case, Warnie had a shrewd grasp of things. In his letters home, he gave a clue as to how his relationship with Jack had deteriorated since Jack went to Malvern. Warnie almost always asked about news from Jack, who had almost completely ceased writing to Warnie.[13] In his bid for independence, Jack had distanced himself not merely from his father but also from his older brother, under whose protection and in whose shadow he had once stood.

Concern over conscription grew, and on May 24, 1916, Kirkpatrick's prediction came true when Parliament passed the Military Service Act.[14] The terms of the act, which was introduced in Parliament the first week of May 1916, were still unclear to Albert the lawyer. Albert read the new act in light of the previous Military Service Act, which drafted young men "ordinarily resident in Great Britain" but exempted those "resident in Great Britain for the purpose only of their education." Albert hoped that the old terms would still apply.[15]

Warnie believed that Jack should stay another year with Kirk rather than risk conscription from Oxford as a private soldier. He thought Jack would make a poor soldier and was better out of the war. Though Trinity College might be an option as far as the war was concerned, it would be a poorer option for Jack's future career.[16] Albert was inclined to take Warnie's advice about keeping Jack with Kirk for one more year. Kirk was surprised, since he saw no need for any further preparation by Jack for his scholarship examination. Clive had read more of the classics than anyone else Kirk had ever heard of, except perhaps people like Addison and Macaulay, whom one might read about but never actually meet. The war, on the other hand, might constitute for Kirk a legitimate reason to keep Jack at Gastons for one more year. He reasoned that conscription was inevitable if the government proposed to stop the greatest military machine in history. The war could never be won with a volunteer army.[17]

Kirkpatrick made clear in a letter to Albert his view that Irish exemption from military service did not apply to a resident of England, so that Jack would be liable to conscription a month after his eighteenth birthday in 1916. A possible case for exemption might be made to the local tribunal if Jack stated his intent to be preparing for entrance to Sandhurst like Warnie. Such a plan was sure to fail, however, since Jack had none of the necessary background in math and science, both of which he loathed intensely. If Jack gained his scholarship to Oxford as a result of the entrance exams in December, he could never attend lectures, for he would be drafted before the Hilary term began in January 1917. The great question behind Kirk's repetition of matters about which Albert had already thought was not really about conscription but about how Jack could enter military service as an officer instead of as a common enlisted soldier.[18] By May 1916 the question of how to keep Jack out of the war became a moot point, for while home over his Easter holiday Jack had made up his mind to serve.

Albert wrote to Kirk with the news of Jack's decision to volunteer for military service. Nonetheless, Jack planned to follow Warnie's advice and try for the Oxford scholarship before he entered the army. Albert supported this scheme, but he also wanted him to try for Sandhurst on the off chance that desperation for cannon fodder would relax the math and science expectations for raw junior officers. In any event, Albert saw the need to find a way for Jack to secure a commission as an officer. If all else failed, he intended to seek the help of one of his many political friends.[19] Kirkpatrick agreed that a temporary commission arranged by whatever means Albert had at his disposal would be a better option for Jack than a try at Sandhurst, where he would be expected to handle tools "utterly alien to his temperament."[20] When Albert finally got a copy of the Military Service Act, he was relieved to find that the new act preserved the position that those in Great Britain for educational purposes were not considered "ordinarily resident" and would not be subject to conscription. This did not affect whether Jack would serve because he had already decided to serve. It did, however, affect when he would begin his service. He had the freedom to pursue his Oxford scholarship before entering the army. Just in case, Albert the lawyer thought it wise to secure a certificate of exemption from the local tribunal.[21]

Kirkpatrick continually resisted Albert's plan for him to teach Jack enough math to gain entrance to Sandhurst, but he never gave Albert a satisfactory reason. Albert demanded a solution to this mystery from Jack. Kirk had taught Warnie enough to gain entrance with a nice scholarship. Why not Jack? Albert, who thought himself a master at reading between the lines, simply could not read between the lines of Kirk's repeated subtle declarations that Jack simply would not learn math or science and there was no point in wasting his valuable time trying to make something happen that would never happen on this earth, thank you very much. Kirk also informed Jack that he should be free from conscription unless the new Home Rule Bill made Ulster part of Great Britain.[22] Jack declined to answer Albert's demand for the real reason Kirk would not teach him the math he needed for Sandhurst. It fell to Kirk to explain that Sandhurst wanted practical geometry, which Warnie had been exposed to at Malvern. It also meant the practical use of measuring instruments with which Warnie had played at Gastons in his free time. To a certain degree, Warnie had been lucky with the scoring of the exams. Kirk stated emphatically to Albert as regards teaching math to Jack, "I never undertake anything for which I am not fit."[23]

Assuming Jack could win a scholarship to Oxford, he still would have to find a place. As to which college Jack should seek, he had mentioned Christ Church, but Albert knew that prestigious college as the home of "the bloods," who were the very sort of people Jack had abominated at Malvern.[24] Conversely, Albert regarded Balliol as a grand college with a grand reputation, but perhaps too grand for Jack. He advised Jack to look at the second-rung colleges with good reputations, such as New College and Oriel.[25] Christ Church, after all, would be too expensive, and Jack could never keep up with the bloods.[26] Kirkpatrick took Albert's side and observed that Christ Church was too aristocratic and wealthy a place for Jack.[27]

Jack was attracted to the glamour of Balliol College, but Eric Dodds, a correspondent with Kirk who was reading classics at

University College, advised him that its prestige had declined. New College and Christ Church had the growing academic reputations. New College had the advantage from Jack's point of view because it allowed applicants to translate poetry instead of prose for their entrance examinations.[28] His only reason for placing Christ Church first in his order of preference was that it had the biggest reputation of the six colleges on his list. University College did not make his list of the best colleges.[29]

Repairing the Breach

As the war droned on with massive casualties and no progress to show for the mounting death toll, Warnie appears to have developed a desire to repair the breach between Jack and him that had come as a result of their differences over Malvern. The primary manifestation of this desire was the effort to which he went to ensure that he would have both his brother and his father together with him for the duration of his leaves from the front. It was not enough to have some time with his father in Belfast and some time with his brother in Great Bookham. He wanted all of his time on leave spent with both father and brother.

After Warnie's earlier experiences with Kirk's insistence that he was the head of his own house and that Jack was his charge, Warnie planned out his next invasion of Gastons and secured Albert as his ally. Rather than another surprise attack in hopes of catching Kirk off guard, Warnie practiced the art of strategic alliance in advance of his Christmas 1915 leave. In October, Warnie had written to his father to make arrangements with Kirk ahead of time so that he could bring Jack home with him on his next leave in December without having to waste a day arguing with Kirk.[30] Warnie was particularly anxious that Jack be with him at home because he told his father that he expected it would be his last leave before the end of the war, though he could not explain why. The explanation was that Warnie's unit had been designated to accompany the proposed French-led Salonika expeditionary force, which never materialized.[31] In the end, all Christmas leave for 1915 was canceled, and Jack went home by himself.[32]

Warnie expected his next leave to come during April 10–20, 1916, with hopes that it would coincide with Jack's Easter holiday.[33] No sooner had he made these plans known than he revised his plans to arrive at Gastons on April 15.[34] It did not suit Kirk for Jack to change his Easter holiday this time because Kirk had agreed for Oswald Smythe's brother, then a captain in the artillery, to stay at Gastons with his mother beginning on April 4, when Kirk had expected Clive to leave for Belfast, in keeping with the public school holidays. Smythe was the former pupil of Kirkpatrick who had suffered a shattered arm at the front. He was to be released from the hospital at Luton, but his mother wanted him to have a few days of convalescence at Gastons. As far as Kirk was concerned, the desires of wounded officers took precedence over the desires of mere officers home from the front.[35]

Jack told his father that he had been "kicked out."[36] In due order, Jack left Gastons on April 4, as Kirk had always planned, and arrived in Belfast the next day.[37] As it turned out, Warnie's leave appears to have been canceled again due to the war, which continued to be an inconvenience to the family.[38] After many fits and starts over comings and goings for the Easter holiday of 1916, Jack returned to Bookham on May 11, completely missing Warnie, who arrived in Belfast on May 19 for a leave that ended on May 25.[39] Still, the brothers managed to rendezvous in London for a brief visit on Warnie's return trip to France.[40]

The Battle of the Somme opened on July 1, a little over a month after Warnie's leave. By July 16, Kirkpatrick and Albert, apparently oblivious to what Warnie was enduring in France, were consulting on the best route for Jack to take home to Belfast for his summer holiday. With the scholarship examinations coming in December, Kirk said that he had done all that he could do for Jack. From then on, it would be review.[41] From France, however, Warnie had written to Albert on July 7 with a description of the Somme:

Do you remember the Biblical phrase "the abomination of desolation"? I never realized before what it meant: in a strip of ground perhaps three miles broad, there is no living thing—not a blade of grass, not a tree, not a building which stands more than three feet high: one cannot walk over it without difficulty, for there are no two square yards which do not contain a shell hole: and all around are men who look as if they were asleep, and things which were once men.[42]

The war had ceased to be something that Jack could keep at arm's length.

The Pleasure of Music

In the New Year, Jack continued his adolescent, rebellious male habit of presenting one face to his father and another face to his friend Arthur. This was his method of assuring his independence from Albert. Upon returning to Great Bookham, Jack had gone up to London to see the matinee of *Carmen* at the Shaftsbury Theatre. Though he panned the performances of the singers to both father and friend, he told Albert that he liked the opera itself nonetheless. To Arthur, however, he declared the opera a great disappointment. He gave his father a favorable review of the "tunes," and though he told Arthur that the opera had plenty of beautiful music, he allowed that he was sick of the "sticky tunes."[43] Did he posture for his father or his friend? Probably both. He was a little too positive with his father, but a little too cynical and caustic with Arthur. This quasi-critical assessment of the opera for Arthur, mixed as it was with slang and jargon, reflects Arthur's superior musical attainments as a pianist and one whose critical musical opinions left Jack in second place. To Arthur, Jack railed against the music and performers as fiendish, tedious, blustery, ghastly, clowning creatures in a steady flow of sarcastic invective suitable to a teenage intellectual snob set on impressing his counterpart.[44]

The love of music formed yet another bond between Jack and Arthur, as it had done once with Warnie. Jack's holidays at home involved long interludes with Arthur, the phonograph, and their growing record collections. In many ways, the youthful love of music has not changed in a century. Musical forms and styles may have changed, but not the youthful love of music. In January 1916, Jack anxiously awaited the arrival of the records he had ordered from T. E. Osborne's store, which included Enrico Caruso's "E Lucevan le Stelle" from Puccini's *Tosca*. He hoped the records would be a success.[45]

While Jack worked away at his lessons with Kirk, Arthur apparently spent the end of January and beginning of February 1916 at the opera, where he possibly saw John Edward Barkworth's *Romeo and Juliet*, as well as *Pagliacci*, *Cavalleria Rusticana*, and *Rigoletto*. Though Jack felt justified in cascades of disparaging remarks about *Carmen*, he chided Arthur for calling *Romeo and Juliet* "blustery," since the same might be said of Wagner's *The Flying Dutchman* and *The Valkyrie*, with the obvious implication that any criticism of Wagner was unthinkable.[46]

The mutual pleasure of enjoying gramophone records, however, made Jack and Arthur aware of something that would become a progressive problem in the twentieth century. Gramophone records spoil a person for listening to live musical performances by any but the greatest of musicians since gramophone records only represent the greatest musicians. The records created an elevated expectation for quality that represented an unrealistic standard for most performances and all but killed amateur performance.[47] By the middle of the twentieth century, the ancient practice of singing and playing instruments in homes among friends for mutual enjoyment and pleasure would all but disappear. By the end of the twentieth century, the common experience of piano lessons would be in serious decline in the general population.

To his credit, Jack regularly acknowledged that Arthur had the greater knowledge of music. Jack had even wondered if he had lost his love of music, but by March 1916, he could happily report to Arthur that he was enthralled by the preludes of Chopin that Mrs. Kirkpatrick had been playing lately. Though she did not play them well from Jack's point of view, the music itself had such passion that it carried her along.[48] This discussion of music, however, prompted a return of another subject that Lewis the boy and Lewis the man would ponder into old age: the relationship of love and friendship. Eventually, C. S. Lewis examined this relationship in *The Four Loves* (1960), which he published in the year that his wife, Joy, died. He had already introduced the outline of *The Four Loves* in *The Allegory of Love* (1936).[49] In his March 16 letter to Arthur Greeves at the age of seventeen, however, Jack laid out his early thoughts on the subject long before he knew what it meant to be in love but after he knew what it meant to be and to have a friend. The subject arose in a discussion of the difference between books and music:

> I think (to get back to an old argument) it is just the same difference as between friendship and love. The one is a calm and easy going satisfaction; the other a sort of madness: we take possession of one, the other takes possession of us: the one is always pleasant the other in its greatest moments of joy is painful.[50]

Like Edgar Allan Poe, Jack Lewis thought that music was the highest form of art. He thought it began where the other arts left off. Painting expresses the visible; poetry expresses what can be analyzed; but music—here he stopped and changed the subject, perhaps unsure of how music was different. That it was different, however, he had no doubt.[51] He made these views perfectly clear when he wrote *An Experiment in Criticism.*[52]

Mrs. Kirkpatrick continued to have an active social life and never appears to have missed an opportunity to help young Clive develop socially. One evening in June 1916, the neighbors visited Mrs. Kirkpatrick and brought a girl staying with them who was studying to sing opera. She sang two operatic pieces that suited Jack, but the rest of the evening was devoted to old ballads like "Annie Laurie" that Jack simply hated. He expounded on this hatred in *An Experiment in Criticism* some forty-five years later.[53] As for the singer, romance was not in the air, for Jack asked Arthur why singers are always so plain.[54]

As July wore on and Jack's cares mounted over his prospects for a scholarship to Oxford, admission to a good college, and the real possibility of death in the trenches, he lost his interest in music. It annoyed him that he could no longer take comfort in the world of pleasure he once enjoyed, but even the thought of going up to London to see *The Magic Flute* at the Shaftsbury or *Tristan and Isolde* left him thinking depressively that he would probably be disappointed.[55]

Reading as a Critic

In his reading, Jack began 1916 deeply immersed in *The Faerie Queene*, ecstatic over his new red-leather Everyman edition, which looked so splendid on a shelf with two or three other books in the same binding. The mature C. S. Lewis would have been horrified by such an attachment to a pretty binding, but the mature Lewis lay on the other side of youth. In the meantime, he had also reread *Jane Eyre*. What struck him at this time about the "magnificent" novel were the long dialogues between Jane and Mr. Rochester, which had the effect of duets from a "splendid" opera.[56] Given his sarcastic criticism of *Carmen* in the same letter, the contrast in tone suggests the high romance that affected young Lewis—the duet would obviously be a love duet. He had also begun reading Algernon Blackwood's *The Education of Uncle Paul* (1909). The passage that most deeply touched Jack was one in which Uncle Paul and Nixie find themselves in a dream together where they experience the waking of the winds at dawn within a primeval forest and visit the crack between yesterday and tomorrow.[57] Jack claimed to Arthur that he had never read anything like it, but the underlying effect of the male-female encounter in a mysterious setting is the stuff he had been devouring for several years, though in different literary styles and quality produced in different places over the previous thousand years.

Finally, Jack was reading Layamon's *Brut*, part of the vast body of Arthurian literature of the medieval period. It bears noting that C. S. Lewis wrote an introduction to a new edition of the *Brut* translated and edited by G. L. Brook in 1963. What we repeatedly see about the adolescent Jack Lewis is that his pleasure reading would provide him a career and a reputation as scholar and literary critic that would last far beyond his death, independent of any of his popular or religious writings. Without his pleasure reading at Gastons, Jack Lewis the classicist and philosopher would never have had the option of doing a second degree in English literature at Oxford when his dream of a philosophy position at Oxford never materialized.

By the end of January 1916, Jack Lewis had also become self-conscious of a habit of mind that he would carry throughout his life, and which would inform his critical theory. In fact, it became the foundational idea in *An Experiment in Criticism* (1961). To Arthur Greeves, he wrote, "You really lose a lot by never reading books again."[58] In *An Experiment in Criticism*, C. S. Lewis built the case that literary people are those who read books over and over. They know the plot, so nothing is a surprise, but the fact of rereading indicates a quality of reading that satisfies the conscious or unconscious literary taste of the reader. Such a reading habit suggests a qualitative difference in literature ranging from good to bad. The possibility that such value judgments could be objective statements would haunt the doubts of Jack Lewis's atheism/ agnosticism in the 1920s and would animate his apologetics in the 1940s, all the while informing his literary judgments. The ability to make value judgments about right and wrong forms the heart of his radio broadcast talks that became *Mere Christianity*, also known as his moral argument for the existence of God. The ability to make value judgments about literature lies at the heart of *A Preface to Paradise Lost*, *The Abolition of Man*, and *An Experiment in Criticism*. It all began with the observation that a chap loses a lot by not reading a magnificent book more than once. Throughout his time at Gastons, Jack kept Arthur abreast of what he was reading again and what he had learned or discovered or understood as a result.

For Kirkpatrick, Jack was reading John Ruskin's *A Joy Forever*, originally published as *The Political Economy of Art* (1857). He asked Arthur if he had read it—a regular pattern, for it gave Jack the opportunity to comment immediately that he was sure Arthur had not.[59] For his pleasure reading at the beginning of February, Jack was down to the last three books of *The Faerie Queene*, and upon completing it, he expected to return to a William Morris book, such as one of the romances or a translation of one of the Norse sagas.[60] Instead, something new would take him by surprise.

Finding George MacDonald

In *Surprised by Joy*, C. S. Lewis described how he first became acquainted with George MacDonald on an October evening at the train station in Leatherhead, the town where he went to have his hair cut. Browsing through the bookstall while waiting for his train, he chanced upon a grubby copy of George MacDonald's *Phantastes, a Faerie Romance* in the Everyman edition.[61] It is a lovely memory, but memory often fails us. Lewis actually first came upon MacDonald at the train station on Saturday, March 4, 1916, as he explained to Arthur immediately after it happened.[62]

Jack's reading took a critical turn when he stumbled across the copy of *Phantastes*. As usual, Jack asked Arthur if he had read it, and answered his own query as usual in the negative. This serendipitous discovery would play a huge part in eventually changing Lewis's life forever. At the time, Jack recognized that MacDonald belonged to a circle of writers who wrote a certain kind of story that he loved to read. He believed that MacDonald was as good as Malory or William Morris, who heretofore had been the gold standard.[63] In *Phantastes*, Jack found the same plot he had come to love in Malory, Spenser, Morris, and Yeats, but with one twist that he did not recognize at the time, though it had a profound effect on him that he could not shake. The mature C. S. Lewis said that *Phantastes* had introduced the idea of holiness to him completely unawares.[64]

Jack appears to have plowed into *Phantastes* as soon as he finished *The Faerie Queene*. By the time he wrote to Arthur three days after buying the book, he could already say that he enjoyed the book more than anything he had read since Morris's *The Well at the World's End*.[65] After giving a sketch of some of the most moving passages in the book, Jack warned Arthur not to be put off by the conventional fairy-tale style of the opening chapter. Jack promised Arthur that after the first chapter he would not be able to put the book down until he finished it, which suggests that Jack did not put the book down until he had finished it.[66] To Jack's great relief, Arthur liked *Phantastes* as much as he did. Jack thought the best parts were the forest scene and the fancy palace. He was now ready to rush out and buy all he could find of George MacDonald, for the titles of his books were alluring and gave him a thrill like music.[67]

The Kind of Story Jack Loved

In his pleasure reading after Easter, Jack devoured *Sir Gawain and the Green Knight* in short order. He considered the fourteenth-century poem "absolutely tophole."[68] He particularly liked the winter landscape around an old castle that contrasted so splendidly with the blazing fireplace in the castle.[69] Jack expressed a number of times his marked love of winter scapes and warm hearths, both of which figure prominently in *The Lion, the Witch and the Wardrobe*. Such a preference in youth lasted all his life and simply provided more of the rich tapestry of life that informed his later storytelling.

Sir Gawain, one of the tales associated with the King Arthur stories, is yet another of the same kind of story that Jack so loved. In future years, J. R. R. Tolkien, together with E. V. Gordon, edited the long poem. Lewis heavily annotated his copy of their edition and made a drawing of knight's armor in the margin, as a key to the vocabulary of chivalry from the period.[70] As usual, the hero that enchanted young Lewis is a solitary figure on a quest for an elusive prize—in this case, combat with the Green Knight.

From *The Green Knight*, Jack moved on to Sir Walter Scott's *Rob Roy*. He chanced upon it in Kirkpatrick's library and reveled in it. He loved the descriptions of the wild county of Northumberland and Scott's treatment of Die Vernon, the heroine of the tale.[71] Jack loved a well-drawn heroine, especially Charlotte Brontë's Shirley from the novel of the same name. Set in the period following the Napoleonic Wars, *Shirley* is a social commentary on the upheavals of the industrial revolution. Shirley herself is a wealthy philanthropist who hopes to use her wealth to relieve some of the suffering caused by the unemployment that arose from mechanization. It is not the kind of story that would normally have drawn Jack's attention, but perhaps he explained the attraction perfectly well by simply mentioning Shirley as such a good heroine. His letters to Arthur would repeatedly refer to Shirley, and it may be that Jack developed a crush on the fictional character the way boys of sixteen or seventeen develop crushes on female movie characters today.

Jack and Arthur disagreed about Jane Austen's *Persuasion*. Arthur appears not to have liked the departure from Austen's usual style, and Jack admitted that it was more romantic and less humorous than *Emma* or *Mansfield Park*. Instead of being a sideline to the story, however, the love interest was the point of the story. Jack liked the departure from what he had once come to expect from Austen, but perhaps that was because the love story itself had a charm for the romantically inclined Jack that involved the fulfillment of a great longing. The story "worked" on Jack. In his first great scholarly work, *The Allegory of Love*, C. S. Lewis examined the relationship between the quest story and the love story critically, but he had learned from his own experience how these stories "work" on a person.

While reading *Rob Roy* for pleasure, Jack also read a French edition of *Tristan and Isolde* as part of his French study with Mrs. Kirkpatrick.[72] The story is one of the great love stories that emerged in twelfth-century France and played an important role in the development of medieval romantic love literature. It was taken up in several countries where the names of the adulterous lovers appear alternatively as Tristram and Isolde, Yseult, Isolt, or Iseult. Eventually, the story became entwined with the King Arthur stories, as Tristan became a knight of the round table. In the meantime, Jack struggled with the technical problem of how to send his fictional character, Bleheris, off on his adventures.[73] He was coming to grips with the arduous element of writing. As he would remark in his last interview in 1963, once the stage has been set, something actually has to happen.[74]

Having finished reading *Rob Roy*, some of which he extolled as on par with the writing of William Morris, Jack moved on to Chaucer's *Canterbury Tales*.[75] He felt "awfully bucked" by the book, but perhaps as much by the quality of paper, the boards, and two bits of tissue paper at the front as by Chaucer's poetry. In later life he would leave Chaucer to his friend and fellow Inkling Nevill Coghill, but at seventeen he adored the first stories he read.[76]

Arthur had mentioned in a letter that he found that books could get tiresome halfway through the story. Arthur, who was not as literary as Jack, appears to have had this feeling most of the time, but while acknowledging that it does happen, Jack insisted that it does not always happen. In fact, some books just begin to get exciting halfway through, like *Shirley*, which he adored. He also suggested that *Jane Eyre* and *Phantastes* did not get tiresome.[77] Before long, however, Jack had joined Arthur in the ranks of those who find books tiresome halfway through when he gave up on *The Canterbury Tales*, which he now found "impossible," having read as many of the tales as he ever expected to read. He thought that Chaucer had the faults of the medieval world without the romantic charm of the Green Knight or Malory.[78] He would expound on these views in *The Allegory of Love*, but for a boy of seventeen, he had judged Chaucer's *Tales* garrulous and coarse.[79] All of these observations make their way into the critical imagination of the C. S. Lewis who spent his adult life making critical judgments about the quality of writing and plot and character development.

While Jack was reading *Rob Roy*, Arthur had read *Frankenstein*, a book Jack had never read. Arthur gave it a poor review, and Jack was surprised that its author, the wife of Percy Shelley, was not a woman of taste; or perhaps he spoke ironically, not trusting Arthur's judgment.[80] After saying that he thought *Frankenstein* badly written in one letter, Arthur asked in the next letter that Jack tell no one he had made such a judgment. Jack would have none of it. With the same fervor with which he would attack T. S. Eliot years later for claiming that only great poets could judge poetry, Jack insisted that Arthur should rely on his own judgment in the matter of books unless he were out for self-improvement, which Jack regarded as nonsense.[81] C. S. Lewis developed these same ideas in a more organized way in *An Experiment in Criticism*.[82]

With Chaucer behind him, Jack plunged into Sir Philip Sidney's *Arcadia*, a sixteenth-century prose romance in a pastoral setting. He thought Sidney was an extraordinary writer—sometimes like Malory but more connected, and sometimes like Spenser, yet different from either. *Arcadia* had everything in just the right proportion: a great deal of lovemaking, which had become increasingly important to Jack, not too much fighting, which had grown tedious to Jack, a definite set of characters, and comic relief. Sidney and Spenser would be major figures that C. S. Lewis examined in his monumental *English Literature in the Sixteenth Century, Excluding Drama* (1954).

When Jack wrote to Arthur about his favorite parts in *Arcadia*, he was drawn to the sections that deal with sexual attraction and desire. Jack was a seventeen-year-old boy whose hormones were exploding. He described a section in which Philoclea finds herself falling in love with a girl who, unbeknownst to her, is actually a man in disguise. From *Twelfth Night* to *Some Like It Hot*, this comic device has always pleased audiences. When Jack tried to explain Philoclea's inner wrestling with her feelings to Arthur, he realized that he could not. He was now in uncharted territory that his intellect alone could not navigate.[83] His guide and touchstone for stories that touched his growing interest in females, however, had become the Brontë sisters with their powerfully moving explorations of romantic attraction.

By early July, Jack was reading the *Argonautica* by Apollonius of Rhodes, while Arthur was reading William Morris's retelling of the same story in *Jason*. Jack thought that the story of Jason and the Golden Fleece was a perfect tale that could not be spoiled by the retelling. Again, Jack was enchanted by a tale that involved a journey with multiple unexpected obstacles and challenges on the way of a quest for an unattainable goal.[84] In his preface to *George MacDonald: An Anthology*, which he edited in 1946, C. S. Lewis repeated almost the same words that he had written to Arthur Greeves thirty years earlier. In a myth like the story of the Golden Fleece, the pattern of events, and not the precise words, holds the power.[85] At seventeen, Jack Lewis knew but did not yet understand why this should be so.

By the age of seventeen, Jack had already developed a deep appreciation for poetry and how it works on the feelings of its audience. He had arrived at the same views as Edgar Allan Poe regarding the importance of meter as a musical component of poetry that words alone could not accomplish. Though prose works on the reader, poetry can create a greater effect because it has more tools at its disposal than prose, and it can express more by the musicality of meter than by words alone.[86]

Jack ordered *Letters from Hell* by the Danish priest Valdemar Adolph Thisted, but it took a long time arriving. He had built himself up with the expectation that it would be a tale of the "phantastic type," which he loved the most, but he put it away unfinished because it turned out to be just a novel. Hell served only as a vehicle for exploring the former life. Ironically, C. S. Lewis used hell in the same way when he wrote *The Great Divorce* (1946). More ironically, Jack liked the description of paradise most. Still, he wondered if he had missed something because both his new idol, George MacDonald, and Arthur liked the book.[87] In the end, he donated it to a jumble sale.[88] In thinking about the next book he would read, Jack asked Arthur what *Guy Mannering* by Sir Walter Scott was like. Meanwhile, *The Astrologer* appealed to Jack, who was now in his "occult phase," but he feared the novel might not be about astrology at all.[89]

The Occult!

The interest in the occult began innocently enough. Lewis admired the poetry of his Irish compatriot William Butler Yeats. Yeats, who was not a Christian, seemed to believe in spirits! For his philosophical views on life, Jack had learned from Kirkpatrick to rely on the authority of science, but Yeats represented an authority that Jack secretly held in higher esteem. Yeats was a poet![90] About the same time he was reading Yeats, he had turned to Maurice Maeterlinck to improve his French. Jack had never intended to develop an interest in the occult, but in reading Maeterlinck, he had encountered spiritualism, theosophy, and pantheism. The Belgian was a recognized intellectual and not a Christian, but he believed in something beyond the physical world. Just the possibility that Maeterlinck might be right had the effect of shaking Jack's confidence in materialism.[91]

From October 1916 until February 1917, Jack mentioned Maeterlinck with regularity to Arthur and told him that even if one did not accept his views, they had a certain romantic attraction to them.[92] Of course, with Jack Lewis a certain romantic attraction was all it took. In the end, Jack's rationalism led him to discard the hocus-pocus magic of the occult approach to reality, but the idea that something existed beyond the physical world had stuck in his brain and, worse, was confirmed by his experience of the feelings he had from reading the stories he loved.[93] One kind of story seemed to be speaking to him.

All the while, Jack honed his critical reading skills. He regarded Arnold Bennett's book *Literary Taste: How to Form It* with contempt. The very idea that Bennett thought a person could learn literary taste the way a person learns golf only told Lewis that Bennett was no true booklover at all. Jack believed that people should develop their literary tastes by reading what they like and finding their way by trial and error, instead of reading books because they are the classics or because they are the books that everyone should read.[94] C. S. Lewis explored this idea of forming literary taste at the end of his life in *An Experiment in Criticism*.[95]

Reading Christian Books

In November 1916, when Jack was rereading Malory's *Le Morte d'Arthur*, he tried to explain to Greeves the uselessness of comparing Malory to *Beowulf*. The two stories belong to entirely different worlds or cultures, even though they came from the same geographical territory. Malory wrote in the medieval world, but *Beowulf* came from the pre-Norman, Anglo-Saxon world. Malory wrote as a Christian, but *Beowulf* came from the pre-Christian, pagan tradition. Furthermore, Arthur tended to judge both works from the perspective of the norms of British literature of the recent 150 years, which Jack regarded as a very small world. To help Arthur appreciate a book from another age, Jack advised him to lay aside all of his notions of what a book should be and put himself back in the culture that produced the book. He *imagined himself* into the world for which *Beowulf* was originally told and finally written.[96]

Later, C. S. Lewis began *The Allegory of Love* and *A Preface to Paradise Lost* by expanding on this youthful insight.[97] For the mature scholar and critic of literature, understanding the world in which a piece of literature was written, and not imposing modern prejudices and assumptions upon it, was the starting point for reading any work. In his own case, on the eve of his eighteenth birthday, it meant laying aside his prejudice against Christian faith, because all the stories he liked the best were written from a Christian perspective with the Christianity latent.

As examples of what Jack meant by laying aside his prejudice against Christian faith, consider the Christian classics that he read during the second half of 1916. Jack journeyed home to Ireland on July 31 and returned to Great Bookham on September 22.[98] Just before the end of the long vacation, he went with Arthur for a getaway at Portsalon by the sea. For his pleasure reading during this period, he reread Jane Austen's *Sense and Sensibility*.[99] In future years, C. S. Lewis had a high regard for Austen as one of the preeminent exemplars of Christian writing. He was entranced by John Milton's poem "Comus" for its abundant magic, ladies in distress, and haunted woods, not for its latent Christianity.[100] In November, Warnie received a field promotion or a temporary promotion to captain, a rank he would hold until his retirement. Their father was proud, and Jack was delighted when he heard the news as he prepared for his Oxford entrance exams. He told his father that he was reading *The Pilgrim's Progress* in the weeks leading up to his exam, a remarkable matter, given his views on religion.[101] He justified the choice to himself on the grounds that it is unsurpassed as a romance and as an example of "real English."[102] Jack loved *The High History of the Holy Graal*, an old French romance, because of its eerie, mystical quality, even though this quality stood at odds with his materialist philosophy.[103] Eventually, what he liked to read and what he liked to think would stand in such obvious opposition that he would have to choose between them for the one that made the most sense. That choice, however, would have to wait fourteen years.

As the time for his exams drew near, Jack found himself arguing with Arthur over almost everything, from music to books. He would begin a letter with extreme sarcasm only to conclude it with profound apologies and pleas not to fall out over trifles. He continued to feel that he had lost his love of music, which had meant so much to him for such a long time. Still, he had his books.[104]

Surprisingly, Jack's latest discovery was Nathaniel Hawthorne's *The House of the Seven Gables*, which he thought was almost the most glorious novel he had ever read. He loved the idea of a house with a curse and a brooding sense of horror hanging over events. Given that C. S. Lewis became extremely popular in the United States, it is interesting that Jack lamented that Hawthorne was a "beastly American."[105] His prejudice against Americans appears to have been as strong as his prejudice against the French. He did not care for Woodrow Wilson and his set, dismissing the Yanks to Warnie as "squatters and damned money grubbing puritans."[106]

The Worship of Pretty Books

Shortly after finding *Phantastes*, Jack ordered a copy of *British Ballads* in the Everyman edition with a chocolate binding, a style of book binding that Arthur liked but Jack formerly did not. He joked to Arthur about being converted to all of Arthur's views and then, adding to the joke, suggested that Arthur might even make a Christian of him.[107] Jack's jokes had a way of being prophetic. The extent to which his lust for beautiful editions of books had gotten the better of him is evident from an episode shortly after he had promised himself to read one of William Morris's translations of the Icelandic sagas as soon as he finished *The Faerie Queene*. He found the very book he wanted in the cheap Walter Scott Library edition, but decided not to buy it because the edition simply was not pretty enough.[108]

At a time in his life when Jack had developed a reverential adoration of beautiful books with fine paper, gilded edges, and finely tooled leather bindings, he was particularly horrified that Kirkpatrick would grab a book and bend the boards back to break the spine, which made it easier to keep the book open without pages turning. Jack complained to Arthur that Kirk committed this sacrilege with "filthy hands." Kirkpatrick loved to work in the garden, and it appears that from time to time he went directly to his lessons with Jack from the garden without bothering to clean up.[109] Mrs. Kirkpatrick did not handle books quite as badly as her husband, but she would hold them so close to the fire that the boards warped, to Jack's utter horror.[110]

As part of his book veneration, Jack decided to have his paperback edition of *Triston and Iseut* bound in brown leather. It took weeks and weeks for the book to come back from the binder, and when it did, it was the "abomination of desolation." Instead of the artistic delight he had imagined, it looked like a bank ledger book. Where the edges of this French book had been rough and untrimmed, giving it what Jack thought to be an artistic flare, the binder had trimmed the edges and colored them with speckled red ink. He consoled himself in the fact that the book itself gave him great pleasure.[111]

Writing

In May of 1916, following his Easter vacation at home, Jack began writing his own romance, *The Quest of Bleheris*. In contrast to the titles of George MacDonald's romances, Jack acknowledged that he had given his story a "rotten title" but that he hoped to think of a better title with a more poetic ring.[112] With Jack attempting to write a fantastic adventure story about his hero Bleheris, Arthur decided to write a sequel to *Alice in Wonderland*.[113] Jack encouraged his friend to write anything, but warned him off humor as a dangerous thing to try. By this time, two years into their friendship, Jack would have had a grasp of Arthur's narrative strengths and weaknesses. He probably did not shine at humor. Jack encouraged him to write something weird, beautiful, passionate, or homely instead. The extent of Jack's encouragement was that Arthur's "Alice" could not be more boring than Jack's "Bleheris."[114] Jack had the self-awareness of one determined to make his mark as a writer. Even as he struggled with "Bleheris" and urged Arthur to continue his sequel to *Alice*, Jack viewed his writing as practice for what would come later. No matter what he wrote, even if bad, it moved him further along and improved his writing. He needed the experience of effort in order to learn how to write.[115]

By October, Jack confessed to Arthur that he had no stomach to finish "Bleheris," though he would find bits and pieces of it to use later, such as the name Jadis, who was a young man in "Bleheris" but would become a witch queen in *The Magician's Nephew*. He gave a brief lament that all the great plans that he and Arthur had for operas, plays, stories, and poems had come to naught, but the lament did not last long. It had all been good practice, and perhaps he had learned that he should focus on shorter pieces for the time being.[116]

Jack explained to Arthur that he composed his poetry and prose fiction in his head during walks because he believed his imagination worked only when he was walking. In a sense, when he sat down to write, he was only taking dictation from what his imagination had been working on for some time.[117] He found that the creative process does not usually happen at the desk; rather, it is recalled at the desk.

Jack had slipped his new, vibrant atheism into his romance of "Bleheris," and Arthur did not like what he read. Jack warned him that he would like it even less if he grasped the inner meaning.[118] Jack admitted to Arthur that "Bleheris" was an anti-Christian story and that the heroine would contrast sharply with the saintly Alice of Wonderland, with whom Arthur had to deal.[119]

Many years later, C. S. Lewis used this idea of the subtext of a book as his ultimate statement on effective apologetics. At the end of World War II, a group of youth ministers asked him to address them on how to go about apologetics. He published his talk as an article, "Christian Apologetics." He explained that the best apologetic was not a frontal attack on rival beliefs. It was not little Christian books that were most effective as apologetics but books by Christians on every subject undergirded by their faith perspective. He suggested that this idea came to him from experiencing rival ideas in reading.[120]

Jack carefully planted rival ideas in Bleheris that he intended to remain unexamined but accepted. During World War II, this mix of rival ideas in a high school literature text prompted C. S. Lewis to deliver the lectures later published as *The Abolition of Man*. By September, however, Jack was losing confidence in "Bleheris." He realized that he had made a mistake in imitating an old-fashioned style of English. He gave serious consideration to abandoning the project and starting over. He deplored the idea of not finishing what he had begun, but he thought it at least had been good practice.[121]

From extolling the sensual bits in the great literature of the English language, Jack and Arthur moved on to discussing the introduction of sensuality in their writing. In one episode of Arthur's story, the hero went swimming. Jack asked whether he wore a bathing suit or swam naked. Arthur, who by now had identified his homosexuality to Jack, asked if Jack were implying that the character should be wearing a bathing suit. Jack insisted that he merely wanted a clear picture.[122]

Self-Awareness

In a moment of frank self-awareness, confession, and contrition, Jack expressed his regret that he rarely invited Arthur to spend time at Little Lea. Arthur entertained Jack royally at his house, but Jack failed to reciprocate for the simple reason that he wanted to avoid his father's intrusion into their friendship. Albert Lewis had always assumed that his sons would want his constant companionship and wit to entertain their friends, but such was not the case. Jack dreaded his father's ubiquitous flare for being in the way. In a telling admission, Jack acknowledged to Arthur that he tended to hide the uneven nature of their hospitality with "silly jokes."[123] Jack had learned the art of masking his feelings and any unpleasantness with humor. An example of such humor was Jack's suggestion that the best solution to Albert's unending intrusions would be for the boys to find him a wife. Perhaps they should poison old Mr. Stokes, a regular object of joking, and then Jack's father could marry the widow.[124]

Once he opened the confessional door, Jack continued this mood throughout his March 21 letter. He opened the door wider and wider to his inner thoughts and feelings. He had the feeling that something strange and wonderful ought to happen to him, but he could not bring himself to believe, as Arthur did, that it could actually happen. If something mystical really did happen, Jack wondered if he would not prefer the dull everyday world. He even coined the term "Terreauty" to describe the world of terror and beauty that might be available to everyone every day, except that people like him lack the courage to open the door. Then, in a flash, Jack dismissed this line of spiritual thinking as nonsense, which he attributed to his recent interest in the mystical philosophy of Maurice Maeterlinck, the Belgian writer whom Jack had been reading to improve his French.[125]

By the end of July 1916, Jack showed a keen interest in the occult. He was reading *John Silence* and *Paradise Lost*, but not from the perspective of faith. He loved the passages that referenced "Ancient Sorceries" and "the old, old incantation." He particularly liked Milton's reference to "Leopard witches." While reading these books, he had come across *Letters from Hell*, the title of which excited him.[126]

As a teenager, Jack had learned to enjoy the most simple pleasures of life. He could go on and on in his letters to Arthur about the joy of seeing the moonlight on a winter's evening, the feel of snow falling on his face, the taste of Irish soda bread, or the immense pleasure in simply falling asleep. He loved the comfort of curling up in a nice warm bed surrounded by darkness and slowly drifting off to sleep. He wondered if the pleasure of falling asleep was enhanced by working late into the night as he often did.[127]

The Inevitability of War

While recalling a holiday at home in Ireland when he and Arthur went for a long walk and sprawled on the moss drenched in sunshine, Jack suddenly grew melancholy. He reflected that he would only have two more holidays before his eighteenth birthday, when he would reach military age and go off to the fighting fields of France, which he had no ambition to do.[128] As we have seen, however, during the Easter vacation between April 5 and May 11, Jack had made the momentous decision that is not reflected in any of his correspondence with his father or Arthur Greeves during the previous months. Nor is there any indication that he had previously discussed the issue with Kirk, as evidenced by the many letters between Kirk and Albert Lewis on the subject. Jack Lewis decided by himself that he would enter the war and fight.[129] The extent to which duty, the noble obligation, and the chivalric tradition had influenced Jack can be seen in a curt remark to Arthur when he expressed the view that Ireland would soon have conscription. He added that he would be glad to see some of their relations finally forced to act like men.[130]

Having determined to enter the army, Jack quickly realized, as his father and Kirk had done, that he must enter as an officer and a gentleman. The Sandhurst scheme seemed too remote to him. Even if Kirk had been willing to teach him mathematics, which he was not, other obstacles presented themselves. He would emerge from Sandhurst as a permanent officer after the war, and he could not simply tell the army that he had decided to leave to become a poet. Jack thought the most promising option lay in his father using political influence to obtain a commission.[131]

Jack had mustered all the denial possible to ignore the war for two years, but as his eighteenth birthday and the certainty of military service drew nearer, thoughts of the war crept into his correspondence. His earlier comments on the war had been with flippant detachment, but now he wrote with grave seriousness. He was glad to hear that his cousin Dick Lewis had been wounded and was out of the war. Jack pitied the men in the trenches who endured the misery of war only to be killed in the end, probably after returning from leave. In the cold light of day, Jack thought the war was going badly and now Kitchener was dead. It all made a fellow think . . . and grow up.[132]

As far as the effect of the war on Jack's decision about Oxford colleges, he reasoned that in a college as large as Christ Church, there would have to be a literary group, no matter how small. Besides, he suspected that all the old "bloods" had died in the war. He thought Oxford would be a vastly different place after the war than it had been before. England after the war would not be conducive to a return to the old ways.[133]

The Christian Myth

In early October 1916, Jack finally spelled out to Arthur in detail his views on religion. After two years with Kirkpatrick, Jack had drunk deeply of the materialist explanations for the phenomenon of religion. Together with Kirkpatrick and materialist philosophy, Jack believed in no religion for the simple reason that there was no proof for any of the world's religions.[134] By "proof" Jack meant empirical evidence or knowledge acquired though the senses— what we can see, hear, taste, touch, and smell. One of the growing philosophical trends of the day was logical positivism, or the view that only what can be verified by sensory evidence actually exists and has meaning; otherwise, talk about it is literally nonsense. From a philosophical point of view, and philosophy was the only point of view that really mattered to him, Jack did not think Christianity was even the best religion.[135]

Jack accepted the view made popular by the approaches of history of religion, comparative religion, and phenomenology of religion that all religions are human inventions and should properly be called mythologies. The story of Jesus is just another mythology, like the Norse story of Loki. Jack accepted the idea that religion had several stages of development. In the first stage, primitive humans associated the powerful forces of nature such as storms, disease, and dangerous animals with evil spirits who posed a danger. These supposed spirits were placated by cringing before them, offering them sacrifices, and singing songs to them. In the second stage of the development of religion, these spirits were aggrandized into the gods, who took on more elaborate identities. Finally, in the third stage, as human society became more refined, the gods became good as well as refined.[136]

Jack explained that by this process of development, the Christian mythology came about. Just as great men among the Greeks, like Heracles, or among the Celts, like Odin, came to be regarded as gods, a Jewish philosopher named *Yeshua* (Jack took great delight in telling Arthur that *Jesus* was a corruption of the real name) came to be worshiped as a god with a cult that associated him with the old Hebrew god *Jahweh*. To this account for the origins of Christianity Jack added that it was simply the religion of the culture in which he and Arthur had grown up.[137]

Jack then made a serious error that he would spend a number of bottles of ink refuting in his later life. He called his point of view on religion the accepted "scientific" view.[138] The view he proposed had nothing to do with science, which depends upon empirical evidence. Jack accepted a philosophical theory without any empirical evidence. Science does not have the conceptual framework or method to study the possibility of spiritual reality. Science is limited to describing the behavior of the physical world and makes no statements about whether or not anything else exists. For a number of years, however, Jack Lewis would continue to confuse philosophy and science, as many do today.

Jack then made a second serious error. He said that a person's point of view about religion made no difference about morals. His reason for this view was that any good member of society must make the effort to practice the recognized civic virtues of honesty, charity, thoughtfulness, kindness, and similar accepted values. He said that we must do this because we owe it to our manhood and dignity.[139] What he failed to take into account was how to explain the moral values apart from religion, or why moral values matter if religion does not. He had not considered that value has no place in a brute universe of matter where things are not good or bad; they just are.

In years to come, refuting the two major errors that Jack held about religion and morals would become the basis for the moral argument for the existence of God proposed by C. S. Lewis. He had begun to explore these questions in *The Problem of Pain*. He would make use of the three stages of the development of religion, but to these he added a fourth—the historical event of God making himself known in the flesh as Jesus Christ.[140] The origin of moral values eventually posed an insurmountable logical problem for the atheism of Jack Lewis. When nature seemed so red with tooth and claw, why would any human have ever thought that God was good? And how could an idea like goodness or justice or kindness ever occur to a human if these ideas work against the idea of the battle for preeminence in natural selection? This is the first problem he would address in his radio broadcasts during World War II, later published as *Mere Christianity*.[141]

In 1916, however, Jack had not yet mastered the art of self-criticism. He had mastered patronizing condescension instead. He told Arthur that they must not fall out over a difference of opinion over a theoretical idea like religion, and that if any evidence for religion should ever turn up, he would happily change his mind. Some fourteen years or so later, the evidence he dredged up out of his own brain forced him to change his mind, but he was not happy about it. In his spiritual autobiography, he said that he was "the most dejected and reluctant convert in all England."[142]

Jack was willing to believe that a real person named Jesus once lived and was executed. After all, Tacitus mentioned the fact in his *Annals*. But Jack did not believe in the virgin birth, the healings, the resurrection appearances, or anything else about Jesus that he regarded as mythology. He put the miraculous aspects of the Jesus story on the same footing with all other mythologies. He had no remorse that everlasting life had no basis, nor did he fear being tortured in hell forever. Arthur had hoped Jack felt sad that he had no hope of heaven, but Jack replied that he only felt sad that Arthur was still captive to the old beliefs.[143]

Jack was not as blunt with his father about his attitude toward God and religion as he had been with Arthur. With his father, he chose to maintain the facade of respectability, perhaps to spare his father's feelings or, more likely, to avoid a row. Nonetheless, as father and son commiserated over the death of Lt. Donald Hankey, whose prose had been published in the newspaper, they were struck by the extent to which his article seemed to foreshadow his death. Jack could not quite leave it there. He added that the article called for a reappraisal of Christianity as he applauded the recent trend to get back to the original teachings of Jesus before they were overladen with traditions by his followers. Albert, who prided himself in reading between the lines, failed to read between the lines.[144] Jack had accepted the idea that the Jesus of history had nothing to do with the Christ of mythology.

The Eighteenth Birthday

Just before leaving for Oxford to take his exams, Jack went into Leatherhead with Kirkpatrick to consult a solicitor about his status with respect to conscription. He was advised to submit his situation to the chief recruiting officer at Guildford, who determined that Jack was exempt from service but that he should register immediately.[145]

Jack traveled to Oxford on December 4, 1916, and took his exams in the icy cold great hall of Oriel College from December 5 through 9.[146] He left Oxford not knowing how well he had done on the exams upon which his future depended. He returned to Gastons and then left for Belfast and the Christmas break on December 11. On December 13, he received a letter at home advising him that he had received a scholarship. Jack would also receive an exhibition, which meant an additional stipend.[147]

New pupils normally matriculate at Oxford at the beginning of Michaelmas term in October. As 1916 came to a close, Jack faced an uncertain future. Though exempt from the draft, he had decided to serve, but he did not know in what capacity. Oxford was a ghost town with most fit dons and students serving in the army and navy. Kirkpatrick advised delaying any decision about military service until after he had taken the Responsions examination, required for entrance into Oxford University. Though he had been granted a scholarship and a place in University College, he had not yet actually been admitted to the university. Kirkpatrick wanted that matter settled before Jack went off to war. In the meantime, Albert Lewis wanted to be sure that Jack had a commission as an officer before he went off to fight.[148]

During his seventeenth year, Jack was moving out of that period of middle adolescence when teenagers struggle for independence. He had distanced himself from his father and brother. Though he was devoted to Kirkpatrick's thinking about philosophy and logic, he did not let Kirk intrude on his romantic territory. He did not accept his teacher's views on literature. Furthermore, he would not accept the dictates of literary taste from any established literary critic. He had become his own man. He made up his mind about what he liked and what he believed. This adolescent drive for independence had played its own part in his rebellion against the idea of God. He had found God inconvenient because, as he would observe many years later, he did not want to be "interfered with."[149]

All the while, Jack continued to be drawn to the same kind of story about a quest for an unobtainable goal by a "gallant knight" who encountered insurmountable obstacles along the way and a beautiful woman who either helped or hindered the hero. This story fed his imagination and elicited a deep longing in his heart. The plot of this kind of story was working on him as much as or more than the lessons of Kirkpatrick. As we shall see, the plot of this great story proved to be the life of the rapidly maturing Jack Lewis.

8

Oxford and War

1917–1918

Jack Lewis's eighteenth year proved to be a monumental one. In 1917, he came of age in many ways. The final stage of adolescent development involves the formation of one's identity apart from parents and other associations. At eighteen, he had to decide who he was and what he would do with himself apart from what anyone else had to say. He went up to Oxford as a member of University College, which he loved. He entered the Officer Training Corps (OTC) and gained a commission as second lieutenant, in which capacity he entered military service and went to fight in the trenches of France. He developed a perverse interest in sexual bondage, which he would later discard. Finally, he met the mother of a fellow cadet, and she would come to live with him until her death in 1951. In his nineteenth year, Lieutenant Lewis served with distinction at the front in 1918 and received severe wounds that kept him in the hospital for the duration of the war. By the end of the war, Jack Lewis had grown up.

Forbidden Thoughts

During the Christmas vacation of 1916, Jack and Arthur must have had serious discussions about sex and their particular proclivities. Arthur's preference was with men. Though Jack had a clear attraction to women and preferably beautiful women, he also had developed an erotic fascination with sadism expressed as a deep desire to take a lash to the women who aroused his interest. He referred to this love of the whip by its Greek name, *philomastix*.[1] Jack first mentioned the subject in a letter to Arthur after having visited University College on his way back to Gastons in January 1917. While visiting the master of the college, he met the master's wife and niece. He confided to Arthur that the niece was nice and would make a good subject for the lash.[2] He explained that if the object of his desire lay across his knee, he would not be able to get a good swing with the whip, but that the torture of a brush would work well. The advantage of the brush is that it would combine the childhood intimacy of its association with the nursery with humiliation for the victim.[3] Jack liked the idea of inflicting pain and humiliation on the object of his sexual desire.

Arthur was not interested in inflicting pain, but he appears to have had at least passing interest in receiving pain. Jack said that he had once had the same interest, but he realized that the victim would only focus on the pain while the "operator" would only grow more aroused. How this bizarre perversion arose, one cannot say, but Jack alluded to a passage in Morris's *The Well at the World's End* that he had been rereading before Christmas. In it, a man remarks that the advantage of slave girls over wives is that it does not matter how they feel, as long as they are regularly whipped.[4]

Jack realized that his obsession with whipping beautiful women was not normal, and he was surprised that Arthur could even engage him in conversation about it when it did not appeal to him.[5] On the other hand, Arthur may have been attracted to the topic from the other way around. Jack suggested that Arthur would enjoy being whipped by "some Eastern queen."[6] Jack did not mind telling Arthur that he would enjoy whipping Arthur's sister and that it would do her good.[7] Though he spoke most of the whip, Jack assured Arthur that it had no special virtue for him and that hundreds of other methods of torture would suit him just as well.[8] In his French reading, he came across Rousseau's *Les Confessions*, and Jack was delighted to find that he had a soul mate in Rousseau as far as a love of the rod, though the Frenchman preferred to receive instead of to give.[9]

When Jack was home in Belfast over Christmas, he and Arthur apparently had discussed a specific girl that Jack longed to have at his disposal. She was a vision of physical perfection, especially where he wanted to lay on the lash. She would have been more than a casual acquaintance, someone both boys knew and with whom they had social involvement to the point that they observed her in the same room with them. Jack imagined laying on the lash and covering her body with stripes enough to discipline her.[10]

Between early March and early June, by which time Jack had gone up to Oxford, the subject disappeared from the correspondence when it suddenly appeared again with the revelation from Jack that the authority on his special interest was the eighteenth-century Frenchman Comte de Sade.[11] Jack knew nothing of de Sade until informed of him by his new great friend at Oxford, Theobald Richard Fitzwalter Butler, who unsurprisingly was also an Irishman. Jack did not reveal his sadist inclinations to his new set at University College, though he feared he may have given the game away one night when he became roaring drunk and went around offering a shilling to all who would let him whip them. Following that episode, Theobald took Jack aside and explained sadism and its history to him. After that conversation, the interest in the whip disappeared from Jack's correspondence, and he seems to have moved on in his development.[12] George Sayer reminds us that Lewis would view sadomasochism with disdain in maturity, but he was far from maturity in 1917.[13]

This abnormal mode of arousal and sexual gratification should not be entirely surprising, given Jack's adolescent experience. He had virtually no experience with girls his own age. He had no occasion for conversation, much less the playful flirting that goes with teenage years and often leads to more explicit acting out. The females he knew were older. He had older female cousins who had shown him attention, but this was of the mothering sort. Arthur had older sisters, but of the dismissive sort. He had witnessed brutality at the hands of Capron at Wynyard School, where the whip was a normal part of daily life. He was left with no idea what to do with girls, and the brutal treatment of women in the Greek and Latin texts he had studied did not help.

While Jack's private sexual fantasies played out, he had begun the final transition from life at Gastons to life at Oxford in University College. In a letter to Warnie in early January 1917, Jack confided or confessed that he had owned up to his time at Malvern as a necessary expedient to his acceptance at Oxford and had even begun to grow sentimental over his time there after receiving a letter from his former teacher, old Smugy.[14] In January, Jack did not yet expect to go up to Oxford until October and planned to spend the next few months with Kirkpatrick preparing for Oxford's Responsions exam.

When he visited Oxford on the way back to Gastons in January, Jack learned from Reginald Macan, the master of University College, that if he passed Responsions in March, he would be allowed to matriculate and come up to Oxford in Trinity term, which began after the Easter vacation. This also meant that he could join the Oxford OTC in order to enter the army as an officer. Unfortunately for Albert, the scholarship would not begin until October, so he would have to bear the expense of half a year in Oxford.[15] After this visit, Jack made clear to all his correspondents that he loved Oxford and appears to have rejoiced that it was a dangerous place for book lovers, with its many new and used bookstores.[16]

After laying "Bleheris" aside, Jack had begun a new story he named "Dymer," but it was not the book he would publish in 1926. He sent regular installments of this new adventure story to Arthur for comment and praise with the expectation that he would finish it quickly.[17] Somehow, it did not go quickly. One week he did not write because the snow was too enticing for him to stay inside, so he walked through the thick snow to Wisley, where he skated on a lake. He gloried in the snow-covered landscape and thought the long, cold walk absolutely "topping."[18] By late February, however, he thought he was making such good progress that he would soon finish, yet he feared not finishing. He had started too many projects that went unfinished, and he feared it would happen again with "Dymer."[19] Like the quests of romantic literature that Jack had been devouring for several years, Dymer encounters a beautiful girl at night and they make love. In the morning, however, Dymer leaves her alone sleeping without her ever having seen him in the light.[20]

In preparation for Responsions, Kirk had decided to teach Jack Italian in addition to his study of German. Thus, he began reading Dante for Kirk, while during his pleasure reading time he continued to read Milton's *Paradise Lost*. Jack fully expected to have mastered Italian before going up to Oxford in May. It was not an arrogant boast so much as an expectation based on previous performance.[21]

The adult C. S. Lewis expressed few political opinions in his public writing. Yet, the experimental atheist Jack Lewis took an interest in socialism as he prepared to enter Oxford. He lamented the sorry plight of factory workers who labored twelve hours a day. They faced monotonous work in horrible conditions with few pleasures in life besides getting drunk. He felt ashamed of his luxuries and idle life when half the population lived as little more than slaves without any hope of improving their lot. He had no proposals to make about the situation, but he felt bad for the poor. He and Arthur had their books and music while the working poor only had the freedom to starve. He mentioned his social concern to Arthur before moving on to a discussion of books and music.[22] Perhaps even more indicative of a change in his outlook toward the world than the development of a social conscience was his changing attitude toward those around him. In an uncharacteristic moment of generosity of spirit, Jack told his father that he was beginning to like Terry Forde, who had been called up for service but had managed somehow to get an exemption.[23]

The harsh conditions of the poor were not merely a matter of social and economic theory. The German submarine attacks had severely damaged the sea trade that Britain depended upon for survival. Food had grown scarce by the winter of 1917, and Jack complained to his father that potatoes were no longer on the table every day at Gastons and that they had disappeared from the diet of the poor.[24] As he prepared to leave Gastons to take Responsions in Oxford, he looked forward to returning home after Oxford and the prospect of an unlimited supply of potatoes, for Ireland did not experience the shortage that afflicted England.[25] He also hoped he might see his old Malvern friend Cooper along the way, which may seem surprising, given his bad experience with all things Malvern. Harry Richard Lucas Cooper would have been an exception to what Jack regarded as the norm at Malvern. He mentioned him in several letters home and always as a decent fellow. In all events, leaving Gastons prompted an uncharacteristic nostalgic mood in Jack.

Life in Oxford

On March 20, 1917, Jack arrived in Oxford to take his Responsions exams. As he feared, he did not do well in algebra, which under ordinary circumstances might have kept him out of Oxford, but circumstances were not ordinary in 1917. The flower of English manhood lay dead in the mud of France. The university authorities looked the other way and allowed Jack to take up residence in Oxford in Trinity term to read algebra with John Edward Campbell of Hertford College in hopes of passing Responsions later.[26] In the meantime, his presence in Oxford, though of an ambiguous nature, permitted him to enter the Oxford OTC. He signed his papers on April 30, just three days after arriving in Oxford following the Easter vacation.[27]

Cadet C. S. Lewis

Jack's application papers for acceptance into the Oxford OTC included several letters of reference from former teachers. Robert Porch, house master of School House at Malvern College, where Jack had resided, wrote a letter of reference on April 28, 1917, in which his most glowing comment was that the conduct of Mr. C. S. Lewis "was entirely satisfactory."[28] W. T. Kirkpatrick signed as reference for the moral character of Jack for the previous two and a half years, and Arthur C. Allen, schoolmaster of Cherbourg School, attested to his moral character for the period September 1911 to July 1913. The certification that Jack had achieved a standard of education suitable for a commission was signed by the dean of University College.[29]

On his application for admission to the Officer Training Corps, Jack had indicated his preferences for the branches of service with artillery listed first, according to his father's wishes, which he scratched through, followed by infantry, and finally the Royal Army Service Corps, in which Warnie had spent the war.[30] On his form, the admitting officer wrote the comment that Jack was "likely to make a useful officer but will not have had sufficient training for admission to an O.C.U. [Officer Cadet Unit] before the end of June—INFANTRY."[31] During the month of May, Jack took part in daily drills, which constituted his training before admission to the No. 4 Cadet Battalion of the Oxford OTC on June 7, 1917.[32] At the time of admission, he stood 5 feet, 10 3/4 inches tall and weighed 138 pounds.[33]

Until his assignment to a cadet unit in June, Jack lived at University College. His most vivid immediate impression of University College was the enormous size of the rooms. The college buildings dated from a time when undergraduates came almost exclusively from the great families of the kingdom. The young men of noble birth who had spent their early lives in great houses were provided with rooms in college befitting their station in life. College rooms in the old colleges consist of a large sitting room and a bedroom, and possibly another smaller room. In other words, each undergraduate had a suite that would have been furnished in keeping with his style of life. At first, Jack was shown to a large suite of rooms with oak paneling that astonished him, but it was a mistake. Jack was not grand enough for that suite. He was taken to a smaller suite full of expensive furniture that belonged to its previous occupant who had gone off to the war. Jack was merely minding the furniture until the true occupant returned. Jack described the true owner as a "tremendous blood," and, to make his point, he mentioned that the furniture included a grand piano![34]

The Oxford Way

Jack also had to learn a new way of behaving. Oxford has its own way of doing things and a special, private vocabulary for describing all that it does. It also had traditions that were allowed to lapse during the war. Normally, meals should have been taken in the great hall, but with only twelve undergraduates still in college by the third year of the war, the undergraduates took their meals in a small lecture hall without the fellows, who presumably ate in the Senior Commons Room (a glorified version of a faculty lounge).[35] Jack also had the new experience of a college servant, known as a "scout," who waited on him. The scout brought him his breakfast in his room each morning. The scout would also clean his room. It was a new way of life for Jack, who had known maids at Little Lea, but this was different.

Of the twelve men in college, only three were freshmen, and Jack learned that the older men did not condescend to talk with the "freshers" at first except to ask for the salt. Neither of the other freshmen could be a friend to Lewis in the way that Arthur had been. Of the two other freshers, one was "impossible," and the other did not read.[36] At least Jack found the OTC full of friendly chaps who were interested in learning and not simply there to be bullied by the drill sergeants. Jack drew a strong distinction between the Oxford OTC and the mob from outside Oxford, other Officer Training Corps units from other places assigned to Oxford for training. The worst of these, in his opinion, were the cadets in the Flying Corps, now heralded as the RAF. Jack regarded these fellows as too preoccupied with living out the "eat, drink, and be merry for tomorrow we die" stereotype. His old study companion Hardman from Malvern was numbered among the flying cadets, and Jack spent some time with him reminiscing about the good old days at Malvern. But he observed to Arthur that some books and people do not read as well after a long passage of time.[37] This was the same Hardman who would later take C. S. Lewis to task for his description of Malvern in *Surprised by Joy* after his distinguished career as air chief marshal and a knighthood.

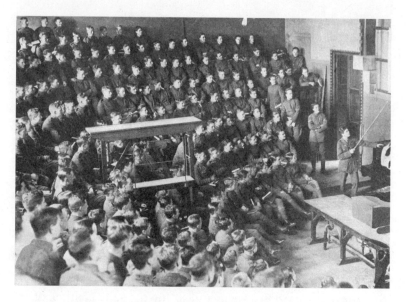

Oxford Officer Training Corps lecture

Surprisingly, the nonathletic Jack Lewis took up rowing. Unlike most team sports, rowing requires a level of cooperation that leaves no room for a "star" or the kind of competitiveness that leaves some players looking bad. Jack found that his fellow fresher who did not read, Edgell by name, actually knew a great deal about rowing. Together they created havoc on the river as Jack tried to learn to row. Nonetheless, Jack referred to Edgell as a companion rather than a friend in a letter to Arthur in which he complained that Edgell's piety was unendurable. His piety took the form of regular lectures on Jack's lack of moral fiber.[38] In later years, Laurence Fayrer Arnold Edgell was ordained in the Church of England and served for many years as a missionary in Persia before returning to England, where he served several parishes.[39]

After a few weeks, the barrier between upper class and freshers began to subside when a senior man invited the freshers to breakfast in his rooms. Theobald Butler, the man who would educate Jack about de Sade, impressed Jack on two accounts. His shelves had books that Jack approved, and he was not only Irish but an Irish nationalist. Jack liked Butler more than anyone else he had met at Oxford, largely because he could carry on a conversation about books and Ireland. Butler probably influenced Jack in other ways. By the end of July, Jack informed Arthur that if he had any interest in politics, he would probably be an Irish nationalist.[40] Another thing Jack liked about Butler was that he could carry on a conversation in which Edgell could not take part.

After breakfast, they all rode bicycles to Parson's Pleasure on the Cherwell River, where they swam in the nude. After swimming, Jack went to the Oxford Union, the great debate club with its own assembly room and library. It was his own private club and he reveled in it. It was his retreat and happy abode for reading and writing. As he described his adventures to Arthur, he added a line that would become characteristic of C. S. Lewis in years to come. He wanted Arthur to visit Oxford after the war because the wartime Oxford was not the real Oxford; it was only a shadow.[41] This contrast between the real and the shadow, a device of Plato, would mark the philosophical idealism that Lewis adopted.

The Rhythm of Life and the Circle of Friends

At first, the demands of OTC required little of Jack. Morning parade lasted from 7:00 until 7:45. In the afternoon, parade resumed from 2:00 until 4:00. Lectures on map reading and other military matters took place from time to time in the evenings. Jack feigned disappointment to his father that he could not attend college chapel due to the early hour of parade. He also regretted that he had not yet attended a Sunday service at St Mary the Virgin, the university church. He had heard that it was not a very good service and involved a lecture more than a sermon. He claimed that the best service to be had was at the cathedral within Christ Church—the large aristocratic college of which the monarch is the patron—known colloquially as "The House." By making this declaration, he implied that he had actually been to a service. Jack had managed to continue to shield his father from knowing his true views on God and religion.[42]

Butler had become Jack's great friend by the end of May. They often ate breakfast together in each other's rooms, followed by swimming at Parson's Pleasure. They talked of books and poetry, Ireland and the ghastly English. With Butler he could talk about the improbability of God, but Edgell continued to annoy him with talk about his brother and cousin who had been killed in France. In contrast to these two college men, Jack marveled at John Robert Edwards, who had decided to become a Catholic after life as a confirmed atheist.[43] What surprised Jack was how interesting Edwards was, because he could talk on every subject that interested Jack, even though he now believed in God![44]

Without any real tutorials, Jack had plenty of time to read whatever he wanted. He continued to lecture Arthur on what he was reading, usually comparing everything to *Phantastes* or *The Faerie Queene*. By early June he had come across William Fletcher Barrett's *Psychical Research*, which refueled his old interest in the occult. Though the book did not prove to his satisfaction the existence of spirits, he reserved judgment that scientific proof might yet come. He was only beginning to come to grips with how such an idea might conflict with the materialistic views he had adopted from Kirkpatrick. To add to the excitement of this reading, Jack learned that Butler's good friend Dodds would visit Oxford soon, and he was a great enthusiast for the subject of the occult.[45]

The Move to Keble College

By the beginning of June, the number of undergraduates at University College had fallen to nine, and they had their class photograph taken together. By June 7, the number had fallen even more, because Jack Lewis was assigned to a cadet battalion billeted across Oxford at Keble College. He quickly became friendly with several of the other cadets. His chief friend was Martin Ashworth Somerville, who attended Eton before gaining a scholarship to King's College, Cambridge. Somerville was the sort of person that Jack liked, because he was bookish and interesting, which to Jack meant that he knew how to talk about what Jack liked to talk about. Alexander Gordon Sutton had attended Repton School and was acknowledged as the humorist of the company. The third person, whom Jack regarded as too childish to be a real companion, was Paddy Moore, who had attended Clifton College. Moore and Jack shared a room at Keble.[46] In addition to these three, Jack mentioned to his father two others with whom he kept company: Denis Howard de Pass of Repton School and Thomas Kerrison Davey of Charterhouse School.[47] Perhaps it bears noting that as much as Jack hated the public school system, he identified everyone in terms of where he had attended public school. People were their school, even to Jack Lewis. He was, after all, an intellectual snob at this stage of life, something that would have horrified him in his maturity.

Keble College, Oxford

As Jack moved to Keble College, his great friend Butler took a first in law and went down, which is to say that he graduated with the equivalent of magna cum laude and left Oxford. Thus, after little more than a month, Jack started fresh with new friends. He repeated to Arthur that Somerville was the first among his friends and that his roommate Paddy Moore was too childish for his tastes. His opinion of Moore began to change by the middle of June when he wrote to his father that Moore's mother was staying in Oxford and that they had met several times. She was Irish.[48] Nothing more commendable needed to be mentioned than her Irish background.

Female company of a regular sort broke the tedium of Jack's existence while he was in Oxford. The last week of May, Jack's cousin Gundreda Ewart visited Oxford with their aunt Kittie Robbins. They had come to see Aunt Kittie's daughter Cherry. Though Jack did not regard his second cousin Cherry as pretty, he thought she was the best kind of company, and he saw a great deal of her during the summer. Cherry served in the Voluntary Aid Detachment as a nurse at the military hospital in Oxford.[49] When she came to tea, she played the grand piano in Jack's room. Jack told Arthur that she was just the sort of person he liked—a real sport. Even though her figure did not fit her personality, Jack thought she was plain in a pleasing sort of way.[50] When he left University College for Keble, he told Arthur that he was glad he would still be close to his new university friends *and to Cherry*.[51] During an afternoon that he spent with her on the river, he discovered that she shared his interest in Wagner's music and Arthur Rackham's illustrations. She had seen *Die Walküre* performed at the Royal Opera House in Covent Garden, and she had read the entire *Ring* libretto. To go from the beautiful to the sublime, Cherry also loved Norse mythology!

Cherry appears to have been the perfect mate for Jack, who thought it a pity that she was not beautiful, even though he now realized that she was not as plain as he had originally thought. The greatest obstacle he told Arthur facetiously was that she liked the poetry of Robert Browning and loved photography.[52] Cherry was away on leave during the middle week of July, and Jack felt her absence had created a hole in his normal life, which suggests that he had been seeing her regularly every week since May. He told Arthur that she had been a great relief to him as he adjusted to his new military life.[53]

Though Jack and Cherry did not discuss religion, Jack thought that her comments on Norse mythology implied that she might *also* be agnostic. The interesting point here is that Jack now identified himself as agnostic rather than atheist, a significant shift. In his pleasure reading, he had taken up Bishop Berkeley's *Principles of Human Knowledge*. Berkeley was one of the great Christian philosophical apologists in the eighteenth century, and he had the virtue to Jack of being Irish. Jack was now focusing his reading on metaphysical questions related to the existence of God. He planned to read David Hume and Descartes after he finished Berkeley.[54] The atheism of young Jack Lewis had given way to the agnostic's open question. At this point, he probably regarded the question of God as settled and thought he was only exploring the arguments out of intellectual curiosity and the obligation of a scholar to know the intellectual history behind the controversy before science had made all things clear.

Enter Mrs. Moore

Jack managed to have a brief holiday at home in Belfast for only a few days in the second week of August before he went on maneuvers with his unit at Warwick. He was billeted with an undertaker in a small house where six cadets shared three beds. He said it was a horrible experience, with no bath and terrible food. Following the week in Warwick, Jack spent a week with his roommate Paddy Moore at the Oxford home of his mother. Jack's opinion of Moore had risen from childish to decent, but he told his father that he liked Mrs. Moore "immensely." For the cynical, opinionated Jack Lewis, who rarely had a good word to say about anyone over the previous ten years, this was high praise indeed.[55] By September 10, Jack referred to Mrs. Moore as his friend. Jack rarely called anyone a friend who did not meet the most rigorous standards of acceptability. He had not called Paddy Moore a friend.[56] In *Surprised by Joy*, C. S. Lewis remembered that his algebra tutor, John Edward Campbell, had been a friend of his "dear friend Janie M."[57] It is not surprising that Lewis would call Mrs. Moore a dear friend in 1955 after having lived with her for over thirty years, but his awareness of her association with John Edward Campbell suggests a high level of familiarity and personal conversation in 1917. In fact, Jack had a great deal to say about Butler, Cherry, and a few others he liked in Oxford, but virtually nothing about Paddy, who appears not to have been a great friend as much as a means to an end.

In mid-September, the army arranged for Jack and his fellow cadets to bivouac in the rain-soaked Cumnor Hills near Wytham, outside Oxford. The rain filled the trenches so that the cynical Jack could reflect on how authentically the mud resembled Flanders Fields. By the time the bivouac began, however, the rain had subsided and Jack had two nights of pleasant sleep on his waterproof mat and bracken-stuffed bed.[58] After the army training experience, Jack took Responsions again on September 25. The next day, he received his temporary commission as a second lieutenant. Now an officer in the regular army, Jack began service with a month's leave before he would have to report for duty and service in France. From September 29 until October 12, he stayed with the Moore family at their home in Bristol. He wrote to his father that he had a cold and Mrs. Moore had put him to bed, which was his explanation for why he stayed so long in Bristol rather than coming home to Belfast.

On October 12, 1917, Jack's commission was confirmed in the Third Battalion of the Somerset Light Infantry.[59] Before deployment, however, Jack was transferred to the First Somerset Light Infantry, Eleventh Brigade, Fourth Division, which would soon leave for France without further training.[60] Alister McGrath has argued persuasively that Lewis sought the Somersets because

Paddy Moore had been assigned to that unit, only to discover later that Paddy had been reassigned to the Rifle Brigade.[61] Jack remained with his father at Little Lea until October 18, when he left to join his regiment at Crownhill, South Devon.

Portrait of Jack Lewis at the time of his entry into military service, 1917. Used by permission of the Marion E. Wade Center, Wheaton College, Wheaton, IL.

Jack gave his father a report on life in camp that smacked of his usual facetious view of life. The barracks were really only huts. He declared authoritatively that only about 65 percent of the officers were gentlemen. His work involved walking around for several hours while the non-commissioned officers drilled the recruits. He thought that being an officer would be hard on the legs. On the whole, he thought army life would be rather dull as long as he was in England.[62]

To Arthur Greeves, Jack wrote an entirely different kind of letter from Crownhill. In his most serious prose, he asked Arthur to forget all that he had told Arthur about "a certain person" that he had seen since returning to England. Jack had traveled to Crownhill by way of Bristol, and he appears to have been referring to Mrs. Moore. Jack had told Arthur more than he thought he should have. Of course, after discussing his sadomasochistic fantasies, Jack might have been entitled to believe that he could tell Arthur anything. This time, however, another person was involved who did not know Arthur. Whatever Jack confided to Arthur was of a most sensational nature, such that he insisted the subject never be raised again between them and should be forgotten if possible.[63] The letter suggests that Jack's connection with the Moore family went beyond the three months that he and Paddy Moore had shared a room at Keble. The letter suggests that Jack had a much stronger connection to Mrs. Moore than to Paddy. Mrs. Moore was separated from her husband, Edward Francis Courtenay Moore, whom she called "The Beast," beginning in 1907, but never divorced. Mr. Moore outlived her by five months.

Jack and Janie

Biographers and champions of Lewis are divided over what to make of the relationship between Jack and Janie Moore. His brother, Warnie, who lived with them for the better part of twenty years, had no idea what to make of them.[64] George Sayer, who knew them both, believed that Jack had loved Mrs. Moore. But Sayer based this on his interpretation of this letter to Arthur, not on personal knowledge.[65] According to Sayer, Owen Barfield took the view that there was a fifty-fifty chance that Lewis and Mrs. Moore were lovers at some point. From his own experience beginning in the 1930s after Lewis's conversion, Sayer always viewed the relationship as more like a mother and devoted son.[66] Walter Hooper expressed the view that a sexual relationship may have existed before Lewis's conversion.[67] Janie Moore, the daughter of a clergyman, did not share Jack's faith following his conversion. Alister McGrath explored the complexity of the relationship in his biography of Lewis and concluded that the relationship was much more complex than merely sexual, for it also involved the nurturing dimension of a mother for a lost son and a son for a lost mother.[68] It is also possible that the relationship involved unexpressed feelings that were never acted upon by either party.

In 1917, Janie King Moore was forty-five years old. The idea that Jack Lewis might have been attracted romantically to a woman that age when he was only eighteen may seem unlikely at first blush. Such a relationship would not be normal. Yet, at the age of forty-five, Sandra Bullock starred in *The Blind Side*, and Jennifer Aniston starred in *Cake, She's Funny That Way*, and *Horrible Bosses 2*. At forty-five, Nicole Kidman starred in *The Paperboy*, and Julia Roberts starred in *August: Osage County*. The point is that some women continue to be remarkably attractive to young men during the middle years. When Jack first met her, Janie Moore was a vivacious and energetic woman. For a young man to have a crush on her would not be terribly strange, especially if he had not been accustomed to pretty, vivacious women who paid him lots of attention and laughed at the funny things he said. Whatever Jack may have told Arthur about him and Janie Moore, he insisted on Arthur's most solemn discretion and vow to keep the secret.

In the meantime, rumors spread about the camp that the Third Somerset would soon be sent to Ireland to bolster the English presence there against the Sinn Féin. As it turned out, the rumors had no basis. Instead, Jack's unit was reassigned to the First Somerset Battalion, already stationed in France. He sent a hurried and uninformative telegram to his father on November 15 advising Albert that he had a forty-eight-hour leave and would be departing from Southampton following the leave. He asked if his father could come to Bristol. With so few lines to read between, Albert Lewis was at a loss. He did not understand the telegram. Albert wired back to Jack asking for clarification. Jack sent a second wire on November 16 informing his father that he must report to Southampton, the embarkation point for France, on the following day. By then, it was too late for Albert to get to Bristol to see his son before he left for France. Jack had spent the two days with Mrs. Moore, whose son Paddy had been in France since October.[69]

Albert Lewis took immediate steps to have Jack transferred from the infantry to the artillery, which he thought would be a safer branch of service. He wrote to Colonel James Craig, member of Parliament, for the East Division of County Down, requesting his help.[70] Craig said that he would need a letter from Jack requesting a transfer. Jack informed his father that he had no desire to leave his regiment, and he thought that the artillery was not a particularly safe assignment since the Germans worked hard to knock out the guns. He also thought that his commanding officer would not think highly of the idea. No, Jack would stay with his regiment and take what came, like Beowulf.[71]

The end of 1917 found Jack in a village in France completing his training so that he could go to the front to fight in the worst war in history. When he wrote to Arthur in mid-December, he thanked him for writing to Mrs. Moore because the two of them mattered most to him of all the people in the world. He also asked that Arthur not show the letter to his father.[72] Neither Albert nor Warren would be pleased by the turn of Jack's affection. It is also noteworthy that Paddy did not figure in the small group of those who mattered most to him in the world. The taboo appears to have lifted, and Arthur was now in the confidence of Jack and Mrs. Moore. Jack and Mrs. Moore had carried on a steady correspondence for she had asked frequently that she be allowed to read the poetry collection Jack had been working on for several years. It was in Arthur's keeping, and Jack wrote to him and asked that he send it on to Mrs. Moore on New Year's Eve 1917.[73]

Trench Warfare

Second Lieutenant C. S. Lewis arrived at the front on his nineteenth birthday, November 29, 1917. Further training had occupied the rest of the year, but in the New Year he began to experience the miseries of trench warfare. For Lewis, the primary enemy was not the Germans but the cold and the wet of the French winter. The winter of 1918 witnessed a worldwide influenza pandemic that killed twenty million people. In a letter to his father on January 4, 1918, Jack lied about how comfortable conditions were in the trenches: Deep down in their trenches, the men had warm, snug bunks where they could sleep quietly. The only real discomfort in the trenches in the dead of winter was that it might get too hot. Jack had a very pleasant time in the trenches and was never in any real danger.[74] He might have been describing a Hobbit's hole, but his description was just as imaginary as Tolkien's description of Bag End.

What C. S. Lewis remembered of the winter of 1918 was how cold, wet, and tired he was through it all. While marching through the mud, he could fall asleep in mid-step only to waken and find himself still marching. The trenches filled with water above the knee, and boots filled with ice-cold water. Dead bodies lay strewn everywhere, and one grew familiar with the sight, which reminded him of his mother's corpse when he was a little boy.[75] The trenches were not warm and cozy, but Jack did not want his fretful father to know just how bad war really was. By February 1, the winter had taken its toll on Jack, and he found himself in No. 10 British Red Cross Hospital at Le Tréport, a fishing village not far from Dieppe, where Jack had spent the summer vacation of 1907 with Warnie and his mother.[76] He would remain at the hospital for the entire month with a severe case of "trench fever."

Jack explained to his father that he only had a mild case of pyrexia, which was no more serious than influenza. His brief note emphasized what a little thing his illness was.[77] To Arthur, however, he explained that he had endured a long period with a high temperature during which he could do nothing, meaning he could not even read.[78] After two weeks in the hospital, he confessed to his father that his illness involved a high temperature, that he had a relapse, and that he had been seriously ill for a time.[79] He was so ill, he could not get up from bed for three weeks.[80] In his light-hearted effort to alleviate his father's fears, Jack emphasized what good luck he had to get so much good rest, so many comforts, and the possibility of leave as a result of his illness.[81] To Arthur, he cynically remarked that the gods hated him.[82]

Before leaving England, he had heard his good friend Laurence Bertrand Johnson talk about the important contemporary writers, including G. K. Chesterton, but Jack knew nothing about any of them.[83] He felt a bit ignorant. During his stay in the hospital, however, he began to rectify the deficiency, beginning with reading Chesterton. He made no mention of Chesterton in his few letters to Arthur during this period, but in *Surprised by Joy*, he acknowledged that reading Chesterton at this moment in his life played an important part in who he would become. He liked Chesterton's humor and logic, even if he did not like his Christian outlook.

What surprised Jack was that he liked Chesterton's goodness.[84] Goodness had a certain charm for Lewis that he had not expected, and he famously reflected a lifetime later, "A young man who wishes to remain a sound Atheist cannot be too careful of his reading."[85] The mature Lewis thought of Chesterton as a trap, but he felt the same way about his friend Johnson, who journeyed on a parallel spiritual path as he, only a few years farther along. Johnson had almost come to believe in God, but he had already come to accept the traditional virtues of truthfulness and sexual morality. Jack was ashamed of himself when he realized that Johnson was not joking about such matters and assumed that Jack agreed with him. Jack, never one to let a lie stand in his way, pretended to agree with Johnson . . . until he actually did agree.[86]

Among the officers in his unit, Jack began to learn something that he had never experienced before. He began to realize the value, the comfort, the pleasure and delight of the *camaraderie* of officers thrown together who then drew together and cared about each other. He now knew companionship of a sort different from what had been inflicted on him at Malvern. He met generosity of spirit and kindness on the part of older officers who took him under their wing. He wondered if that facial expression that prompted older boys to tell him to wipe that expression off his face had somehow been replaced by an expression that elicited pity or amusement. The misery of the war managed to breed in Lewis the ability to enjoy the company of other people in a way he had never done before.

This capacity would blossom in later years until Jack Lewis was known as someone who collected friends like other people accumulate pennies. His chapter "Friendship" in *The Four Loves* includes an important section on the company of friends that alludes to his literary circle, the Inklings.[87] This capacity for a circle of friends, however, began in the mud of France with officers who showed kindness to a young officer. What surprised Jack, perhaps most of all, was how good the conversation could be with a gang of farmers, lawyers, career soldiers, and university men.[88] The younger Jack with all his snobbery could not have participated.

Wounded in Action

Jack was out of the hospital for barely three weeks when the massive German spring offensive began on March 21, 1918. Several of his best friends were killed in the carnage, and by April 3, Jack and the Somersets found themselves in the Battle of Arras. Jack's friends were killed in the action during the first few days. On April 8 he wrote to his father a brief note to say that his unit had had "a fairly rough time."[89] Given Jack's long habit of sugarcoating all bad news for his father, it is safe to assume that the battle was hell on earth. On April 15, Jack and his sergeant were wounded by shell fragments fired by English guns![90] Sergeant Ayers died, but Jack was taken to a military hospital for treatment.

Upon admission, Jack was reported to have suffered injuries from shell fragments that caused three wounds: The first wound was to the left chest, past the ancillary region, and included a fractured rib. The second wound involved a superficial injury to the left wrist. The third wound injured the back of his left leg just above the knee.[91] On April 16, a brief note from Jack written for him by someone else informed Albert that he was "slightly" wounded and was in the hospital. A note the next day in Jack's handwriting gave the address as Liverpool Merchants Mobile Hospital in Étaples.[92] For Albert, however, wounded always meant severely wounded and at death's door. Upon receiving a telegram from Albert with the news of Jack's severe wounds, Warnie rode fifty miles on a borrowed motorcycle to see Jack. He reported to his father, "A shell burst close to where he was standing, killing a Sergeant, and luckily for 'It' he only stopped three bits: one in the cheek and two in the hands."[93]

Jack soon gave his father a different story. His story agreed with the admissions record.[94] Nonetheless, he assured his father that he had only suffered flesh wounds and nothing serious. Warnie's story, with its errors, can probably be accounted as his attempt to reassure his father that Jack was in no mortal danger. His wounds would not be reclassified by the army as "very severe" until June 6, 1919, following a medical inquiry.[95]

The severity of Jack's wounds is a more complicated matter. On June 11, a medical evaluation concluded that he had received only slight wounds and that he would be ready to return to active duty after four months in the hospital. In fact, Jack had suffered a very serious wound to the chest and would remain in the hospital and then military convalescence for the duration of the war. Though his father hoped that Jack could spend his convalescence at a facility in Ireland, Jack went to Ashton Court at Bristol in June, where he would be near Mrs. Moore.[96] Paddy Moore had gone missing during the action at Pargny on March 24 and was presumed dead. His death was not confirmed until September.[97] Jack would remain close to Mrs. Moore until October 4, when he was sent to a convalescent camp at Ludgershall, Hampshire.[98] Six weeks later he was reassigned to a facility at Eastbourne, Sussex, until he was discharged from the hospital and demobilized on Christmas Eve 1918.[99] Jack's war was finally over.

Albert Lewis wrote a letter of sympathy to Mrs. Moore following the death of Paddy. In her reply, she told Albert that Jack was the only one of her son's friends who had survived the war. Furthermore, she said that Paddy had asked Jack to look after her if he did not return from the war.[100] In a letter to A. N. Wilson, Maureen Moore, who by then was Lady Dunbar of Hempriggs, expressed her clear memory of Paddy and Jack making a solemn oath that if one of them should die in war, the survivor would care for the deceased's parents.[101] This account of an oath provided the explanation for why Jack and Mrs. Moore would live together for the rest of her life after the war. A solemn oath for one who lived within *Beowulf*, the *Iliad*, *Le Morte d'Arthur*, and *The Faerie Queene* was life itself. The chivalric ideal in service to a lady in need would be Jack's future.[102]

In reflecting on his experience of the war to his father, Jack made the point that nearly all the friends he had made in his battalion had been killed, including Laurence Bertrand Johnson, who was cut down by the same shell that injured Jack.[103] Johnson had won a scholarship to Queens College, Oxford. Jack had enjoyed his company and conversation, and he had expected to have many good conversations with him in Oxford when the war was over. Surprisingly, he had little to say about the death of Paddy Moore except to express sympathy for Mrs. Moore. Jack's cynicism had also mellowed into a faint reflection of his father's sentimentality. In June, while convalescing in London, he was allowed to visit the Kirkpatricks in Great Bookham. He saw familiar faces in the street as people walked home from church, but no one recognized him. In the year since he had gone away, he had become a man. He entered the garden at Gastons, and he thought about the good time that he and Terry Forde had ice-skating during the hard frost of 1916.[104]

9

The End of Youth

Almost forty years after World War I, C. S. Lewis tried to recollect his first battlefield experience of that dreadful war. With his first encounter of hearing bullets whizzing past his head, a voice inside him seemed to say: "This is War. This is what Homer wrote about."[1] Why did Jack decide to serve when he could have avoided the draft? After living with the heroic ideal of the Greeks in the *Iliad* and the medieval ideal of the chivalrous knight in *Le Morte d'Arthur* and *The Faerie Queene*, he probably could not do otherwise. He had entered the story. He had accepted the values. Like *Beowulf*, he would be loyal and go to his death in battle. He was a romantic at heart, and Kirk's materialism could never provide him with a philosophy to live by.

In trying to capture that feeling of his first taste of battle, C. S. Lewis summed up the adventure that had been his life from childhood through adolescence to young adulthood. His closest companion in the absence of parents or friends on a daily basis was a collection of stories that he cherished and that nurtured him. Though W. T. Kirkpatrick instilled in Jack a love and passion for logic that would stay with him all the days of his life, the philosophy of materialism, with its emphasis on empirically observed facts as the only real knowledge, did not even survive Jack's stay at Gastons. By the time he left for the war, Jack had already come to the conclusion that some kind of metaphysical reality must exist beyond the physical world of sensory observation; otherwise there would be no accounting for the ideals that had gripped him so firmly.

The Story of a Journey

During his days at Gastons, Jack Lewis fell in love with a story that never grew old for him in the retelling. He made this remark about the various versions of the story of Jason and the Argonauts from Greek mythology. He made the same observation of the rich tradition of the King Arthur legends that have been retold by dozens of storytellers for a thousand years. The kind of story that captured the imagination of young Jack Lewis was a broader, richer, more personal tale than either of these. He fell in love with the story that involved a difficult journey and a quest for an elusive thing. We find this very thing expressed in William Morris's *The Well at the World's End*, Maurice Hewlett's *Pan and the Young Shepherd*, George MacDonald's *Phantastes*, Edmund Spenser's *The Faerie Queene*, and *Sir Gawain and the Green Knight*. These were the stories that touched him deeply and that he read over and over again.

When Jack Lewis first tried to write his own grand story at Gastons, he had in mind this same tale of a quest, first with "Bleheris" and then with "Dymer." His first prose work after he became a Christian took up this form in *The Pilgrim's Regress*. He then told the story of the journey over and over again in *Out of the Silent Planet* (1938), *Perelandra* (1943), *The Great Divorce* (1946), *The Lion, the Witch and the Wardrobe* (1950), *Prince Caspian* (1951), *The Voyage of the Dawn Treader* (1952), *The Silver Chair* (1953), *The Horse and His Boy* (1954), *The Magician's Nephew* (1955), and *The Last Battle* (1956). In his academic life, Lewis's most important book was *The Allegory of Love* (1936), because almost everything else he did of a scholarly or popular nature came from its overflow. The entirety of this book explains why the journey is the best plot for exploring the inner conflict of the heart. He then explores this theme across the great English literature of the allegorical courtly love tradition from the eleventh century until the dawn of the modern era.

In many ways, the adolescence of C. S. Lewis is the story of a journey that began when he left home after his mother died. His journey took him to good places and bad, and all the while he was growing into the man he would become. He was always conscious of the separation from home as he journeyed to Wynyard School in Watford or Malvern College in Worcestershire. The separation from home and the longing to be in a better place became metaphors for his spiritual condition. Jack Lewis identified with the tales of journey in search of the great elusive something, he knew not what. After his conversion, he understood why this story of journey had been so important to him, because it was his own story. More than that, it is a story common to people all over the world, and one especially important to the biblical message. Whether in the journey of Abraham and Sarah out of Ur to the land that God had promised them, or of the children of Israel as they trekked out of Egypt through the wilderness to the promised land, or of Jesus on his way from Galilee to Jerusalem and Golgotha, the journey exemplifies the spiritual condition of human existence. Life is never stagnant. Thus, the quest for something pricked the heart of young Jack Lewis, and he would not know why until he was many years older than where this book ends. The point is that his life story would not have had the same plot had he not fallen in love with this story.

The journey motif that Lewis fell in love with was the version he found in the medieval literature of England. The courtly love tradition he explored in *The Allegory of Love* is indeed the tradition of Malory's *Le Morte d'Arthur* and Spenser's *The Faerie Queene*. The stories that captivated him at Gastons were the ones he would devote his entire academic life to expounding in lectures to undergraduates and in his scholarly writing. The world that Malory and Spenser opened to him became a world that he brought to life, not only in *The Allegory of Love* but also in *The Discarded Image* (1964); *English Literature in the Sixteenth Century, Excluding Drama* (1954); and the scholarly articles and papers collected in *Studies in Medieval and Renaissance Literature* (1966) and elsewhere. The story of the noble quest and the knight who risked all to fulfill that quest, often in the service of a great lady who remained unapproachable, was a story that gripped the heart of Jack Lewis and would hold his heart for the rest of his life. The story that the teenager loved became the one that C. S. Lewis would tell himself. Almost all of his fiction dealt with the journey, and some of his fiction also involved the courtly love tradition but without the adultery of Lancelot and Guinevere. In *Perelandra*, Ransom battles the demonic Weston to protect the great lady who will become the mother of her world. In *Prince Caspian* and *The Voyage of the Dawn Treader*, the noble mouse Reepicheep represents the glory of the chivalric tradition in his courtesy toward Queen Lucy when, for her sake, he is willing to forgo his honor and not skewer her cousin Eustace. All the books of The Chronicles of Narnia are set in the tradition of the world of Malory and Spenser, with the pageantry and ceremonial that young Jack Lewis loved.

Courtly Love

Whatever may have been at the heart of the relationship between Jack Lewis and Janie Moore, the courtly love tradition was how Jack lived it out. He found himself in the midst of a medieval drama with a lady who had no defender and protector. Here was his chance to do the noble thing and provide for the lady who could not provide for herself. He wrote his life into the medieval romance he loved. In so doing, he would only later learn the cost of courtesy that runs through all of the medieval romances. This costliness is the necessary ingredient of *agape*, that divine love that transcends human self-interest. If *eros* had drawn Jack Lewis to Janie Moore in 1917, it was *agape* that led him to care for her long after the fire had gone out. He had decided to follow the path of noblesse oblige, the noble obligation.

In reading the stories of William Morris, Sir Walter Scott, Jane Austen, Edmund Spenser, and the Brontë sisters, Jack Lewis found himself agreeing with the values they espoused. He accepted the traditional virtues of a society that had come under the influence of Jesus Christ without recognizing the source of those values. The stories had worked on him not through logical argument but by portraying life in such a way that made a longing appeal to Jack's deepest desires. The life these stories described was what he longed to experience. He liked the feeling that arose in his heart when he read the stories of these authors. They were not evangelists, and some were not even people of faith, but they presented a world in which a certain set of values about people, courtesy, relationships, and society had grown to be accepted even by people for whom religion was optional. Thus, Lewis experienced what it meant to read a book with its Christianity latent long before he understood what had happened to him by reading. Then he read books with all of these same elements, plus something more. In Chesterton's writing he found goodness, and in *Phantastes* he found holiness. He did not realize that he had found these at the time of reading, but after his conversion he understood what had happened.

From W. T. Kirkpatrick, Jack had learned to think critically and logically, but from his pleasure reading he had learned something else. Kirkpatrick taught him that opinion counted for nothing and that only facts mattered. Kirkpatrick taught him that only the physical world that we know through our senses actually exists. From his pleasure reading, however, Jack gradually came to believe that Kirkpatrick was mistaken. Jack knew some things through his feelings. He knew some things to be real even though intangible. The values that he had come to accept had to have some source other than the physical world, and so a crack in his atheism appeared that he could not mend. It would grow wider and wider, but the fissure began in his teenage years. It would make it impossible for him to hold on to his rejection of God, but that final crisis lay in his future. The important thing to note about his conversion is that it began with the irreconcilable cognitive dissonance that grew between the philosophy of materialism he had accepted from Kirkpatrick and his own experience from reading stories.

The Path to Conversion and Career

During his adolescence, Jack Lewis laid the tracks on which his conversion to Christianity would run. By the choices he made in his reading, by the values he imbibed with his reading, by the critical skills he developed that enabled him to disagree with his revered mentor W. T. Kirkpatrick, and by receiving the friendship of a boy like Arthur Greeves, Jack Lewis virtually assured his own eventual conversion, however unwittingly. It was not a single, isolated event or decision that set him on his journey, but the totality of all the aspects of his life that moved him almost inevitably toward faith in Jesus Christ. Looking back on his life journey in later years, Lewis would see the hand of God present all along the way.

Most people ask how pain and suffering can exist if a good, all-powerful God exists. Jack Lewis asked the question and opted not to believe in God. Most people who take this option usually leave it at that, but not Jack. He had other questions that he could not avoid. He thought he had settled the God question by the time he left Gastons for the war, but his time at Gastons only led him to ask other questions that would inevitably lead him back to the question of God several years later. As soon as he began trying to find a place for values like right and wrong, he was on a collision course with his easy dismissal of God.

Even if the course he set as a teenager had not led to his conversion, it certainly led to his academic career. With his adulation of Kirkpatrick, Jack thought he would become a philosopher, but in the end he could not find a place at Oxford as a philosopher. All the plans and work and sacrifice it took for him to survive the war and earn a first-class honors degree while supporting Janie Moore and her daughter, Maureen, behind his father's back would all come to naught. Because of the way he spent his leisure time at Gastons, however, Jack Lewis would be able to pick himself up and do a second degree in English literature in one year and thus secure a fellowship in English at Magdalen College. Because of the stories he read for pleasure, C. S. Lewis emerged as a literary scholar of the medieval and Renaissance periods.

What he thought about the things he read as a teenager became the seminal ideas that guided the development of his critical theory. Ideas that lie at the heart of his critically acclaimed *The Allegory of Love* first began to percolate in his bedroom at Gastons on cold winter evenings. His ideas about how to read a text from a different time and culture, which became hallmarks of his critical reputation, began while he explained to Arthur Greeves why he could not so easily compare *Beowulf* and *Le Morte d'Arthur*. His views on literary taste that he expounded in *An Experiment in Criticism* were ones he developed as a teenager. His concepts of friendship, romantic love, and affection were matters he talked about with Greeves as he tried to understand them and find his way through the emotional maze of adolescence. These matters found their way into his popular and scholarly books, from *The Allegory of Love*, to *The Screwtape Letters*, to *The Great Divorce*, to *That Hideous Strength*, to The Chronicles of Narnia, to *Till We Have Faces*, to *The Four Loves*, to *A Grief Observed*. Love and how to account for it was always the big question. It simply did not fit into a materialistic universe.

What a Fellow Likes

In big matters and in small, so much of what went into making C. S. Lewis the person goes back to preferences he developed when he was a teenager. The things he liked and the things he hated were fairly well established, with few changes after World War I. What brought him pleasure and what brought him discomfort remained fairly constant after he made up his mind as a teenage boy with strong opinions on everything. He liked tea, but he hated grown-up talk. He loved to walk for miles and miles across the wild countryside in the most appalling weather, but he hated to dawdle along the way. He loved to swim and to take a long hot bath, but he hated to play card games. He loved the company of friends, but he hated the kind of clique that he called "the inner ring." He loved vigorous exercise like rowing, but he hated team sports. He loved to read books, but he hated reading a newspaper. He loved to write, but he hated math. He loved his experience with fellow officers in the misery of the war, but he hated his experience with fellow students at Malvern College.

None of this means that C. S. Lewis did not change his opinion on many things during his adult life. It does mean, however, that Jack Lewis set a general course that made all the difference in his daily life, his career, and his conversion. Yet, despite a strong prejudice against the French, the English, and the Americans, he at least managed to spend his adult life in England and marry an American, so that indicates some ability to adjust to circumstances.

Jack Lewis managed to weather the difficult quest of adolescence with its three heroic tasks. First, he developed a sense of self-respect in spite of the insults and injuries inflicted upon him for his clumsiness. He found what he was good at, and he did not let peer pressure rob him of the delight he took in what made him happy. Second, he established his independence as a person. He learned to think for himself and to make his own decisions about what he would do with himself. This independence involved an emotional distance from his father and even from his brother until it was achieved, but it left him with the ability to stand alone, if necessary, against all pressures. Third, he developed an identity of his own. He would pursue an academic career, but identity involves so much more than how one earns a living. His identity involved who he was at his core. It involved the values that drove him and determined the choices he would make. It involved how he would treat other people. It involved what he would be and not just what he would do.

C. S. Lewis would not become a Christian and find his true identity until long after he passed from adolescence into adulthood. The process of his conversion, however, had begun before he left the safety and comfort of Gastons. The preferences, opinions, convictions, and values that Jack Lewis developed as a teenager became the skids on which his conversion took place. They established the trajectory of his early adult life and focused the questions he would ask once he went to Oxford. In the last thirty-seven pages of *Surprised by Joy*, C. S. Lewis described the path of his conversion between 1919 and 1931. In many ways, his adult conversion represented a series of logical conclusions that Lewis drew based on the values he had come to accept as real as a result of reading the stories that had occupied his free time in his teenage years.

The Value of Values

In a telling remark in *Surprised by Joy*, Lewis credited Johnson— his friend from the army who was killed but not before teaching Jack how admirable it was to lead a truthful, chaste life devoted to duty—with preparing Lewis to be drawn to and influenced by his new Oxford friends. The first Oxford friends—A. K. Hamilton Jenkin, Owen Barfield, and A. C. Harwood—were not Christians, but they would engage him in the kinds of conversations that assumed the reality of the values he had accepted. In these conversations, Lewis gradually came to refine his objection to and rejection of Kirkpatrick's materialist understanding of reality.

C. S. Lewis, the young Oxford intellectual who assumed the "New Look," tried desperately to rid himself of his love of the romantic and thirst for the supernatural, but it did not work. At first, he dismissed as mere "aesthetic experience" those troubling

267

feelings that he had associated with the old Norse mythologies and the music of Wagner that gripped him from time to time.[2] With the new psychology all the rage, Lewis could discount all his previous experience as a projection on the universe or mere fantasy. But it was no good. No sooner had Lewis written off all he loved as just wishful thinking than his new Oxford friends turned to the anthroposophy of Rudolf Steiner, with all of its "gods, spirits, after-life and pre-existence, initiates, occult knowledge, meditation," which should not have fit into a modern Oxford man's thinking.[3] His experimentation with the occult as a teenager made Lewis too wary to join the band that accepted Steinerism, but the whole episode rattled and horrified him. Disgusted though he was, Lewis could not and would not give up his new friends. Barfield in particular would not cease his argument for the validity and supernatural origin of those values and experiences that Lewis had come to cherish in his youth. Lewis referred to this ceaseless debate as "The Great War," and he lost it.[4]

In many ways, Barfield did not introduce Lewis to new arguments against a ruthless materialism that only recognized the existence of things knowable through the senses. Instead, he revived in Lewis a troubling observation about Kirkpatrick's realism that Jack had made before he left Gastons. Barfield defeated Lewis by stressing what the younger Lewis had already begun to notice but had managed to suppress. He helped Lewis accept an idea that was alien to his independent spirit but that he had flirted with along the way. Barfield helped Lewis accept the logic that for values to exist independently of matter, some kind of mind must lie behind the matter of the universe.[5] At this stage, emphasis must be placed on the idea of "some kind of." Lewis certainly did not think the kind of mind behind the universe was in any sense personal. The Hegelians, and even the Marxists, had some kind of something behind the universe driving the march of progress. The "Absolute" would do for Lewis for the time being. The absolute never intrudes into a fellow's private affairs. At least Lewis came to accept the idea of something ultimate that stands above the physical world and transcends it. Lewis remarked, "The Norse gods had given me the first hint of [glory]; but then I didn't believe in them, and I did believe (so far as one can believe an *Unding*) in the Absolute."[6]

Pleasure Reading Saved the Day

Failing to get a job teaching philosophy at Oxford when he finished his degree in 1922, Lewis stayed on a fourth year to do a second degree in the English School. As has been suggested, without his free time reading as a teenager, the task of completing an Oxford degree, even in English, in only one year would have been impossible. Once in the English School, however, Lewis met a new kind of friend. The first really bright friend he made was Nevill Coghill, another Irishman, who was both a supernaturalist and a Christian. In many ways, Coghill embodied the traits of chivalry and honor that Lewis had loved most in the stories of knights, quests, and duty. Whereas Barfield challenged Lewis on the idea that anything modern is better than anything old, Coghill actually manifested the old virtues in his life. With Coghill, Lewis in effect met one of the archaic figures that he had loved.[7]

Everything went back to the books he had read as a teenager, and once he was in the English School, he had to deal with them all over again. "All the books were beginning to turn against me," he wrote.[8] Another way of looking at it would be to say that all the books were leading him in another direction. He found himself enlivened by George MacDonald, Chesterton, Johnson, Spenser, Milton, Donne, Thomas Browne, and George Herbert, all of whom were maddeningly Christian. On the other hand, he found himself bored by George Bernard Shaw, H. G. Wells, John Stuart Mill, Edward Gibbon, and Voltaire. He rationalized the situation by explaining to himself that the "Christian myth" merely allowed an author to convey some elements of truth to minds incapable of grasping philosophical ideas. Belief in a god was simply a step along the way to grasping the idealistic concept of the absolute.

Christianity could be easily handled as only a myth. He had explained it all to Arthur Greeves years ago.

Coghill was not the only intelligent Christian Lewis met in the decade after the war. H. V. D. (Hugo) Dyson, who had been at Exeter College with Coghill, went on to teach at the University of Reading. J. R. R. Tolkien, who had been at Exeter College before the war, came back to Oxford in 1925 as professor of Anglo-Saxon. Lewis joined these three in a weekly group that drank beer and read Old Icelandic together. In Tolkien he had found a boon companion who also loved the old northernness that had first drawn him to Arthur Greeves and had drawn out of him a deep longing for something, he knew not what. Lewis was doomed. At least the comfortable secularism of the modern man in Lewis was doomed. He was now only a few steps away from faith.

The Final Steps

In the first step, he found himself rereading the *Hippolytus* of Euripides, a work he may have first read with Kirkpatrick. All the attraction of the journey to the world's end that he had found in William Morris, Edmund Spenser, and so many others came rushing back to him. With his postwar sophistication, he had dismissed all the stories that roused the sense of longing in him, but all of his modernity came crashing down as he began to revel once again in the favorite story. He observed, "I was off once more into the land of longing, my heart at once broken and exalted as it had never been since the old days at Bookham."[9]

In the second step, he came to accept Samuel Alexander's distinction between enjoyment and contemplation. Alexander was a Jewish philosopher who became interested in psychology and might be called one of the first evolutionary philosophers. By enjoyment, Alexander actually meant engagement with something, so that the act of seeing a table is the enjoyment of the table. Contemplation, on the other hand, involves reflection on or thinking about seeing the table.[10] Lewis immediately recognized the implications of this distinction. It is impossible to attend to something and think about attending to something simultaneously. To think about attending is to cease attending and move to a different kind of activity. In his own experience of the longing and desire that he would eventually name Joy, Lewis realized that he had been making the mistake of trying to contemplate or think about the experience, which had proven impossible, since to contemplate the experience necessarily meant to cease having the experience. Here was Lewis, a grown man, still preoccupied with a recurring experience of his childhood and youth, and that experience instead of his adult preoccupations was driving his conversion.

In the third step, he realized that all desire has an object. Desire does not arise in the absence of an object. Something causes the desire. The longing and desire that he would call Joy is not the thing desired. It merely points to the thing desired. The erotic desire for a woman or a man is not the woman or the man. It is the experience of longing for the woman or the man. Lewis realized that his lifelong experience of longing was pointing to something else, and he would never know what it was by thinking about the longing.[11]

The fourth step came during the period 1924–1925, when Lewis had a temporary philosophy teaching post at University College and gained his first appointment teaching English at Magdalen College.[12] During this time, he had the difficulty of explaining what he meant by the absolute to undergraduate students. He tried using the idea of the "God of the philosophers," but certainly not a personal being with whom one might have a relationship. Then he read G. K. Chesterton's *Everlasting Man*. Chesterton was a holdover from the waning days of his youth, and he had thought him a splendid fellow apart from his Christianity. Now, Lewis was confronted with a grand Christian outline of history that made perfect sense. In a way, it was the first time he had seen the Christian faith presented as a whole.

Almost a hundred years later, Christians rarely think to present the story of Jesus in a comprehensible whole that makes sense. Evangelism in the West has certainly failed to do this since it began focusing almost exclusively on an explanation of how the penal substitutionary view of the atonement works. Chesterton, however, made sense of Jesus, Lewis thought. Riding a bus up Headington Hill away from Oxford toward the home he kept with Mrs. Moore and her daughter, Maureen, Lewis became aware that he was keeping something at arm's length. The whole of his meaningful life up to that point seemed in conspiracy against him. All the books he enjoyed and the most important friends were lined up against him. Something or, worse, Someone was pursuing him. In retrospect, they may have been lined up for him. Ever the logician, he concluded that the something he was keeping at arm's length was God, whom he reluctantly chose to believe in.[13]

Belief in God, however, is not the same as faith in Jesus Christ, the manifestation of the Creator within the creation. That idea was still a bit much to swallow as Lewis entered his thirties. Just as the story he loved about the journey and quest for the great prize at the world's end had led him to believe in God, the mythologies that he had loved since his days at Malvern College would lead him to believe in Jesus. After he came to believe that God exists, Lewis went on his way without any expectation of reward or punishment for his deeds. God simply was God, and God did not do things for people or interfere in their lives. God explained the existence of values in the universe but not a great deal more. He may be absolute power as well as Creator, but he did not meddle. Lewis went to church each Sunday and to college chapel during the week out of a sense of duty, but not because he believed the Christian doctrines. More than anything, it signaled that he had thrown his lot in with the people who believed in God.

Mythology as Preparation for Christ

In the end, Lewis's love of mythology, which at one time had led him to dismiss Christianity as just one of many religions, led him to take religion seriously. His conversations with Owen Barfield and his former student Dom Bede Griffiths resulted in a view that the history of religion had as much to do with growing to maturity as with conflicting views of God. In many ways the human constructs of religion obscure the vision of God that comes from religious experience when people try to preserve the experience in ritual, sacred offices, and speculation upon the original prophetic experience. The myths, however, preserved the original experiences in a different way—in a story. In *Surprised by Joy*, Lewis confessed that his memory was blurry about exactly how he came to see what marked the story of Jesus as different from all the other stories. We know what happened, however, because Lewis wrote to Arthur Greeves about it immediately afterward.

In a letter on September 22, 1931, Lewis told Arthur of a late-night walk with Tolkien and Dyson on Addison's Walk, within the grounds of Magdalen College. They had spoken at length about Christianity and myth.[14] Then, in another letter on October 18, he explained what they had talked about on their walk. His problem with Christianity had not so much been that he had difficulty believing. It was more that he had no idea what redemption meant and in what sense the life and death of Jesus saves people. He understood how sin might keep people from God, but he did not see what Jesus actually did about it. Why would the death of Jesus affect him two thousand years later?[15] At this point, his love of mythology showed him the way.

Lewis loved the story of a dying and rising god wherever he found it . . . except in the Gospels. What Tolkien and Dyson helped Lewis understand, based on his own experience with myths, is that the story of Jesus is a *true* myth in the sense that "it really happened." It was different from other myths in that they were myths constructed by humans, while the story of Jesus was constructed by God.[16] Then he told Arthur something amazingly profound that many Christians do not understand after years in the faith. The doctrines of Christianity, or the many different theologies, are less true than the true myth because they are only attempts to translate the story, while God has expressed it all more adequately in the real incarnation, crucifixion, and resurrection.[17] He was almost certain that the story of Jesus had actually happened. The end of the journey was in sight.

A few days after the late night walk, Warnie took his little brother in a motorcycle sidecar to the Whipsnade Zoo. Of this excursion Lewis wrote at the end of *Surprised by Joy* that when they left for the zoo, he did not yet believe that Jesus Christ was the Son of God, but when they arrived at the zoo, he realized that he did. He had not spent the time speculating, thinking, or contemplating the gospel. He said it was more like waking up.[18]

It is appropriate that Jack's brother, Warnie, home on leave from his army posting in China, should be with him when he finally came to the world's end. Warnie had been with him at the beginning of his journey and had periodically met with him along life's way. Warnie had first introduced Jack to the experience of beauty and wonder with the miniature garden he had created in the top of a tin cookie box when they were children. At the end of Jack's great quest, Warnie drove as Jack sat in unselfconscious reverie while they bumped along the road from Headington to Whipsnade in John Bunyan's Bedfordshire—or, allegorically, along the Pilgrim's road from the City of Destruction to the Heavenly City. He was on the Pilgrim's journey that he had loved to read about at Gastons. At the close of *Surprised by Joy*, Lewis described his conversion in terms of the quest story that had captured his imagination as a teenager. He wrote of the experience of being lost in the woods, like the figures in the stories of Morris and Spenser and MacDonald, when suddenly a signpost appears. His experiences had not been the great thing itself but were merely signs along the way to point him in the direction of the great prize, the true destination, the garden at the end of the world.[19] He would come to believe that God had erected the signs along his path.

The Importance of Youth

Biographers of Lewis have regularly wondered why he devoted so much of *Surprised by Joy* to his school days. It seems such a waste of time and space. Studies of Lewis have tended to move quickly from the nursery to Oxford, where the important things happened. Lewis did not view his life that way. In *Surprised by Joy*, he mentioned that episodes or events or relationships that the curiosity seeker might be interested in did not really play a major role in his conversion. Lewis acknowledged that matters such as his father's death, important friends, the influence of Oxford dons, or his taking sixty prisoners during the war, his first experience of *eros* with a nurse during his convalescence, and "one huge and complex episode" that involved a great deal of emotion—probably involving Mrs. Moore—did not play a major part in his journey.[20] If anything, they were only sights along the way. His teenage years, on the other hand, played an enormous role. They paved the road on which he trod. They formed the boundaries from which he would never wander far. They cleared the path he would walk his entire life.

As has been demonstrated throughout this study, Lewis not only devoted the major part of *Surprised by Joy* to his youth but also referenced the importance of his youth in a number of his other books, including *An Experiment in Criticism*, *The Abolition of Man*, the Narnia tales, and more. His youth provided C. S. Lewis with a trajectory for his life of which he remained aware until the end of his life. The story of his youth and its significance suggests the importance of this period of life for everyone. Adolescence is a fertile time of formation or deformation for each person, yet it is a time of great neglect by society. Teenagers struggling with self-image, independence, and identity need significant older influences in their lives as they unknowingly put together the pieces that will form them for the rest of their days. Friends and teachers play an increasingly important role in the direction a young person's life will take as parents fade in significance.

As Jack Lewis lay in his hospital bed convalescing in 1918, he had not only survived the war to end all wars. He had survived adolescence and lived to tell the tale. He was a man. His adolescence, however, had gathered all the material out of which the man would build his life. His adolescence provided the values, the longings, and the questions that would eventually result in his conversion. His adolescence gave him a career and taught him to be a writer.

Notes

Chapter 1: Young Jack Lewis at Wynyard School: 1908–1910

1. C. S. Lewis, *Surprised by Joy* (London: Bles, 1955), 73. In making this comparison, Lewis first had to belabor what he meant by the term "renaissance," because he had taken the professional position that the Renaissance had never happened. The events and achievements that historians and critics now call the Renaissance certainly took place, but Lewis insisted that the achievements of the Renaissance belonged to a gradual progression of achievement that dated back centuries.

2. Lewis, *Surprised by Joy*, 73.

3. Roger Lancelyn Green and Walter Hooper, *C. S. Lewis: A Biography* (New York: Harcourt Brace Jovanovich, 1974), 21.

4. Walter Hooper, ed., *The Collected Letters of C. S. Lewis*, vol. 1 (New York: HarperSanFrancisco, 2004), 190, 205.

5. "Memoirs of the Lewis Family, 1850–1930," ed. Warren Hamilton Lewis (Marion Wade Center Collection, Wheaton College), 3:140–41, 199.

6. "Memoirs," 3:92.

7. Hooper, *Letters*, 1:98n76.

8. Clyde S. Kilby and Marjorie Lamp Mead, eds., *Brothers and Friends: The Diaries of Major Warren Hamilton Lewis* (New York: Harper & Row, 1982), 263–64.

9. Hooper, *Letters*, 1:178. In a letter to Albert Lewis, Kirkpatrick repeatedly refers to young Jack as Clive.

10. George Watson, "The Art of Disagreement," in *C. S. Lewis Remembered: Collected Reflections of Students, Friends and Colleagues*, ed. Harry Lee Poe and Rebecca Whitten Poe (Grand Rapids, MI: Zondervan, 2006), 82.

11. Hooper, *Letters*, 1:71.

12. Walter Hooper, ed., *The Collected Letters of C. S. Lewis*, vol. 2 (New York: HarperSanFrancisco, 2004), 454, 494, 496, 497. Lewis then began signing himself "Bro. Ass" before settling in as C. S. Lewis, the way he signed his letters to all but the most intimate of family and close friends.

13. Hooper, *Letters*, 1:996–97.
14. "Memoirs," 3:20.
15. "Memoirs," 3:199.
16. "Memoirs," 3:6–7.
17. "Memoirs," 3:25–26.
18. "Memoirs," 3:26.
19. "Memoirs," 3:27.
20. "Memoirs," 3:28–29.
21. "Memoirs," 3:30.
22. "Memoirs," 3:19–20.
23. "Memoirs," 3:72.
24. "Memoirs," 3:72, 73.
25. "Memoirs," 3:20.
26. "Memoirs," 3:74.
27. "Memoirs," 3:80.
28. "Memoirs," 3:82.
29. "Memoirs," 3:83.
30. W. H. Lewis, "C. S. Lewis: A Biography" (unpublished manuscript, Marion Wade Center, Wheaton College), 151.
31. W. H. Lewis, "Biography," 151.
32. "Memoirs," 3:94–95, 97–98.
33. "Memoirs," 3:99.
34. "Memoirs," 3:103.
35. "Memoirs," 3:112–13.
36. "Memoirs," 3:119.
37. "Memoirs," 3:120.
38. "Memoirs," 3:136.
39. "Memoirs," 3:202.
40. "Memoirs," 3:214.
41. Hooper, *Letters*, 1:6.
42. Hooper, *Letters*, 1:67.
43. Kilby and Mead, *Brothers and Friends*, 47.
44. Kilby and Mead, *Brothers and Friends*, 56.
45. Walter Hooper, ed., *All My Road before Me: The Diary of C. S. Lewis, 1922–1927* (New York: Harcourt Brace Jovanovich, 1991), 15.
46. Hooper, *Letters*, 1:982–84.
47. W. H. Lewis, "Biography," 25.
48. Hooper, *Letters*, 1:6.
49. Hooper, *Letters*, 1:983.
50. "Memoirs," 3:34.
51. "Memoirs," 3:95–97.
52. "Memoirs," 3: 97.
53. "Memoirs," 3:109–10.
54. "Memoirs," 3:146.
55. "Memoirs," 3:148.

56. "Memoirs," 3:139.
57. "Memoirs," 3:151.
58. "Memoirs," 3:152.
59. "Memoirs," 3:169.
60. "Memoirs," 3:170.
61. "Memoirs," 3:65.
62. "Memoirs," 3:66–67.
63. "Memoirs," 3:68, 69.
64. "Memoirs," 3:86.
65. "Memoirs," 3:149, 153, 170, 179.
66. "Memoirs," 3:172–73.
67. "Memoirs," 3:174.
68. "Memoirs," 3:180.
69. "Memoirs," 3:180.
70. "Memoirs," 3:175.
71. "Memoirs," 3:175–76.
72. "Memoirs," 3:183.
73. Hooper, *Letters*, 1:2.
74. Hooper, *Letters*, 1:3–5.
75. Hooper, *Letters*, 1:12–13.
76. C. S. Lewis, *God in the Dock*, ed. Walter Hooper (Grand Rapids, MI: Eerdmans, 1970), 16. *God in the Dock* was published the next year in London by Bles with the title *Undeceptions*.
77. Lewis, *God in the Dock*, 224.
78. C. S. Lewis, *The Problem of Pain* (New York: Macmillan, 1944), 128–31.
79. Hooper, *Letters*, 1:9.
80. C. S. Lewis, "The Inner Ring," in *They Asked for a Paper* (London: Bles, 1962), 149.
81. "Memoirs," 3:154.
82. Hooper, *Letters*, 1:14.
83. Lewis, *Surprised by Joy*, 40.
84. Hooper, *Letters*, 1:105.
85. Lewis, *Surprised by Joy*, 40.
86. C. S. Lewis, *On Stories and Other Essays on Literature*, ed. Walter Hooper (New York: A Harvest Book, 1982), xix.
87. Lewis, *On Stories and Other Essays*, 55.
88. Lewis, *On Stories and Other Essays*, xviii, 9. The volume involving Lewis, Sayers, and others is *Essays Presented to Charles Williams*, but the essay was originally presented by Lewis as a talk to a Merton College literary club in 1940.
89. These reflections occur in chapter 5. See C. S. Lewis, *Out of the Silent Planet* (New York: Macmillan, 1977), 35.
90. "The Establishment Must Die and Rot . . . C. S. Lewis Discusses Science Fiction with Kingsley Amis and Brian Aldiss," *SFHorizons*, no. 1 (Spring 1964): 5–12; reprinted in Poe and Poe, *C. S. Lewis Remembered*, 235–44.

91. Lewis, *Surprised by Joy*, 40.
92. Lewis, *Surprised by Joy*, 41.
93. Hooper, *Letters*, 1:10.
94. Lewis, "The Inner Ring," 141.
95. C. S. Lewis, *The Four Loves* (London: Bles, 1960), 97.
96. Lewis, "The Inner Ring," 148.
97. "Memoirs," 3:194.
98. "Memoirs," 3:165.
99. "Memoirs," 3:195.
100. "Memoirs," 3:194.
101. "Memoirs," 3:195.
102. "Memoirs," 3:195.
103. "Memoirs," 3:194.
104. "The Ulsterior Motive" is the title of an unpublished essay by Tolkien in which he offered a critique of Lewis's *Letters to Malcolm*, which was published after Lewis died. See Humphrey Carpenter, *The Inklings* (Boston: Houghton Mifflin, 1979), 50–52, 265.
105. Hooper, *Letters*, 1:14.
106. "Memoirs," 3:195. See also 3:205, where Jacks describes playing games over a period of several days during which he found bowlers "good fun."
107. "Memoirs," 3:45, 46, 49.
108. "Memoirs," 3:35.
109. "Memoirs," 3:177.
110. "Memoirs," 3:204.
111. Lewis, *Surprised by Joy*, 38.
112. Ironically, Lewis appears to have had a great capacity for mathematics, which he might have inherited from his mother, who earned a first in mathematics at Queen's College in Belfast. Matt Lunsford has argued persuasively that Lewis demonstrates a strong capacity for math in his apologetic writings. See Matt D. Lunsford, "Mere Mathematics: The Role of Mathematics in the Apologetic Works of C. S. Lewis," in *Inklings Forever*, vol. 7, *A Collection of Essays Presented at the Seventh Frances White Colloquium on C. S. Lewis & Friends* (Upland, IN: Taylor University, 2010), https://pillars.taylor.edu/inklings_forever/vol7/iss1/.
113. Hooper, *Letters*, 1:264. Hooper quotes from "Memoirs," 5:174.
114. Lewis, *Surprised by Joy*, 36.
115. C. S. Lewis, *The Last Battle* (New York: Macmillan, 1956), 49, 90–91.
116. Lewis, *Surprised by Joy*, 41.
117. Lewis, *The Last Battle*, 173.
118. W. H. Lewis, "Biography," 18–19.
119. "Memoirs," 3:200.
120. "Memoirs," 3:206.
121. George Watson, "The Art of Disagreement: C. S. Lewis (1898–1963)," in Poe and Poe, *C. S. Lewis Remembered*, 83.

Chapter 2: Off to Malvern: 1910–1914

1. C. S. Lewis, *Surprised by Joy* (London: Bles, 1955), 57.
2. Lewis, *Surprised by Joy*, 73.
3. Lewis, *Surprised by Joy*, 56.
4. Alan Jacobs, *The Narnian: The Life and Imagination of C. S. Lewis* (New York: HarperSanFrancisco, 2005), 27.
5. Jacobs, *The Narnian*, 27.
6. Lewis, *Surprised by Joy*, 138.
7. "Memoirs of the Lewis Family, 1850–1930," ed. Warren Hamilton Lewis (Marion Wade Center Collection, Wheaton College), 3:222.
8. A brief clarification of terms might prove helpful for American readers. In the context of institutions like Wynyard School and Cherbourg School, a school in England would be what might be called a middle school or junior high school in the United States. Campbell College, Malvern College, and the like would be called high schools in the United States. To confuse matters, the great English universities of Oxford and Cambridge are composed of self-governing colleges.
9. Walter Hooper, ed., *The Collected Letters of C. S. Lewis*, vol. 1 (New York: HarperSanFrancisco, 2004), 16n.
10. Hooper, *Letters*, 1:16.
11. Walter Hooper, ed., *The Collected Letters of C. S. Lewis*, vol. 2 (New York: HarperSanFrancisco, 2004), 242.
12. Hooper, *Letters*, 2:934.
13. Lewis, *Surprised by Joy*, 61.
14. Lewis, *Surprised by Joy*, 126.
15. Hooper, *Letters*, 1:16.
16. Hooper, *Letters*, 1:17.
17. Hooper, *Letters*, 1:17.
18. Hooper, *Letters*, 1:17.
19. "Memoirs," 3:229.
20. Hooper, *Letters*, 1:16.
21. Hooper, *Letters*, 1:17.
22. W. H. Lewis, "C. S. Lewis: A Biography" (unpublished manuscript, Marion Wade Center, Wheaton College), 26.
23. Hooper, *Letters*, 1:28.
24. "Memoirs," 3:310–11. No known copies of these issues of the *Cherbourg School Magazine* are known to exist, but Warnie Lewis included copies of his brother's first article in his "Memoirs," the project that occupied his early years after retiring from the army.
25. "Memoirs," 3:318–19.
26. "Memoirs," 4:51.
27. Hooper, *Letters*, 1:31.
28. Hooper, *Letters*, 1:18.
29. Hooper, *Letters*, 1:22.
30. Hooper, *Letters*, 1:22.

31. Hooper, *Letters*, 1:25.
32. Hooper, *Letters*, 1:26.
33. W. H. Lewis, "Biography," 28.
34. C. S. Lewis, "Kipling's World," in *Literature and Life: Addresses to the English Association* (London: George G. Harrap, 1948), 57.
35. Lewis, "Kipling's World," 63.
36. Lewis, "Kipling's World," 69.
37. Lewis, "Kipling's World," 70.
38. Lewis, "Kipling's World," 71, 72, 73.
39. Hooper, *Letters*, 1:19.
40. Lewis, *Surprised by Joy*, 61.
41. Lewis, *Surprised by Joy*, 65.
42. Lewis, *Surprised by Joy*, 64, 67.
43. C. S. Lewis, "The Norse Spirit in English Literature," 78 rpm record (London: Joint Broadcasting Committee, [1941]). This unique recording is part of my private collection.
44. Lewis, "The Norse Spirit," 40.
45. Hooper, *Letters*, 2:242.
46. "Memoirs," 3:233.
47. "Memoirs," 3:234.
48. Hooper, *Letters*, 1:26.
49. Clyde S. Kilby and Marjorie Lamp Mead, eds., *Brothers and Friends: The Diaries of Major Warren Hamilton Lewis* (New York: Harper & Row, 1982), 204.
50. Hooper, *Letters*, 1:25.
51. Hooper, *Letters*, 1:23–24.
52. Hooper, *Letters*, 1:28.
53. "Memoirs," 3:190.
54. "Memoirs," 4:58.
55. "Memoirs," 4:125.
56. "Memoirs," 4:59.
57. "Memoirs," 4:69.
58. "Memoirs," 4:107.
59. Hooper, *Letters*, 1:46–47.
60. "Memoirs," 4:123–24.
61. "Memoirs," 4:126.
62. Hooper, *Letters*, 1:36–37.
63. Lewis, *Surprised by Joy*, 59.
64. Lewis, *Surprised by Joy*, 102.
65. Hooper, *Letters*, 1:50 (emphasis added).
66. Hooper, *Letters*, 1:43.
67. Lewis, *Surprised by Joy*, 30–31.
68. "Memoirs," 4:93.
69. "Memoirs," 4:12–14.
70. Hooper, *Letters*, 1:51–52.

71. Hooper, *Letters*, 1:55.
72. Hooper, *Letters*, 1:60.
73. Hooper, *Letters*, 1:31.
74. Hooper, *Letters*, 1:29, 31, 35, 37, 49.
75. Lewis defined a blood simply as one of the aristocrats of the school. They were the prefects and the star athletes who lorded it over everyone else, especially the weak. See Lewis, *Surprised by Joy*, 85.
76. Lewis, *Surprised by Joy*, 85–86.
77. Lewis, *Surprised by Joy*, 91.
78. Lewis, *Surprised by Joy*, 19.
79. C. S. Lewis, preface to *Essays Presented to Charles Williams*, ed. C. S. Lewis (London: Oxford University Press, 1947), ix.
80. Kilby and Mead, *Brothers and Friends*, 252–53.
81. W. H. Lewis, "Biography," 31.
82. W. H. Lewis, "Biography," 204.
83. Lewis, *Surprised by Joy*, 66.
84. Lewis, *Surprised by Joy*, 91–92.
85. Lewis, *Surprised by Joy*, 95.
86. In his letters, Jack spelled this nickname a variety of ways. The spelling chosen here is from *Surprised by Joy*, 110.
87. Hooper, *Letters*, 1:39.
88. Hooper, *Letters*, 1:39.
89. "Memoirs," 4:156–57.
90. Hooper, *Letters*, 1:59.
91. W. H. Lewis, "Biography," 36.
92. "Memoirs," 4:156–57.
93. "Memoirs," 4:160.
94. W. H. Lewis, "Biography," 35.
95. "Memoirs," 3:208.
96. "Memoirs," 3:209.
97. "Memoirs," 4:62.
98. "Memoirs," 4:165, 167.
99. Hooper, *Letters*, 1:54.
100. Lewis, *Surprised by Joy*, 123.
101. Lewis, *Surprised by Joy*, 127.
102. George Sayer, *Jack: A Life of C. S. Lewis* (Wheaton, IL: Crossway, 1994), 327.
103. Alister McGrath, *C. S. Lewis: A Life* (Carol Stream, IL: Tyndale, 2013), 25.
104. Roger Lancelyn Green and Walter Hooper, *C. S. Lewis: A Biography* (New York: Harcourt Brace Jovanovich, 1974), 37.
105. Lewis, *Surprised by Joy*, 217.
106. Hooper, *Letters*, 1:55–56.
107. Hooper, *Letters*, 1:55.

Chapter 3: Making a Friend: Spring 1914

1. Clyde S. Kilby and Marjorie Lamp Mead, eds., *Brothers and Friends: The Diaries of Major Warren Hamilton Lewis* (New York: Harper & Row, 1982), 266.
2. C. S. Lewis, *Surprised by Joy* (London: Bles, 1955), 74.
3. Lewis, *Surprised by Joy*, 23.
4. J. R. R. Tolkien, *Tree and Leaf* (Boston: Houghton Mifflin, 1965), 68.
5. Lewis, *Surprised by Joy*, 75.
6. Lewis, *Surprised by Joy*, 76.
7. Roger Lancelyn Green and Walter Hooper, *C. S. Lewis: A Biography* (New York: Harcourt Brace Jovanovich, 1974), 32.
8. Green and Hooper, *Lewis*, 77.
9. Lewis, *Surprised by Joy*, 78.
10. Walter Hooper and Roger Lancelyn Green corrected the titles given by Lewis in *Surprised by Joy* and added the authors. See Green and Hooper, *Lewis*, 39; cf. Lewis, *Surprised by Joy*, 79.
11. Lewis, *Surprised by Joy*, 112.
12. Lewis, *Surprised by Joy*, 78–79.
13. Walter Hooper, *Through Joy and Beyond: A Pictorial Biography* (New York: Macmillan, 1982), 87.
14. Kilby and Mead, *Brothers and Friends*, 10–11.
15. Kilby and Mead, *Brothers and Friends*, 190.
16. Kilby and Mead, *Brothers and Friends*, 189.
17. Kilby and Mead, *Brothers and Friends*, 224.
18. Kilby and Mead, *Brothers and Friends*, 266.
19. C. S. Lewis, *The Four Loves* (London: Bles, 1960), 77.
20. Lewis, *The Four Loves*, 78.
21. Walter Hooper, ed., *The Collected Letters of C. S. Lewis*, vol. 1 (New York: HarperSanFrancisco, 2004), 320.
22. Hooper, *Letters*, 1:324.
23. Hooper, *Letters*, 1:405–6.
24. This sketch was included by Walter Hooper in the introduction to the letters of Lewis to Greeves. See Walter Hooper, ed., *They Stand Together: The Letters of C. S. Lewis to Arthur Greeves (1914–1963)* (London: Collins, 1979), 24–26.
25. Hooper, *They Stand Together*, 25.
26. Hooper, *They Stand Together*, 25.
27. Lewis, *The Four Loves*, 146.
28. Lewis, *The Four Loves*, 147.
29. Lewis, *The Four Loves*, 33.
30. C. S. Lewis, *The Allegory of Love* (Oxford: Clarendon, 1936), 339. In his discussion of *The Faerie Queene*, Lewis remarked, "In the ninth canto Spenser explicitly classifies Eros, Storgē, and Philia as 'three kinds of love.'"
31. C. S. Lewis, *Mere Christianity* (New York: Macmillan, 1952), 67.

32. Justin Phillips, *C. S. Lewis at the BBC* (London: HarperCollins, 2002), 305.
33. Hooper, *They Stand Together*, 25.
34. George Sayer, *Jack: C. S. Lewis and His Times* (New York: Harper & Row, 1988), 75. This information comes from Mrs. Moore, who included it in a letter she wrote to Albert Lewis. Warnie Lewis included a copy of the letter in his "Memoirs of the Lewis Family, 1850–1930."
35. Hooper, *Letters*, 1:481.
36. Hooper, *Letters*, 1:59.
37. Hooper, *Letters*, 1:59.
38. Lewis, *The Four Loves*, 27.
39. Hooper, *Letters*, 1:59.
40. C. S. Lewis, *Transposition and Other Addresses* (London: Bles, 1949), 32–33.
41. Lewis, *Transposition and Other Addresses*, 33.
42. One of the last pieces that C. S. Lewis wrote before he died was an essay on Malory's *Le Morte d'Arthur*. See C. S. Lewis, "The English Prose Morte," in *Essays on Malory*, ed. J. A. W. Bennett (Oxford: Clarendon, 1963), 7–28. The collection was edited by Lewis's fellow Inkling and contains an essay by Lewis's former pupil Derek Brewer.
43. Hooper, *Letters*, 1:75–77. Jack sketched the whole story for Arthur in six scenes.
44. Hooper, *Letters*, 1:77–78.
45. Hooper, *Letters*, 1:80.
46. Hooper, *Letters*, 1:81.
47. Hooper, *Letters*, 1:84.
48. Hooper, *Letters*, 1:81.
49. Hooper, *Letters*, 1:84.
50. Hooper, *Letters*, 1:115.
51. Hooper, *Letters*, 1:134.

Chapter 4: Jack and War Come to Great Bookham: Fall 1914

1. C. S. Lewis, *Surprised by Joy* (London: Bles, 1955), 131.
2. "Memoirs of the Lewis Family, 1850–1930," ed. Warren Hamilton Lewis (Marion Wade Center Collection, Wheaton College), 4:211.
3. Lewis's famous description of his first meeting with Kirkpatrick at the train station, included in *Surprised by Joy*, was first written for Warren's collection of the family papers during the period 1930–1935, when his memory was still fresh and he had commenced his life as a Christian. See "Memoirs," 4:65.
4. Lewis, *Surprised by Joy*, 145.
5. Walter Hooper, ed., *The Collected Letters of C. S. Lewis*, vol. 1 (New York: HarperSanFrancisco, 2004), 74.
6. Hooper, *Letters*, 1:75.
7. Hooper, *Letters*, 1:74n30.

8. Hooper, *Letters*, 1:69.

9. Hooper, *Letters*, 1:69–70.

10. "Memoirs," 4:63.

11. "Memoirs," 4:63.

12. Hooper, *Letters*, 1:72.

13. "Memoirs," 4:223–24.

14. "Memoirs," 4:227.

15. "Memoirs," 4:231.

16. Hooper, *Letters*, 1:69n24.

17. Hooper, *Letters*, 1:70.

18. Hooper, *Letters*, 1:79.

19. Hooper, *Letters*, 1:83.

20. Hooper, *Letters*, 1:79.

21. Hooper, *Letters*, 1:74.

22. Lewis, *Surprised by Joy*, 204–5.

23. Hooper, *Letters*, 1:85.

24. Hooper, *Letters*, 1:83.

25. Lewis, *Surprised by Joy*, 151.

26. By 1917, the public hatred of the Germans had grown so strong that King George V renounced his family name and German titles, taking the new name of Windsor for his dynasty. Prince Battenberg followed suit and changed his name to Mountbatten. When he relinquished the German title of prince, the king conferred on him the new creation of marquess of Milford Haven. His son Louis Mountbatten would receive the title Earl Mountbatten of Burma following World War II. His daughter Alice married Prince Andrew of Greece, the younger brother of the king of Greece, and to this union was born Prince Philip, who married Queen Elizabeth II. Serving in the Royal Navy during World War II, Philip adopted his mother's new maiden name of Mountbatten rather than use his real name of Schleswig-Holstein-Sonderburg-Glücksburg.

27. Hooper, *Letters*, 1:88.

28. Hooper, *Letters*, 1:88.

29. Hooper, *Letters*, 1:90.

30. Hooper, *Letters*, 1:90–91, 91n58.

31. Hooper, *Letters*, 1:90.

32. Hooper, *Letters*, 1:90.

33. Hooper, *Letters*, 1:92.

34. "Memoirs," 4:66.

35. "Memoirs," 4:90.

36. "Memoirs," 4:90, 93.

37. Lewis, *Surprised by Joy*, 135.

38. Hooper, *Letters*, 1:78.

39. Hooper, *Letters*, 1:72.

40. "Memoirs," 3:53, 64.

41. "Memoirs," 4:95.

42. "Memoirs," 4:218.
43. "Memoirs," 4:85.
44. "Memoirs," 4:79, 83.
45. Hooper, *Letters*, 1:140–41.
46. Hooper, *Letters*, 1:72.
47. Hooper, *Letters*, 1:110. Lord Kitchener was secretary of state for war following a distinguished military career. It is his picture that appeared on British recruiting posters with the slogan "I Want You." Kitchener knew well how to fight a nineteenth-century war, as he had done in India and the Sudan. Unfortunately, he used nineteenth-century tactics in a twentieth-century war, having failed to learn the lessons of the Russo-Japanese War, in which the Russians had made the same mistake.
48. Hooper, *Letters*, 1:100.
49. Hooper, *Letters*, 1:95; Lewis, *Surprised by Joy*, 121.
50. W. H. Lewis, *C. S. Lewis: A Biography* (unpublished manuscript. Marion Wade Center, Wheaton College), 28.
51. Lewis, *Surprised by Joy*, 136.
52. Roger Lancelyn Green, "C. S. Lewis," in *Three Bodley Head Monographs*, ed. Kathleen Lines (London: The Bodley Head, 1963), 116.
53. George Watson, "The Art of Disagreement," in *C. S. Lewis Remembered: Collected Reflections of Students, Friends and Colleagues*, ed. Harry Lee Poe and Rebecca Whitten Poe (Grand Rapids, MI: Zondervan, 2006), 79.
54. Watson, "The Art of Disagreement," 79.
55. Watson, "The Art of Disagreement," 79.
56. Hooper, *Letters*, 1:72.
57. Hooper, *Letters*, 1:81–82.
58. Hooper, *Letters*, 1:87.
59. Hooper, *Letters*, 1:138.
60. Hooper, *Letters*, 1:85.
61. I saw my first operas at the Coliseum after Christmas in 1971. It was a grand experience and the ideal way to be introduced to opera, with two light operas: *Die Fledermaus* by Strauss and *Orpheus in the Underworld* by Offenbach.
62. Hooper, *Letters*, 1:87.
63. Hooper, *Letters*, 1:97.
64. Hooper, *Letters*, 1:99.
65. Hooper, *Letters*, 1:144–45.
66. C. S. Lewis, *An Experiment in Criticism* (Cambridge: Cambridge University Press, 1961), 81.
67. C. S. Lewis, "It All Began with a Picture . . . ," in *Of Other Worlds: Essays and Stories*, ed. Walter Hooper (New York: Harvest, 1994), 42.
68. Hooper, *Letters*, 1:95.
69. Hooper, *Letters*, 1:145.
70. Hooper, *Letters*, 1:143.

71. We do not discover his last name until the opening pages of *The Voyage of the Dawn Treader*.
72. C. S. Lewis, *The Lion, the Witch and the Wardrobe* (New York: Macmillan, 1950), 41.
73. Hooper, *Letters*, 1:147–48.
74. Hooper, *Letters*, 1:143, 188.
75. Hooper, *Letters*, 1:188.
76. Hooper, *Letters*, 1:247.
77. Hooper, *Letters*, 1:260.
78. Hooper, *Letters*, 1:273.
79. Hooper, *Letters*, 1:168.
80. Hooper, *Letters*, 1:271.
81. Hooper, *Letters*, 1:191.
82. Hooper, *Letters*, 1:182.
83. Hooper, *Letters*, 1:227.
84. Hooper, *Letters*, 1:226–27.
85. C. S. Lewis, *The Last Battle* (New York: Macmillan, 1956), 173.
86. Hooper, *Letters*, 1:93.
87. Hooper, *Letters*, 1:93, 96.
88. "Memoirs," 4:253.
89. "Memoirs," 4:253.
90. "Memoirs," 4:253.
91. Lewis, *Surprised by Joy*, 153.

Chapter 5: Reading for Kirkpatrick and for Pleasure: 1914

1. C. S. Lewis, *Surprised by Joy* (London: Bles, 1955), 134–35.
2. C. S. Lewis, *A Preface to Paradise Lost* (London: Oxford University Press, 1942), 19–25.
3. Lewis, *A Preface to Paradise Lost*, 20.
4. Harry Lee Poe and Rebecca Whitten Poe, eds., *C. S. Lewis Remembered: Collected Reflections of Students, Friends and Colleagues* (Grand Rapids, MI: Zondervan, 2006), 236. We have included the full text of this conversation, which was originally printed as "The Establishment Must Die or Rot . . . C. S. Lewis Discusses Science Fiction with Kingsley Amis and Brian Aldiss," *SFHorizons*, no. 1 (Spring 1964): 5–12.
5. One of the distinguishing features of the Bible from all the holy books of the world's religions is that it tells one story after another that form one true unified story about the whole world from its beginning until its ending.
6. Walter Hooper, ed., *The Collected Letters of C. S. Lewis*, vol. 1 (New York: HarperSanFrancisco, 2004), 72.
7. Hooper, *Letters*, 71.
8. Lewis, *Surprised by Joy*, 134.
9. Lewis, *A Preface to Paradise Lost*, 19–25.
10. Henry Thomas Buckle, *History of Civilization in England*, vol. 2 (London: Parker, Son and Bourn, 1861), 1.

11. Buckle, *England*, 2:443.
12. Buckle, *England*, 2:444–45.
13. Buckle, *England*, 2:447.
14. Buckle, *England*, 2:458–59.
15. "Memoirs of the Lewis Family, 1850–1930," ed. Warren Hamilton Lewis (Marion Wade Center Collection, Wheaton College), 3:191.
16. John G. West Jr., "*The Abolition of Man*," in *The C. S. Lewis Readers' Encyclopedia*, ed. Jeffrey D. Schultz and John G. West Jr. (Grand Rapids, MI: Zondervan, 1998), 68.
17. C. S. Lewis, *The Abolition of Man* (New York: Macmillan, 1955), 16.
18. Lewis, *The Abolition of Man*, 16–17.
19. Hooper, *Letters*, 1:128.
20. Lewis, *Surprised by Joy*, 137.
21. Lewis, *Surprised by Joy*, 137.
22. Lewis, *Surprised by Joy*, 137.
23. C. S. Lewis, "William Morris," in *Rehabilitations* (London: Oxford University Press, 1939), 37.
24. Lewis, "William Morris," 37.
25. Hooper, *Letters*, 1:92.
26. Hooper, *Letters*, 1:92n60.
27. Alastair Fowler, "C. S. Lewis: Supervisor," in Poe and Poe, *C. S. Lewis Remembered*, 109.
28. Hooper, *Letters*, 1:94.
29. C. S. Lewis, *The Pilgrim's Regress*, 3rd ed. (London: Bles, 1943), 7, 9.
30. J. R. R. Tolkien, "On Fairy-Stories," in *Tree and Leaf* (Boston: Houghton Mifflin, 1965), 68.
31. Walter Hooper, ed., *All My Road before Me: The Diary of C. S. Lewis, 1922–1927* (New York: Harcourt Brace Jovanovich, 1991), 24, 28, 48. See also Don King, "Joy," in Schultz and West, *The C. S. Lewis Readers' Encyclopedia*, 224. King observes that Lewis's poem "Joy," published in 1922, was "one of Lewis's earliest and most successful attempts to capture the essence of joy."
32. Hooper, *Letters*, 1:94.
33. C. S. Lewis, *The Allegory of Love* (Oxford: Clarendon, 1936), 24.
34. C. S. Lewis, *The Discarded Image* (Cambridge: Cambridge University Press, 1964), 210.
35. Hooper, *Letters*, 1:94.
36. Hooper, *Letters*, 1:103.
37. Hooper, *Letters*, 1:106.
38. Hooper, *Letters*, 1:151.
39. Hooper, *Letters*, 1:144.
40. C. S. Lewis, "Edmund Spenser," in *Fifteen Poets* (Oxford: Oxford University Press, 1941), 40. This essay appears as "On Reading *The Faerie Queene*," in Lewis, *Studies in Medieval and Renaissance Literature*, ed. Walter Hooper (Cambridge: Cambridge University Press, 1966).

41. C. S. Lewis, "Edmund Spenser, 1552–99," in Lewis, *Studies in Medieval and Renaissance Literature*, 132. This essay originally appeared in *Major British Writers*, ed. Walter J. Bate, vol. 1 (New York: Harcourt, Brace, 1954).
42. Lewis, "Edmund Spenser, 1552–99," 132.
43. Lewis, *The Allegory of Love*, 298.
44. C. S. Lewis, *Spenser's Images of Life*, ed. Alistair Fowler (Cambridge: Cambridge University Press, 1967).
45. Lewis, *Spenser's Images of Life*, 1.
46. Lewis, *Spenser's Images of Life*, 140.
47. Lewis, *The Pilgrim's Regress*, 8.
48. Lewis, *The Allegory of Love*, 310–11.

Chapter 6: War and Romance: 1915

1. "Memoirs of the Lewis Family, 1850–1930," ed. Warren Hamilton Lewis (Marion Wade Center Collection, Wheaton College), 4:279.
2. "Memoirs," 4:281.
3. Walter Hooper offers this explanation in Walter Hooper, ed., *The Collected Letters of C. S. Lewis*, vol. 1 (New York: HarperSanFrancisco, 2004), 101n1.
4. "Memoirs," 4:280.
5. Hooper, *Letters*, 1:101.
6. Hooper, *Letters*, 1:102.
7. Hooper, *Letters*, 1:104n9.
8. Hooper, *Letters*, 1:105.
9. "Memoirs," 4:298.
10. Hooper, *Letters*, 1:113.
11. "Memoirs," 4:298.
12. Hooper, *Letters*, 1:106.
13. William H. Oakley, *Guildford in the Great War: The Record of a Surrey Town* (Guildford: Billing & Sons, 1934), 146.
14. Oakley, *Guildford*, 147.
15. Oakley, *Guildford*, 149. Oakley's information comes from Joseph Morris's *The German Air Raids on Great Britain*.
16. "Memoirs," 5:18.
17. Oakley, *Guildford*, 149–50.
18. Oakley, *Guildford*, 150.
19. Oakley, *Guildford*, 151.
20. Hooper, *Letters*, 1:148.
21. Hooper, *Letters*, 1:148.
22. Hooper, *Letters*, 1:148.
23. Oakley, *Guildford*, 142.
24. Hooper, *Letters*, 1:79.
25. Oakley, *Guildford*, 142.
26. Hooper, *Letters*, 1:105.

27. Hooper, *Letters*, 1:105, 108.
28. Hooper, *Letters*, 1:108.
29. Hooper, *Letters*, 1:115.
30. Hooper, *Letters*, 1:973.
31. "Memoirs," 4:310.
32. "Memoirs," 5:3.
33. "Memoirs," 4:93.
34. "Memoirs," 5:10.
35. "Memoirs," 5:17.
36. "Memoirs," 5:39.
37. Hooper, *Letters*, 1:121.
38. Hooper, *Letters*, 1:122.
39. C. S. Lewis, *Surprised by Joy* (London: Bles, 1955), 161.
40. Lewis, *Surprised by Joy*, 163.
41. Lewis, *Surprised by Joy*, 162.
42. Lewis, *Surprised by Joy*, 163.
43. Lewis, *Surprised by Joy*, 163.
44. Hooper, *Letters*, 1:122, 124.
45. Chesterton contributed the volume *G. F. Watts* in the Popular Library of Art series (London: Duckworth, 1903). See Rowland Alston, *The Mind and Work of G. F. Watts* (London: Methuen, 1929), opposite plate V.
46. Hooper, *Letters*, 1:124.
47. Hooper, *Letters*, 1:126.
48. "Memoirs," 4:305–6.
49. "Memoirs," 4:306.
50. Hooper, *Letters*, 1:141.
51. Hooper, *Letters*, 1:127.
52. Hooper, *Letters*, 1:128–29.
53. Hooper, *Letters*, 1:133.
54. Hooper, *Letters*, 1:135.
55. Hooper, *Letters*, 1:129.
56. Lewis, *Surprised by Joy*, 160.
57. Hooper, *Letters*, 1:129–30.
58. Hooper, *Letters*, 1:133.
59. Hooper, *Letters*, 1:133.
60. Hooper, *Letters*, 1:141–42.
61. Hooper, *Letters*, 1:143.
62. Hooper, *Letters*, 1:151.
63. Hooper, *Letters*, 1:158.

Chapter 7: A Conflicted Soul: 1916
1. Walter Hooper, ed., *The Collected Letters of C. S. Lewis*, vol. 1 (New York: HarperSanFrancisco, 2004), 159–60.
2. Hooper, *Letters*, 1:167.
3. Hooper, *Letters*, 1:160.

4. Hooper, *Letters*, 1:214.
5. Hooper, *Letters*, 1:164–65.
6. Hooper, *Letters*, 1:172.
7. Hooper, *Letters*, 1:218.
8. "Memoirs of the Lewis Family, 1850–1930," ed. Warren Hamilton Lewis (Marion Wade Center Collection, Wheaton College), 5:42.
9. "Memoirs," 5:43.
10. "Memoirs," 5:47.
11. "Memoirs," 5:43.
12. "Memoirs," 5:47.
13. "Memoirs," 5:48.
14. "Memoirs," 5:58.
15. "Memoirs," 5:79.
16. "Memoirs," 5:70.
17. "Memoirs," 5:74.
18. "Memoirs," 5:78–79.
19. "Memoirs," 5:79–80.
20. "Memoirs," 5:113.
21. "Memoirs," 5:87.
22. "Memoirs," 5:96.
23. "Memoirs," 5:101.
24. "Memoirs," 5:88, 100.
25. "Memoirs," 5:96.
26. "Memoirs," 5:100.
27. "Memoirs," 5:101.
28. Hooper, *Letters*, 1:198.
29. Hooper, *Letters*, 1:198–99.
30. "Memoirs," 5:30.
31. "Memoirs," 5:32.
32. "Memoirs," 5:40.
33. "Memoirs," 5:68.
34. "Memoirs," 5:70.
35. "Memoirs," 5:71.
36. Hooper, *Letters*, 1:177.
37. "Memoirs," 5:72.
38. "Memoirs," 5:75.
39. "Memoirs," 5:81.
40. "Memoirs," 5:88.
41. "Memoirs," 5:108–9.
42. "Memoirs," 5:109–10.
43. Hooper, *Letters*, 1:161.
44. Hooper, *Letters*, 1:161.
45. Hooper, *Letters*, 1:160, 162.
46. Hooper, *Letters*, 1:164.
47. Hooper, *Letters*, 1:164.

48. Hooper, *Letters*, 1:174.
49. C. S. Lewis, *The Allegory of Love* (Oxford: Clarendon, 1936), 339. Lewis took his cue from Spenser, who identified *eros, storgē,* and *philia* as three kinds of love in *The Faerie Queene.*
50. Hooper, *Letters*, 1:174.
51. Hooper, *Letters*, 1:196.
52. See C. S. Lewis, *An Experiment in Criticism* (Cambridge: Cambridge University Press, 1961), 14–26. In his third chapter, Lewis drew on the analogy of pictures and music, a topic that he and Arthur Greeves discussed endlessly.
53. Lewis, *An Experiment in Criticism*, 25.
54. Hooper, *Letters*, 1:191.
55. Hooper, *Letters*, 1:211–12.
56. Hooper, *Letters*, 1:161.
57. Hooper, *Letters*, 1:161–62.
58. Hooper, *Letters*, 1:161.
59. Hooper, *Letters*, 1:165.
60. Hooper, *Letters*, 1:165.
61. C. S. Lewis, *Surprised by Joy* (London: Bles, 1955), 168–69.
62. Hooper, *Letters*, 1:169.
63. Hooper, *Letters*, 1:169.
64. Lewis, *Surprised by Joy*, 169.
65. Hooper, *Letters*, 1:169.
66. Hooper, *Letters*, 1:170.
67. Hooper, *Letters*, 1:175.
68. Hooper, *Letters*, 1:180.
69. Hooper, *Letters*, 1:180.
70. The Bodleian Library holds Lewis's copy in the special collections section.
71. Hooper, *Letters*, 1:180.
72. Hooper, *Letters*, 1:183.
73. Hooper, *Letters*, 1:183–84.
74. Harry Lee Poe and Rebecca Whitten Poe, eds., *C. S. Lewis Remembered: Collected Reflections of Students, Friends and Colleagues* (Grand Rapids, MI: Zondervan, 2006), 236.
75. Hooper, *Letters*, 1:186.
76. Hooper, *Letters*, 1:187. Coghill became the preeminent Chaucerian scholar of the middle decades of the twentieth century. He produced a modern English version of *The Canterbury Tales* and wrote a musical version of the tales that ran in the West End of London and on Broadway.
77. Hooper, *Letters*, 1:189.
78. Hooper, *Letters*, 1:192.
79. See Lewis's chapter on Chaucer, which virtually ignores *The Canterbury Tales*, in Lewis, *The Allegory of Love*, 161–97.
80. Hooper, *Letters*, 1:187.

81. C. S. Lewis, *A Preface to Paradise Lost* (London: Oxford University Press, 1942), 9.
82. Lewis, *An Experiment in Criticism*, 1–39. Almost all of the works of literature that Lewis cites were books he read before he went to war.
83. Hooper, *Letters*, 1:201–2.
84. Hooper, *Letters*, 1:209.
85. C. S. Lewis, ed., *George MacDonald: An Anthology* (London: Bles, 1946), 15.
86. Hooper, *Letters*, 1:210.
87. Hooper, *Letters*, 1:236.
88. Hooper, *Letters*, 1:256.
89. Hooper, *Letters*, 1:240.
90. Lewis, *Surprised by Joy*, 165.
91. Lewis, *Surprised by Joy*, 165–66.
92. Hooper, *Letters*, 1:270.
93. Lewis, *Surprised by Joy*, 167–68.
94. Hooper, *Letters*, 1:246.
95. Hooper, *Letters*, 1:246. See also chapter 2 of Lewis, *An Experiment in Criticism*, 5–13; here Lewis expresses the same views he had held at seventeen.
96. Hooper, *Letters*, 1:244.
97. See Lewis, *The Allegory of Love*, 44–111, and *A Preface to Paradise Lost*, 1–8.
98. Hooper, *Letters*, 1:217, 221.
99. Hooper, *Letters*, 1:223.
100. Hooper, *Letters*, 1:225.
101. Hooper, *Letters*, 1:246–47, 254.
102. Hooper, *Letters*, 1:249.
103. Hooper, *Letters*, 1:249.
104. Hooper, *Letters*, 1:252–53.
105. Hooper, *Letters*, 1:257, 258, 259.
106. Hooper, *Letters*, 1:266.
107. Hooper, *Letters*, 1:170–71.
108. Hooper, *Letters*, 1:168.
109. Hooper, *Letters*, 1:193.
110. Hooper, *Letters*, 1:258.
111. Hooper, *Letters*, 1:195.
112. Hooper, *Letters*, 1:181.
113. Hooper, *Letters*, 1:185–86.
114. Hooper, *Letters*, 1:186.
115. Hooper, *Letters*, 1:193.
116. Hooper, *Letters*, 1:228.
117. Hooper, *Letters*, 1:210.
118. Hooper, *Letters*, 1:216.
119. Hooper, *Letters*, 1:219.

120. See C. S. Lewis, "Christian Apologetics," in *God in the Dock*, ed. Walter Hooper (Grand Rapids, MI: Eerdmans, 1970), 89–103.
121. Hooper, *Letters*, 1:225.
122. Hooper, *Letters*, 1:218.
123. Hooper, *Letters*, 1:176.
124. Hooper, *Letters*, 1:176.
125. Hooper, *Letters*, 1:176.
126. Hooper, *Letters*, 1:214–15.
127. Hooper, *Letters*, 1:241.
128. Hooper, *Letters*, 1:171.
129. Hooper, *Letters*, 1:178; "Memoirs," 5:79.
130. Hooper, *Letters*, 1:250.
131. Hooper, *Letters*, 1:203.
132. Hooper, *Letters*, 1:204.
133. Hooper, *Letters*, 1:208.
134. Hooper, *Letters*, 1:230.
135. Hooper, *Letters*, 1:230.
136. Hooper, *Letters*, 1:231.
137. Hooper, *Letters*, 1:231.
138. Hooper, *Letters*, 1:231.
139. Hooper, *Letters*, 1:231.
140. C. S. Lewis, *The Problem of Pain* (London: Centenary, 1940), 4–12.
141. C. S. Lewis, *Mere Christianity* (New York: Macmillan, 1952), 3–51. The first section of the book formed the first series of radio broadcasts, entitled "Right and Wrong as a Clue to the Meaning of the Universe."
142. Lewis, *Surprised by Joy*, 215.
143. Hooper, *Letters*, 1:234–35.
144. Hooper, *Letters*, 1:242.
145. Hooper, *Letters*, 1:261.
146. Hooper, *Letters*, 1:262.
147. Hooper, *Letters*, 1:263.
148. Hooper, *Letters*, 1:263–64.
149. Lewis, *Surprised by Joy*, 214.

Chapter 8: Oxford and War: 1917–1918

1. Walter Hooper, ed., *The Collected Letters of C. S. Lewis*, vol. 1 (New York: HarperSanFrancisco, 2004), 274.
2. Hooper, *Letters*, 1:268.
3. Hooper, *Letters*, 1:269.
4. Hooper, *Letters*, 1:270–71.
5. Hooper, *Letters*, 1:276.
6. Hooper, *Letters*, 1:272.
7. Hooper, *Letters*, 1:271. George Sayer suggested that Jack had Arthur's sister Lily in mind. She was a beautiful girl but also a selfish person. See

George Sayer, *Jack: C. S. Lewis and His Times* (New York: Harper & Row, 1988), 55.

8. Hooper, *Letters*, 1:281.
9. Hooper, *Letters*, 1:282.
10. Hooper, *Letters*, 1:283–84.
11. Hooper, *Letters*, 1:313.
12. Hooper, *Letters*, 1:319–20.
13. Sayer, *Jack*, 56.
14. Hooper, *Letters*, 1:265.
15. Hooper, *Letters*, 1:267.
16. Sadly, times have changed. When I was at Oxford in 1979, the streets were littered with wonderful bookstores, but today these have all been replaced by souvenir shops. The booksellers have left for cheaper rent in the outlying villages of Oxfordshire, except for Blackwell's, which owns its own property.
17. Hooper, *Letters*, 1:269.
18. Hooper, *Letters*, 1:273.
19. Hooper, *Letters*, 1:285.
20. Hooper, *Letters*, 1:289.
21. Hooper, *Letters*, 1:275, 279n.
22. Hooper, *Letters*, 1:280.
23. Hooper, *Letters*, 1:287.
24. Hooper, *Letters*, 1:291.
25. Hooper, *Letters*, 1:292.
26. Hooper, *Letters*, 1:299.
27. Hooper, *Letters*, 1:294.
28. Bodleian Library, University of Oxford, MS. Facs. b. 98, 1.
29. Bodleian Library MS. Facs. b. 98, 8.
30. Bodleian Library MS. Facs. b. 98, 7.
31. Bodleian Library MS. Facs. b. 98, 2.
32. Bodleian Library MS. Facs. b. 98, 5.
33. Bodleian Library MS. Facs. b. 98, 4.
34. Hooper, *Letters*, 1:295, 297.
35. Hooper, *Letters*, 1:298.
36. Hooper, *Letters*, 1:298.
37. Hooper, *Letters*, 1:300.
38. Hooper, *Letters*, 1:301.
39. Hooper, *Letters*, 1:298n.
40. Hooper, *Letters*, 1:330.
41. Hooper, *Letters*, 1:304.
42. Hooper, *Letters*, 1:305–6.
43. Hooper, *Letters*, 1:303n72.
44. Hooper, *Letters*, 1:307, 310.
45. Hooper, *Letters*, 1:313–14.
46. Hooper, *Letters*, 1:317, 318n.

47. Hooper, *Letters*, 1:318n.
48. Hooper, *Letters*, 1:322.
49. Hooper, *Letters*, 1:310n.
50. Hooper, *Letters*, 1:313.
51. Hooper, *Letters*, 1:316.
52. Hooper, *Letters*, 1:320–21.
53. Hooper, *Letters*, 1:325.
54. Hooper, *Letters*, 1:330–31.
55. Hooper, *Letters*, 1:334.
56. Hooper, *Letters*, 1:335.
57. C. S. Lewis, *Surprised by Joy* (London: Bles, 1955), 177.
58. Hooper, *Letters*, 1:335–36.
59. Bodleian Library MS. Facs. b. 98, 6.
60. Bodleian Library MS. Facs. b. 98, 9.
61. Alister McGrath, *C. S. Lewis: A Life* (Carol Stream, IL: Tyndale, 2013), 65–66.
62. Hooper, *Letters*, 1:338–39.
63. Hooper, *Letters*, 1:339.
64. Clyde S. Kilby and Marjorie Lamp Mead, *Brothers and Friends: The Diaries of Major Warren Hamilton Lewis* (New York: Harper & Row, 1982), 236.
65. Sayer, *Jack*, 70–71.
66. Sayer, *Jack*, 89.
67. Hooper, *Letters*, 1:1022.
68. McGrath, *C. S. Lewis*, 73–76.
69. Hooper, *Letters*, 1:345–46.
70. "Memoirs of the Lewis Family, 1850–1930," ed. Warren Hamilton Lewis (Marion Wade Center Collection, Wheaton College), 5:245.
71. Hooper, *Letters*, 1:347–48.
72. Hooper, *Letters*, 1:348–49.
73. Hooper, *Letters*, 1:350.
74. Hooper, *Letters*, 1:351–52.
75. Lewis, *Surprised by Joy*, 184.
76. Hooper, *Letters*, 1:352, 356n.
77. Hooper, *Letters*, 1:354.
78. Hooper, *Letters*, 1:354.
79. Hooper, *Letters*, 1:356.
80. Hooper, *Letters*, 1:358.
81. Hooper, *Letters*, 1:361.
82. Hooper, *Letters*, 1:358.
83. Hooper, *Letters*, 1:342.
84. Lewis, *Surprised by Joy*, 180–81.
85. Lewis, *Surprised by Joy*, 181.
86. Lewis, *Surprised by Joy*, 181–82.
87. C. S. Lewis, *The Four Loves* (London: Bles, 1960), 73ff.

88. Lewis, *Surprised by Joy*, 182.
89. Hooper, *Letters*, 1:363.
90. Hooper, *Letters*, 1:385; Bodleian Library MS. Facs. b. 98, 10; Lewis, *Surprised by Joy*, 185.
91. Bodleian Library MS. Facs. b. 98, 10.
92. "Memoirs," 5:307.
93. "Memoirs," 5:309.
94. "Memoirs," 5:312.
95. Bodleian Library MS. Facs. b. 98, 21.
96. Hooper, *Letters*, 1:387.
97. Hooper, *Letters*, 1:369.
98. Hooper, *Letters*, 1:403.
99. Hooper, *Letters*, 1:416, 423; Bodleian Library MS. Facs. b. 98, 13.
100. Sayer, *Jack*, 75, citing "Memoirs," 9:44–45.
101. A. N. Wilson, *C. S. Lewis: A Biography* (New York: Norton, 1990), 56.
102. A. N. Wilson reached this same conclusion about what motivated C. S. Lewis in his relationship with Mrs. Moore. See his quotation from *The Allegory of Love* in which Lewis alluded to going shopping in service to a lady in the twentieth century. Wilson, *C. S. Lewis*, 84.
103. Hooper, *Letters*, 1:388n.
104. Hooper, *Letters*, 1:385.

Chapter 9: The End of Youth

1. C. S. Lewis, *Surprised by Joy* (London: Bles, 1955), 185.
2. Lewis, *Surprised by Joy*, 194.
3. Lewis, *Surprised by Joy*, 195.
4. Lewis, *Surprised by Joy*, 196.
5. Lewis, *Surprised by Joy*, 197.
6. Lewis, *Surprised by Joy*, 199.
7. Lewis, *Surprised by Joy*, 201.
8. Lewis, *Surprised by Joy*, 202.
9. Lewis, *Surprised by Joy*, 205.
10. Lewis, *Surprised by Joy*, 205–7.
11. Lewis, *Surprised by Joy*, 207–9.
12. Lewis, *Surprised by Joy*, 210; cf. Alister McGrath, *C. S. Lewis: A Life* (Carol Stream, IL: Tyndale, 2013), 108.
13. Lewis, *Surprised by Joy*, 211–15.
14. Walter Hooper, ed., *The Collected Letters of C. S. Lewis*, vol. 1 (New York: HarperSanFrancisco, 2004), 969–70.
15. Hooper, *Letters*, 1:976.
16. Hooper, *Letters*, 1:977.
17. Hooper, *Letters*, 1:977.
18. Lewis, *Surprised by Joy*, 223.
19. Lewis, *Surprised by Joy*, 224.
20. Lewis, *Surprised by Joy*, 187, 188, 204.

Index

language instruction, 145
Last Battle, The (Lewis), 49,
  139–41, 260
Latin compositions, 181
Latin proficiency, 171
Latin translations, 181
Leatherhead, 116, 186, 211, 229
Le Morte d'Arthur (Malory), 108,
  164–66, 218, 257, 259, 261,
  265
Leslie, Dr., 55
Letters from Hell (Thisted), 217,
  224
Lewis, Albert (father), 17, 19
  on the education of his sons, 20,
    32–35, 103
  encouragement of Jack's reading
    habit, 40–41, 188
  encouragement to his sons, 39
  encouragement to Warnie, 75–76
  enjoyment of Shakespeare, 61
  flare for being in the way, 224
  pride in reading between the
    lines, 48, 203, 229
  sentimentality of, 198, 257
  on Terry Forde, 194
  warning on "dangers of drink,"
    118
  on World War I, 124, 172, 174,
    176–77
Lewis, C. S. ("Jack")
  adolescence of, 87, 275–76
  agnosticism of, 247
  as anti-social, 93, 197
  atheism of, 108, 120, 178, 210,
    237, 247, 264
  capacity for mathematics, 198,
    280n112
  clumsy at sports, 58, 80–81, 82, 88
  commission as second lieutenant,
    233, 248
  confirmation and first Commu-
    nion of, 141–42
  contempt for "grown-up" con-
    versation, 128

conversion to Christianity, 264,
  267
conversion to the "Gastons heresies," 142
development of self-identity, 266
drifted away from the church, 120
friendship with Arthur Greeves,
  90–91, 223
gravestone of, 26
growing self-awareness of, 90
hatred of England, 78
humor of, 224
imagination of, 181, 183, 222
independence of, 84, 174, 185,
  200–201, 206, 230, 266
interest in Belgium girl, 179–80
on interpreting literature, 48
as introvert, 83, 91
knowledge about children, 135
as literary scholar of medieval
  and Renaissance periods, 265
looked after Warnie, 73, 93
love for animals, 36–37
love for music, 131–33, 206–9
love for poetry, 54
love of winter, 136–37
makings of a barrister, 180–81
at Malvern College, 76–89,
  97–98
manipulative manner of, 83
as materialist, 158, 219, 226
military service of, 202, 225–26
names and monikers of, 17–19
oath to Paddy Moore, 104, 257
offended by Terry Forde, 199
prejudice against Americans, 220
prejudice against Christian faith,
  219
prejudice against the French, 24
preparation for Oxford, 171, 199
pride of, 81
as a prig, 84, 101
reading habits at Campbell, 54
received scholarship to Oxford,
  230

theodicy, 27
theosophy, 64
Thisted, Vlademar Adolph, 217
Thucydides, 194
Till We Have Faces (Lewis), 153, 265
Tillyard, E. M. W., 48, 110
Tolkien, Edith, 129
Tolkien, J. R. R., 45, 48, 66, 67, 105, 111, 121, 163–64, 179, 213, 270, 273
Tosca (opera), 207
Tower of London, 24
Trafalgar Square, 23, 131
trains, 23
Trinity College (Dublin), 200–201
Tristan and Isolde (French edition), 214, 221
Tristan and Isolde (Wagner), 72, 209
Trojan War, 150–52
tutorial system, 143–45
Twain, Mark, 139
Twelfth Night (Shakespeare), 216

Übermensch, 120–21
Ulster, 78
"Ulsterior motive" of C. S. Lewis, 45
University Church of St Mary the Virgin, 107–8
University College (Oxford), 230, 233, 234, 240

Valkyrie, The (Wagner), 207
Victoria, Queen, 123, 135
Virgil, 65, 138, 152, 157
vivisection, 36–37
Voltaire, 269
Voyage of the Dawn Treader, The (Lewis), 30, 138, 152, 260, 262

Wagner, Richard, 66–72, 94, 96–97, 100, 110, 120, 190, 207, 246, 268
walks, 58, 105, 130, 186, 194, 222, 266
Watford train wreck (1910), 49, 140
Watson, George, 18, 130
Watts, George Frederic, 187
"Weight of Glory, The" (Lewis sermon), 108
Well at the World's End, The (Morris), 159, 161–64, 183, 195, 234, 260
Wells, H. G., 41–42, 269
Whipsnade Zoo, 274
White, Barrie, 144
Williams, Charles, 41, 99
"will to power," 120
Wilson, A. N., 298n102
Wilson, Woodrow, 220
winter landscapes, 136–37, 212, 237
Wodehouse, P. G., 39
World War I, 17, 20
    formed backdrop of Lewis's life, 122–25
    Lewis's battlefield experience in, 259
    Lewis's war injuries from, 233, 255–57
    realties of, 172–77
    start of, 117
    trench warfare in, 253–55
World War II, 134
Wynyard School (Watford), 19–22, 27, 30–36, 39, 47–48, 78, 81, 236, 260, 281n8
    and development of Lewis's tastes, 50–51
    inner ring at, 43–45

Yeats, William Butler, 104, 212, 217

zeppelin threat, 175–77